Witnessness

Witnessness

*Beckett, Dante, Levi and the Foundations
of Responsibility*

Robert Harvey

continuum

2010

The Continuum International Publishing Group
80 Maiden Lane, New York, NY 10038
The Tower Building, 11 York Road, London SE1 7NX

www.continuumbooks.com

Library of Congress Cataloging-in-Publication Data
A catalog record for this book is available from the Library of Congress.

ISBN: 978-1-4411-0072-6 (hardcover)
         978-1-4411-2424-1 (paperback)

Typeset by Pindar NZ, Auckland, New Zealand
Printed in the United States of America by Thomson-Shore, Inc

for Hélène

di levar li occhi suoi mi fece dono

Contents

0.0　Witnessness: The Coordinates

> Why people have to complicate a thing so simple I can't make out.[1]

Emerging from the forest of survival testimonies published over the past forty years, one may easily come to the disappointing conclusion that being a witness is not for everyone.[2] The forces against which witnesses would otherwise testify all too often kill them or, in cases of survival, they have plenty of reasons to balk at coming forward. All too few live on to speak willingly, let alone eloquently, about hell on earth. And everyone else cherishes them as extreme rarities.

But what if being a witness were predicated not on one's use-value in investigations, trials, or the lesser genre of the testimonial, but rather on a fundamental given of the mind? What if the very structure of consciousness were made up of the self-same elements that constitute everyone's potential for being a witness — witnessing in the broadest ethical sense imaginable?

Ethics — if it is ever to be a universal possibility — can never arise from a set of moral principles either suggested or imposed. Nor can it be the consequence of any of the various relativistic ethical theories since these, by definition, reject as fantasy, fallacy or folly the very notion of ethical universality.[3] Even absolutist ethical systems — whether of the rational variety whose pinnacle is perhaps still Kant, or transcendental ones like Christianity — ultimately fall short of achieving a universal basis for responsible moral behavior. A universal ethics would both eschew the necessity of "ought" statements and succeed in unlocking a realm of human reality yet undiscovered: a power that actually *is*, but unbeknownst to the powerful.

In *Witnessness*, I suggest and describe a universally shared propensity for fellow-feeling and responsible action — an antidote to the despair

---

1　Samuel Beckett, quoted in Knowlson, 416.
2　Besides those by Primo Levi, some of the survival testimonies limned here are those by Filip Müller, Françoise Dolto, David Rousset, Robert Antelme, Bruno Bettelheim, and Jean Améry. See the Bibliography for titles, etc.
3　Examples, here, would be David Hume and Jean-Paul Sartre.

of modern thinkers aligned with the hopelessness expressed in Hobbes' dictum, "man to man is an arrant Wolfe." The universality of ethics being ethics' perennial problem, the working hypothesis of this essay is suggested to me by *Worstward Ho*, a late Samuel Beckett text in English that the author deemed untranslatable. *Worstward Ho* is a literary algorithm for the mind of man viewed as a stage upon which the drama of responsibility is played out in a looping that the death of an individual cannot end. This algorithm for ethics would remain difficult to decipher and present sensibly to a non-specialist without the help of a host of writers — from Dante to Primo Levi and from Kant to Lyotard — that *Witnessness* convenes in a series of coordinates arranged under three headings: witness, wit, and witnessness.

Worstward Ho's seeming idiosyncrasies have major repercussions well beyond the (already vast) world of Beckett studies: simply put, they are the very foundation of an ethics of universal applicability. It has already been established that, from a philosophical point of view, *Worstward Ho* is the richest item in Beckett's literary legacy. Alain Badiou has characterized it as a "short philosophical treatise" in a major essay devoted to the book's intricacies.[4] But whereas Badiou recuperates this crucial Beckett text for his own conceptualization of "event," dubbing it "a treatment in shorthand of the question of being, thus restricting its impact to the realm of ontology," *Worstward Ho* seems to me to be, in and of itself, in its own idiom, a grounding for ethics far firmer and permanent than any translation into metaphysical dialect. Bluntly put, ethics is the domain of philosophy for which we have at least as pressing a need today as for the question of being. So, these ethical dimensions of the little treatise remain to be adumbrated. *Witnessness* takes on the task of working through *Worstward Ho* in its original English while bearing in mind the practice of French that brought Beckett to this spare language, extracting its implications for moral science, completing it.

Why could Beckett write *Worstward Ho* only in English? And why did it remain in English until after his death, despite Beckett's accomplishments in French as well as in self-translation? Several years spent reading and lecturing on and about *Worstward Ho* have convinced me that when Beckett said it was "untranslatable," it was because this text — and, by extension, the text of any individual subject — is *already translated*. One sense of the notion of the already translated text is that *Worstward Ho*, in its original English, is also meant to resonate in French — not only in French (and sometimes, in Hibernian English), but in a Babel of other languages as well. There is no way — just to give one example — to fully understand the various functions attributed to "on" in the text without recognizing

---

4 Alain Badiou, "Being, Existence, Thought: Prose and Concept."

that these two letters spelling a preposition in English also form a French monosyllable with vastly different functions and meanings. So, I begin *Witnessness* on that note: to be able to transform the untranslatable into the always translated is, metaphorically speaking, to already be on the road to solving the conundrum of ethical universality.

Yet while Beckett, with his *Worstward Ho*, provides me with three constellations of lexicographic coordinates for broaching the problems I endeavor to solve, *Witnessness* exposes and explains my ideas about a universal ethics across a wide network of writers and texts. It also extends my own reflection on the witness as "subject position" begun with *Témoins d'artifice*. The idea in that book — whose title, punning on "fireworks," means "witnessworks" — is that a witness always uses the ruse of imagination to formulate testimony. This mobilization of imagination's ruse is akin to the passing of a baton from one runner to another in a relay race — an object whose noun in French happens to be the same as that for witness. Far from a mere convenient homonym, this homology keeps us grounded in the core idea of testimony, from *testis* or *terstis*, a third party. How, then, do we get from two — a victim and a survivor — to three in the "economy" of testimony? *Témoins d'artifice* endeavored to suggest answers to that question by exploring the human capacity for artifice. In the act of witnessing, then, an empathetic bridge between two subjects — functioning like the baton passed from runner to runner — is constructed. The task I am putting before myself in *Witnessness* is to bring into focus the elements contributing to this common potential and the universal nature of that intersubjective move.

In addition to aligning itself in the continuity of my prior work, the weave of *Witnessness* includes major strands from a multiplicity of thinkers, attempting to make them if not more decipherable than they've ever been, at least decipherable in newly imagined ways. *Witnessness* deploys an extensive reading of Primo Levi's *If This Be a Man* and *The Drowned and the Saved* based on a rather astoundingly fundamental contradiction between what these texts — written some forty years apart — say about the so-called *Muselmänner*. This analysis results in an original and powerful theory of the witness in the word's conventional sense — the witness who might be called upon to testify in a court of law. The dynamics of ethical relations between individuals then finds a unique motivation in Dante's *Purgatorio* — a bridging text (or perhaps a *témoin*) between Primo Levi and Samuel Beckett. If *Inferno* informs Primo Levi's work, Dante's book *between* heaven and hell accompanies Beckett throughout. The language and images that Dante used to describe the process by which his partnership with another is relayed from Virgil, through Matelda, to Beatrice not only inspired Beckett in casting his various pairs of sidekicks: they are essential to elucidating the state, condition or potential for being a witness and for which I have forged the neologism, *witnessness*.

Reading enables those of us who have never been victims of crime to nonetheless become witnesses by proxy. To read is, therefore, to empathize and, consequently, the imagination must be at least as important for our potential for witnessing as is reason. The best way to have the crucial part played by the imagination in the formation of a moral subject to be recognized is to elicit help from its strongest advocates. Through the thicket of Kant's writings and commentaries on them, it is easy to forget that for Kant, the imagination enables sensorial data to be converted into reason. This and the psychological dynamic driving the experience of the sublime draw portions of the First and Third Critiques into the *Witnessness* tapestry.

Two further works are of major importance in helping me to recover that perennially denigrated dimension of consciousness known as the imagination in forging an ethics for everyone. No one has more convincingly countered the assumption that some things are altogether unimaginable than Georges Didi-Huberman. The core claim of his powerfully polemical *Images in Spite of All* — that the photographic image can spur the viewer to moral action — is crucial to my own work. Finally, in addition to being the most complete history of philosophy's engagement with the imagination, John Sallis' *Force of Imagination* serves me to argue that certain current neurobiological assertions about the precession of metaphor over language in the human brain complement our search for an ethics based on the imagination.

From a short text made painstakingly by Samuel Beckett at the end of his life, thus, I have built a vocabulary that I believe will enable a move from the particularity of witnessing that we find in survival narratives to a generality that has something for everyone. My intimacy with *Worstward Ho* has suggested a lexicon and a conceptual grid to get us beyond envious admiration for the exceptions among us, to make the untranslatable the generic. Part of this vocabulary I borrow directly from Beckett. Part of it is my own. All of it is illuminated by Beckett's oeuvre. It is a set of concepts and conditions that point from admirable exceptions to a single quality that we all share thanks to the force of imagination.

Why is it important to shatter and disperse all restrictions on membership into the elite club of witnesses? — Because if there is one thing that the library of survival testimonies has taught us, it is that in this particular role, in this function that we call witnessing, there lies the key to the establishment of ethical relations among us. To express this in terms that pay homage to one of the many voices in this study: between names, witnessness alone may save the honor of the name, "human."[5]

While each chapter of *Witnessness* is built around a quote from *Worstward Ho*, it is not a book on *Worstward Ho*. Books *on* books speak to the restricted

---

5 Cf. Jean-François Lyotard, *The Differend* and *The Inhuman*.

audience that longs for a better grasp of what the text of reference means. Nor is *Witnessness* about *Worstward Ho*. Rather, it is resolutely *after* it — braced and spurred by the conceptual bulwark of that difficult, spare text. With no pretense of possessing any skill in dramaturgy, I have strived to serve as *Worstward Ho*'s abstract stage director, trying to render visible a virtual scene of universal moral value inspired by the *play* that *Worstward Ho* also is. In this sense, Beckett's text makes me make something of what aspirations remain for my passage here.

Presuming that only a very few of my readers will have read *Worstward Ho*,[6] I have strived to craft *Witnessness* in a manner that should not require any prior reading of that unique work. If you *have* read it, all the better for you, for you are undoubtedly happier for it. But no one should feel left out for not having read *Worstward Ho*. None need to have made that journey in order to follow what I have to say — inspired by Beckett — about us.

---

6 My references to *Worstward Ho* will be of the form $[x.y]$, where y is the number of the stanza or paragraph or aphorism — whatever one decides to call the blocks of text that make up the whole — and x the number of the groups of blocks, separated not just by blank lines, but by three asterisks.

1.0   ness

Murder on a mass scale has become an archetype of human event and lent the witness the status of most precious among us. And, within that archetype, *Auschwitz* has become the paradigm.[1] What is the precise relationship between the subject status that we name "witness" and the systematic murder of at least six million humans in the middle of the twentieth century? That relationship is clear: in the Jews, Roms, homosexuals, disabled, and others, it was their capacity to bear witness that the SS tried to annihilate by taking their lives.

Since *Auschwitz*, witnessing — being a witness and the being of a witness — elicits a level of respect that can be mesmerizing. When a witness is called to the stand that bears his name, when one of them stands before rendering testimony, the audience falls silent, sensing that a heretofore hidden truth about all of us will now, suddenly, come spectacularly to light. The professional representatives of the culpable try to confound them or stifle them in hopes that the deeds of their clients will remain unverified, unprosecuted, unpunished. Witnesses who are survivors of the most egregious crimes are revered as repositories whose memories might build ramparts against future genocides and ethnocides. Even the witnesses of singular killings stand out in our judgment. These apparently exceptional beings enter the ranks of the righteous among us because they alone have seen or heard or smelled or touched the eventness of the crime meant to destroy them as well. They are honored as much as those forever silenced because they have been in the same criminal harm's way, yet can tell us something of it. Somehow they have eluded the ultimate consequence of victimhood.[2] By escaping death, witnesses enter a precarious brotherhood with those who have succumbed. We grant high distinction to these righteous beings "thanks to" a heinous event committed by the worst among us. Thanks to some such event, there is, as Samuel Beckett writes, "something not wrong with one" of us.

---

1 Since the Auschwitz extermination camp is a common metonymy for what Raul Hilberg most accurately named the "destruction of the European Jews," I will use the italicized form of the name throughout this work when I mean what most often goes by either of the misnomers, Holocaust or Shoah. When I refer to the extermination camp and not the genocide as a whole, I will write Auschwitz in roman typeface.

2 The "somehow" of this escape will be examined in detail in "*al fondo.*"

Something, however, *is* wrong with this ritual of distinction, for by elevating witnesses to a state of exception, a state which we others think we shall never attain, we risk lazily letting ourselves drift to the side of negationists — those fascists ever vigilant for their opportunity to annihilate again. What I ask, therefore, and I believe Samuel Beckett asked is this: Was there not, *is* there not, some exercise of the mind already present in us and to which we might avail ourselves in order to turn our admiration into active emulation, to join our models, join forces with them in the state of being witness? Or must we, as so many twentieth-century narratives have suggested, be subjected to a crime ourselves before adopting the condition of righteousness? In our search for a denominator common to all, might we not subtract the compulsion to testify from the subject position we call "witness?" If so, the remainder would be the witness's potential.

It is just this potential that *Worstward Ho* dramatizes to the point of resolute generalization. The purpose of the generic, deadpan ring of Beckett's spare style is to convince us that there's nothing all that special at all about such mesmerizing individuals as witnesses.[3] After all, "witness" less "ness" leaves "wit," an old English word for consciousness itself. As for modern vagaries of "wit," Primo Levi, in an astounding self-contradiction that we will have occasion to examine, maintains that it was precisely a minimal capacity — let us call it *ness* — to keep his wits about him that kept him from drowning, thus saving him from becoming a complete witness. This nexus of complete (annihilated) witness and surviving witness begs the question at the heart of this essay: What of the apparently innate "witnessness" in each of us and its potential for nurturing ethical intersubjectivity? This "ness" of the witness is in every one of us. Beckett's "minimalist" language is the idiom of a lowest common denominator such that Everyman — expressible as *l'on*, in Beckett's adopted French — can recognize himself as originating in that place of basic morality, of humanity before humanity that I will designate the numbskull. But let us not jump too far ahead to a head we all inhabit.

What's both special and common, both precious yet run-of-the-mill, both arduous and effortless? What is silently eloquent and supremely ethical? To be and remain in a state of consciousness to which we associate one of those nouns equipped with the catch-all suffix for capacity, "witness." By hedging our usual understanding of "witness" and suggesting that there be a name — *ness* — for readiness to assume that role, I do not mean *being* or *becoming* one of those participants in a court proceeding who is

---

3 Studies of Beckett's minimalism are myriad. Some of the best are Leslie Hill's "Poststructuralist Readings of Beckett" and Martin Esslin's "What Beckett Teaches Me: His Minimalist Approach to Ethics." One may also wish to consult Enoch Brater's now classic *Beyond Minimalism: Beckett's Late Style in the Theater* and Sarah E. Cant, "In Search of 'Lessness'."

called upon to testify either for a defense or for a prosecution. I mean *possessing* all the qualities of a witness — especially those that attend the witness's intrinsic empathy with the victim — without there ever necessarily having been a crime committed. Bizarre? Perhaps. Nevertheless, this state of preparedness that Samuel Beckett stages most masterfully in *Worstward Ho* marshals the conditions by which we might all, someday, finally, have become truly human instead of settling for being merely all too human.

Staging a state of ethical consciousness is the achievement of *Worstward Ho*. The scenario the little book maps is that of a mind — more precisely, a skull. The action to which we are witness is the product of reflection, of memory, of cognition, of the translation of feeling into rudimentary reason. The players are the presumed subject of the state of consciousness thus staged and the fellow subjects with whom he interacts. The skull's owner is a mute witness. They are all potential martyrs. Together they produce a philosophical theatre in which the rudimentary drama of ethics unfolds. What Beckett offers us is the crux and crucible of our ethical potential: the *ness* of the witness.

> Something not wrong with one. Then with two. Then with three.
> So on. Something not wrong with all. Far from wrong. Far far from
> wrong. [9.4]

To get it right, once and for all, requires practice, rehearsal, opening night and, perhaps, a curtain call. Try having an accident and getting a witness, though. Good luck! The witness is exceptional to the extreme, reticent. Beckett knew this and sought, for insurance purposes, an ethical stance that all could share, without exception — exceptionless. For each of his characters, there is always a helper who would be there for him through thick and thin.

The chapter titles of *Witnessness* pay homage to Beckett's fondness for compound words ending in -ness. The predilection was not gratuitous: abstract qualities, for which English uses the suffix, are the guarantors of permanency. Beckett's biographer, John Knowlson, recounts how he used to take stones that struck his fancy home with him from the beach in order to protect them from the wearing away of the waves or the vagaries of the weather. He would lay them gently into the branches of trees in the garden to keep them safe from harm (29). The *ness* of the witness in all of us turns out, as we shall see, to be one of the ultimate results of Beckett's lifelong fascination with possibilities for a mineralized permanency to existence.

In a better, a far better, arrangement of relations among us, we would all function as mute and dim witnesses one with respect to the other. In an arrangement of relations that would be "[f]ar from wrong. Far far from wrong," we might indeed finally authorize ourselves to call such relations *human*. In the arrangement that Beckett imagined in *Worstward Ho*, no crime whatsoever (let alone *Auschwitz*) has occurred and yet there is "something not wrong with all" because all are witnesses for one another. One is for all. Mystified? Patience.

The formula that Beckett mapped out in *Worstward Ho* prepares for the arrangement I've just tried to characterize in preliminary terms. Whatever the precise lay of the land in the strange consciousness he surveys there, it is a space available to all, since it is the space of consciousness itself. The inclusive set that moves from one, then to two, then to three, then elliptically, infinitely, to all mathematically expresses the universality of "not wrongness," which is ethics, in Beckett's English. *One* has something "not wrong" with one because *all* ones have something "not wrong" with them. Throughout *Worstward Ho*, and even more insistently than the infinity of the set we have just described, Beckett's poetic language universalizes righteousness.

Any conventional reading, any lexicographical analysis of *Worstward Ho* renders apparent the pervasiveness of the preposition *on* and, thereby, its central importance. *On* modifies verbs, introduces prepositional phrases (explicit and implied), appears on its own, hides (in broad daylight) in key words such as *none* and *gone* and *one*, is made to rhyme with quaint awkwardness with *own*. All of these many occurrences of *on* carry implications for the state of consciousness Beckett offers us as his definitive legacy and these implications will be explored through the three sets of disquisitions, the constellations that make *Witnessness* a book.

For now, however, to honor its richness, to hint at its convergence with the *genericness* of ness, let us turn to contemplate the word formed by those two adjacent letters, in reverse alphabetical order, *on*. And let us look further at the two words by which the English language allows one to express the set theory operator [. . .] — *so on* — not "so, on" but "so on," as in "so on and so forth." At first glance this graphic inscription resembles "soon" with a median space, but deduction corrects this, telling us that "so on" must signify all those integers (metaphorically, individual lives) between "one" and "all" because the phrase, "so on," occurs in that particular place in Beckett's ordering of phrases. Some readers may indulge in musing at how "so on" echoes — as so many other phrases in *Worstward Ho* do — with the incessant movement forth announced in the adverbial "Ho" of the title. Maybe, too, might one for an instant permit the "on" of "so on" to be confused in one's free-floating meditation with its other use as preposition of place, opposed to "under," that the text establishes from the outset as fundamental to the state it describes. As preposition of position or preposition of attitude, not unlike an actor who is "on," it will have nothing whatsoever to do with passivity or waiting for some Godot.

The pervasiveness and prepositional promiscuousness of *on*, moreover, has everything to do with Beckett's insistence about *Worstward Ho*'s untranslatability.[4] The writer's perfect bilingualism, incites necessarily — however incongruously — to also seeing and hearing in those two letters — "o" then "n" — a French subject pronoun. Let us entertain, then, for a quick moment in anticipation of this essay's conclusion, the pronoun's meanings, its origins, and the implications thereof. "I. Who might that be?" the laconic Unnamable asked (336). Like "I," "one" is a shifter whose content quickly spins out of control toward subjective promiscuity. That's why toddlers have a hard time, at first, using "I" to designate themselves in speech. (And that's why our undergraduates persist in using "you" instead of "one" in their term papers.) *On*, as we should really get into the habit of reminding ourselves when we use what we think (only because we have been told) is a pleonastic *l'* when it precedes this pronoun, was once, in fact, a French noun. It's the ancient form of *l'homme*, meaning the species or, as I like to think of it, Everyman. Whomsoever has been stricken by muteness will speak if willing to share the words with all: speechlessness breeds speech. That's how we come to accept the use of "I." Not just one witness, but one *as* witness. An almost innate becoming-witness, but not just in any old way: according to the contours of actual witnesses as close to the death of their fellows as survival permits.

In bearing witness to the witness limned in *Worstward Ho*, this first section of *Witnessness* will glimpse at characteristics (such as vicarious-ness and betweenness) of the conventional witness and conditions (e.g. nothingness, lessness, fitness, and dimness) hinting at the witnessness underpinning an ethics for all. As in the preceding sentence, in "Lessness" (1970), and several other later texts, Beckett went crazy with words ending in "-ness." It is true that speakers of English may attach -ness to just about any adjective or past participle to form substantives that signify states, characteristics, traits or conditions of being.[5] But that odd -ness in witness, where for once — exceptionally — it doesn't seem to indicate a feature, points us toward the necessity of witnessness.

---

4 John Knowlson (1996) reports that Beckett wrote the following note to Antoni Libera on 1 August 1983: "I find I cannot translate *Worstward Ho*. Or with such loss that I cannot bear the thought" (note, p. 827) and that he lamented to him, personally, "How, he asked me, do you translate even the first words of the book 'On. Say on.' — without losing its force?" (684–85).
5 The suffix was already around in Old English for the same purpose. It's so pervasive that there's even a noun, *ness*.

1.1   witness . . .

From the beginning there was the witness, the third party — *testis* or *terstis* — as the slippage went in Latin. No one was there to verify that there was a conscience accompanying the first consciousness, but there was a witness to the first one moved to deprive the second. Even if Cain refused to allow himself to be beside himself — with remorse, for example — over his fratricide and thereby become witness to his deed, there was, as *Text for Nothing 12* tells us, the third party, the testicle, the "texticle," the "unwitnessed witness of witnesses" (1995, 151).

A witness is present, thought to be present, hoped present whenever an event occurs. An integral component in the validation of truth under the law, a witness is sought in the aftermath of an event. A witness answers the victim's appeal, "Can I get a witness?" The event that might, with luck, give rise to a witness is not just any event, but an occurrence where grievous harm has been done. Just being present at the scene of the event is not enough to constitute one as witness: one is required to possess sufficient presence of mind, minimal sharpness of wit, some gift of the gab. And *wit*, as we shall amply discuss, has everything to do with the origins of the word, *witness*. Although to eventually speak and make sense, a witness may not be unscathed by the event, any harm sustained by the victim marks him, often unto a death more or less deferred. Most of the time there's no way for the victim to cry out for a witness to come forth. Such, in any event, is the sense in which "event" will be used from here on out.

We conceive the establishment of juridical truth such that even when the victim of a crime has *survived* the event and can speak of what happened, we require the testimony of a third party — a *testis* who is *terstis* — especially, though not exclusively, in the absence of a confession proffered by the guilty party. What both strikes and worries us post-*Auschwitz* moderns about this structure is that in support of the victim's claim, the witness tends to substitute himself for the victim, speaking for him, acting as his proxy. Critical thinking has developed profound suspicion toward any representation wherein an empowered subject speaks in the place of a weaker one — justifiably to an extent that makes examination imperative. Whatever degree of empathy a witness might have managed to acquire, why shouldn't the plaintiff's word suffice to obtain justice and reparation? Doesn't such substitution actually mask identification and vicarious experience and, thus, descend into pure perversion? At a fundamental level, does a plaintiff-position remain at all in the absence of any plaintiff incarnate?

Just such worry and suspicion led Jean-François Lyotard to write *The Differend*, which he begins daringly with the nearly intractable refusal to deny the radical discomfiture of the collective subject (the "we" subject) under the onslaught of *Auschwitz*. Short of precluding the possibility of a newly born, extremely tentative relationship of solidarity between two subjects, Lyotard toyed with various extant meanings of *témoin* to see if some yet-ill-seen witness could escape the impeccably outrageous logic of historical negationism. It is worth recalling that *témoin* serves not only to convey the same meaning carried by witness in English, as noun it also means testimony, relay baton, outlier (geology), telltale (architecture), dumpling (excavation), boundary marker, and as adjective, control (as in "control subject" or "control animal") and pilot, test or model (as in "model home"). None of these are incidental. All of these contribute to building a sense of witnessness.

At the very same time that Lyotard was putting *témoin* to semantic play in an attempt to checkmate negationism in *The Differend*, Primo Levi, in *The Drowned and the Saved*, was equipping *testimonio* with a margin of ontological free play or error that could only result in vast possibilities for the witness. The practical consequences that emerge from a careful comparison between these two contemporaneous efforts to examine the gaps in the concept of the witness will be elaborated throughout this first part of *Witnessness*. Here, for now, I would ask the reader to trust me on credit that in 1986, albeit at the cost of egregious contradiction, Primo Levi found a way to conquer his survivor's guilt and definitively lift the accusation of perversity from the subject position we name witness.

"Move along," a voice commands, "there's nothing to be seen." What does he mean, "nothing?" I can see it right there: a life is ebbing from a body. Right now, at this very moment (it seems an eternity): *all* is becoming *nothing*, or *almost*. And he says, "there's nothing to be seen?" But there's *everything* to be seen, here and now. Someone ought to be saved from sheer, utter nothingness, from annihilation. But how? Beckett's voice responds with an axiom, still using the verb for the sense of sight.

Where all always to be seen. Of the nothing to be seen. [10.10]

How could he do otherwise, given the culturally evolved primacy of sight? But seeing, in Beckett, is always faintly, in the dimness. Like the mental glance with which Primo Levi both "saw" and guiltily averted his gaze from the *Muselmänner*, the Auschwitz zombies, seeing in spite of all, seeing despite impaired senses is always possible thanks to the mind's eye. Unwittingly or (even) willfully blind? No matter: sight and its consequence, insight, can always be supplemented by the force of imagination

— Kant's *Einbildungskraft*. Although the word "witness" itself is to be found nowhere in the lexicon of *Worstward Ho*, witnessing by proxy — by the uncannily accurate approximation of the imagination — is all that is left in the world of the generic anonymous consciousness.

And this is more than enough. Although not bereft of some hocus-pocus, the following analysis is largely true of the ability to witness staged in *Worstward Ho*:

> A discursive sequence like: "Nothing ever unseen. Of the nothing to be seen" includes in the paradox of a referential coincidence a great semantic difference, linked to the subjectivity of representation. [. . .] Furthermore, in this Beckettian narrative notation is the ambivalent realization of a symbolic missaid which has the unusual power of indicating the expressivity of inexpressivity, that is, the expressivity of what has no desire "to be seen," to express itself through figurality, but which only surfaces through representational figurality as in the pure ontology of "Nothing ever unseen. Of the nothing to be seen." [. . .] Reality is literally and imperatively a "nothing to be seen." (Locatelli 1990, 255)

Fair enough, as I said. But let me put it my way, while we continue to explore what we usually mean — within us and without us — by "witness." Let us observe that in the same breath, the voice of *Worstward Ho* adds, "Dimly seen. Nothing ever unseen." For all Beckett's emphasis on eyes wide open, whatever is seen is always "ill seen," as if through the lenses deformed by cataracts. But this does not prevent the seeing subject — or even a blind one — from seeing all. Clarity of assured vision is not required. How so? — On. If the reader trusts, as he should, the text's nodes of insistence, dimmed perception may actually be better for going on as witness than phenomenological certainty. Items to stock the witness's memory will be more likely "misseen" than seen. "Nothing ever unseen" may consequently be read as an affirmation wherein "nothing" is an infinitesimally small "something" (*res*), "unseeing" merely an invitation for the imagination to kick in where the eyes fail, and this always ("ever").

Meanwhile, the witness willing to talk is called to the witness stand. The spectator of the event in question has turned informant, instrument of truth. When he gets there and performs, he's on as a stage actor is *on*. He's got to be on the ball. *Worstward Ho* begins and ends with the word, "on." The text's very first sentence consists of this word alone, written once, followed by a full stop. "How do you translate even the first *word* of the book without losing its force?"[1] Indeed, "on," in the sense of "after

---

1 See note 4, p. 5.

which" or "beyond here" (which may also be characteristic of the witness: a possibility that I'll consider later), conveys the meaning of both the -ward suffix of "worstward" and the "ho" of the title. "On" is also the simpleton's palindrome of "no" and operates in *Worstward Ho* as the antidote to full negation. All for later. All for later. But say it now.

However slightly idiosyncratic it may be (you may not usually think of how deeply affected the witness may be by what he has witnessed or how giving testimony is like being "on show" and striving to be "on the mark"), this is a fairly conventional definition of the witness — at least in juridical terms, if not in religious ones. And this definition, furthermore, jibes with that which French dictionaries offer for the word *témoin*.

With his well-known resigned insistence on the defective nature of words, Beckett recognizes the limited truth-value to be had from conventional or secular witnessing. *Worstward Ho* and its companion texts — *Lessness, Ill Seen Ill Said*, etc. — all describe and espouse a worsening of the correspondence between meaning's vanity and signifier. Yet the net effect of Beckett's repetitions and alliterative poiesis is to bring us to believe, incongruously, that the more impoverished language is, the *less* it is defective. Congruity, in such a notion, can only be restored if the imagination intervenes in the formation of meaning. Among other functions, *Worstward Ho* serves as rallying cry to anyone who reads it to be "on" — on the lookout, on target (or as close as possible), on the ball. But in the same breath (a syllable) by which Beckett invokes myriad senses of "on" to prescribe a space-time for the subject, he calls upon us to approach the worst with Nietzschean open arms. So a not-so-fun or -easy task will be to figure out how "worsening oneself" and "being on" can possibly coexist, cooperate, interdigitate, have anything at all to do with each other . . .

As I just wrote, all of these definitions and speculations extending from definitions jibe pretty closely with various ones associated with the French word for "witness," *témoin*. Everything, in other words, that I've written so far in this chapter could be quite adequately translated into French. But if I were to try to think like the perfectly bilingual Samuel Beckett might have thought as he was writing out in English the only book in his entire oeuvre that he would deem untranslatable — into French, at least — I would necessarily discover aspects of the word "witness" that are likewise untranslatable.

What do I see in the word, "witness?" I see two syllables: wit-ness. I also see two words — "wit" and "ness" — enlisted to form a compound. Yet I don't see "ness" adding its usual sense to "wit." If anything, "wit" adds nothing to "ness" — especially when I think that one of the usages of *témoin* is to designate a model, or a place-holder, or a reminder. This is the kind of semantic reflection that seems to have preoccupied Beckett, leading him to express the absolutely generic nature of the character presented in *Worstward Ho* with the exclusive aid of English. But with Beckett's English, French is never far off. As we will see, it is so little far off that it's inscribed within that English.

Witness, like wilderness, then, is one of the rare English substantives equipped with the -ness suffix, but where it is not tagged onto an adjective or a past participle. Nor does the -ness in witness seem to indicate a quality, as if wit could have any. Certainly witness, as we know it and use it today, is not thought of as the capacity of one who possesses higher than average amounts of wit: it's wittiness, after all, that's the attribute of the witty. Nevertheless, wouldn't it appear that wit, the noun seemingly infected into a witty capacity by "-ness," bears some relation to witness? I found myself guessing so. But rather than first consult the OED, I took a long route that included an extensive rereading of Primo Levi from one end to the other. I became convinced of the strong tie between being a witness and (if not *being* a wit of the Groucho Marx variety) *having* one's wits about one, always.

Of course, the OED confirms how close the meanings of the two words once were. From the first (currently obsolete) definition of witness there unfurls a string of telling synonyms: "knowledge, understanding, wisdom." Keeping in mind the function of the suffix -ness and restricting the scope of its signification to "knowledge, understanding, [and] wisdom," "witness" appears orthographically pleonastic given that we've got "wit." Yet, again, with the same parameters, since "witness" in any conventional setting conveys no particular capacity, it would seem semantically deficient at the same time.

As often as *Worstward Ho* stresses the wide-openness of eyes, those beady ones are said to be clenched tightly shut or otherwise unseeing. Nothing of the external world may be viewed in these moments. Yet "all always" is seen. How so? Is it a matter of what is seen on the inside of eyelids? This is not always simply due to something as nebulous as the power of the imagination at work (although it may well be), for Beckett reminds us incessantly that when we finally understand, when our mind fathoms (below) or grasps (above) something, we say "I see." With eyes wide shut, then, we may better clasp the hand of the fellow long gone, the complete witness for whom we testify not with words but with acts of conscience — acts that may just prevent our still living fellows from having to give up the ghost to Thanatos.

The book you are reading is in large part out to explore the wit of that witness and the capacity, the *ness* attendant to both. The other main task that the book will attempt to perform is to activate "witness" as a potential of everyone, to put the -ness back into witness, to set the groundwork for a witnessness for all. Wit is not only a semantic component of witness, there's a causal connection: without some modicum of wit, one cannot be a real witness. Every singularity, every one on *this* side of death has some wit on his side. All who are here are not none. Far from it. All are *for one*.

Activating the -ness of witness requires the unmitigated reaffirmation that nothing escapes the "sights" of the skull, the full mobilization of the skull's skills when it is full of life, even if blindness affects the hermit crab occupying the dwelling. To be, or not to be, a complete witness, in Primo Levi's words. And if not, how not? Yet even using the metaphor of "sights" is still not sufficiently on the mark for imagining what the recovery and reactivation of our witnessness would be. For ocular perception, in witnessness, is far surpassed. Witnessness precedes witness and wit, for witnessness dwells within us and lends us contour even before logical connectors between our senses and our intellect set the standards for reasonable life.[2] Witnessness far outstrips the power and pretense of reason. Of words, too, as Samuel Beckett ceaselessly toiled to tell us. Where logos and lexus fail and wither, room must be made for the imagination, for that species of observation for which the likes of schools, courts of law, public opinion have no use. Being this kind of witness — the witness that all can be, even without event — is being someone where there was thought to be nobody, because the nobody has seen or "misseen" (but, then, sensed) something where there was nothing.

Before four furtively snapped shots made in Birkenau's Crematorium 5 by a Greek *Häftling* named Alex, Georges Didi-Huberman employs his skills of observation to enter as far as any survivor can into the concentrationary universe.[3] What craft or knack (other names for *ness*) enables one such depth of empathy? The deep empathy of one, that is, who was never there in actuality — in space, in time, in flesh? Didi-Huberman's observation skills are bolstered, of course, as anyone else's can be, by training in art history and by knowledge of the history of *Auschwitz*. He also espouses a belief in the epistemological power of the image — a philosophical stand whose elaboration can be traced through a dozen books of his published by Minuit. But above all, by Didi-Huberman's own naming, it's the imagination that opens the other — be he dead, obliterated, smoke, oblivion — to my visitation, my understanding.

To show how far we've gone in blindly elevating the witness, while neglecting our fundamental witnessness, I offer, as interlude, a brief cautionary tale — *Dichtung und Wahrheit*.[4] In mid-July 2004, just as France was

---

2 A drama of this acquisition of contour when ethical being is stimulated can be found in Raymond Queneau's 1932 novel, *The Bark Tree* (cf. Harvey 1996). For readings by neurobiologists on the pre-linguistic presence of metaphor, see Modell 2003, Johnson 1987, and Lakoff and Johnson 1999.

3 When quoting Georges Didi-Huberman's *Images in Spite of All*, I shall provide the page reference to the original French first (2003), then to Shane B. Lillis's excellent translation (2008), which I do, however, adjust on occasion.

4 In referencing the subtitle of Goethe's autobiography, I am not only suggesting the

reckoning with an increased number of violent racist incidents — notably anti-Jewish ones — and prepared for the annual solemn remembrance of the Vel' d'Hiv Roundup of July 1942, a young woman riding on the D-line of the RER, a suburban Paris train network, reported a particularly heinous and vicious attack. Six youths — three Black and three Maghrebian — surrounded the 23-year-old and her 18-month-old baby in a stroller. She alleged that taking her for a Jew, they had shorn her hair, drawn a swastika with a felt-tipped pen on her belly, and escaped while knocking over the stroller with her baby in it.[5]

A few days after the true story of Marie L.'s highly developed mythomania become known, a letter to the editor of *Libération* appeared in the same issue as the report of Ariel Sharon's outrageous call for all French Jews to flee immediately to Israel. The letter called for readers not to forget yet another victim of the hoax: the *witness* that each and every rider of the RER might have been if it had all been true! One innocent passerby thus hoisted (i.e. lowered) himself and his cohort to the same degree of victimhood as the *Beur* or the Black and every man of color falsely imprisoned anywhere, who is guilty by virtue of ethnic ancestry.

However idiosyncratic (or even deviant), this chapter has nevertheless been concerned throughout with the witness — that key figure in the realm of legal procedure. Yet the object of *Witnessness* is a state of consciousness emblematized by the witness, *before* witnessing, and accessible to all — a *ness*, therefore, available to *l'on: witness* stripped of the definite article. Witnessness is the state we are about to describe. Witnessness indwells in us. Witnessness is latent or active in all of us already. There will, of course, be characteristics of witnessness shared with those of the traditional witness: it is active when we stand in for another, when we serve as a third party or act as proxy; it may manifest itself through our propensity for chatter, our prolixity. But its features extend beyond the expected, beyond and before the expected: our fundamental potential as witness harkens back to the origins of the concept in languages more ancient than English. Back to Greek, for example, where its sense was interchangeable with that of martyr, where the name *itself* for "witness" was μάρτυρ. Beyond Greek, too, in languages that survive alongside English, like Arabic, in which "witness" is just a long or short vowel away from "martyr." Just as the best of friends must know much of enmity, so

---

part storytelling plays in all cautionary tales, but also anticipating my discussion of Jacques Derrida's *Demeure* pp. 67ff.

5 The incident was reported as occurring on 9 July 2004. The public and official outcry was tremendous and the newspaper reporting copious. The analyses after the discovery of the "victim's" mythomania were more muted. "*L'affaire du RER D*" inspired a play, *RER*, by Jean-Marie Besset which in turn became the scenario for André Téchiné's 2009 film, *La Fille du RER D*.

the witness never goes alone.[6] The witness is produced as a third, just as the etymology of the word suggests, from two — a victim and a survivor. If this chapter carries a title ending with an ellipsis, it is to carry the reader on to the next one, which begins with an ellipsis, and where that reader will meet the witness's inseparable sidekick. Beckett who wrote nothing without Dante's *Purgatory* close at hand and who cast inseparable opposites from Vladimir and Estragon to "I" and "not I" knew much about the inextricable twinning of the witness and the martyr functions within one subject.

> *e ora in te non stanno sanza guerra*
> *li vivi tuoi, e l'un l'altro si rode*
> *di quei ch'un muro e una fossa serra.*
> *Purgatorio* VI, 82–84[7]

---

6 Here, I have in mind, a series of texts that have informed much of this essay: Jacques Derrida's *Politics of Friendship*, Gil Anidjar's *The Jew, The Arab*, and Denis Guénoun's *Un Sémite*.

7 But those who are alive within you now
   can't live without their warring — even those
   whom one same wall and one same moat enclose
   gnaw at each other.

1.2 . . . martyr

In the beginning, there was the witness, inseparable from the martyr. Beside the witness is the martyr. The martyr is the witness beside himself.

> *fece me a me uscir di mente*
>
> *Purgatorio* VIII, 15

One may be beside oneself with grief, but also with elation beyond words. When Levinas, then Derrida, pondered the phrase, "I am your hostage," it was given from the start that the rapture that is love is part of the captivity.[1] Thus it is that there is, sometimes, that one that one takes as one's other half. One sacrifices one half of oneself for that other who reciprocally halves himself. If that half dies, the distress is so great that, as Christianity invented the word "dormition" to euphemize death into a sleep of the righteous, those of us who really die altogether see nonetheless that death is always something like the name Michel Deguy gave it in *À ce qui n'en finit pas*: "morition." Better half, I must be the worse half.[2]

> First the bones. On back to them. Preying since first said on foresaid remains. [7.4]

For the sake of witnessness, a martyrdom of sorts must return to the witness becoming himself, while preserving — nay, enhancing — his life. Following in Samuel Beckett's footfalls, we should ready ourselves to put the martyr back into the witness and be as happy as Larry about it. The Larry of the expression being, according to Murphy, short for Lazarus . . .[3]

---

1 Cf. Emmanuel Levinas, *Totality and Infinity* and Jacques Derrida, *Of Hospitality* and *The Gift of Death*.

2 "*De la coucher tendrement, de l'emmourir comme on endort un enfant, la bordant, caressant, soignant dans la morition* [. . .]" (Deguy, [11]). Of the relationship between the two in *How It Is*, H. Porter Abbott writes: "It is as if the feeling of helplessness cannot reflect on itself without the trope of some malignant other. Yet inside this imagined tyranny is the desire to tyrannize" (2004, 23).

3 Cf. Ricks 1993, 80–81. According to the OED, the expression derives from the disposition of the Australian boxer, Larry Foley (1849–1917). Or it might be from the Irish-Australianism, *larrikin*.

Yet, still, the haggard young man straps ten kilograms of explosive material to his waist, walks into a Pizza Hut and pulls the nylon cord. "Another martyr," gleefully shout the zealots responsible for the perfect opium to distract him completely from his desolate desperation. The witnesses will condemn him post-mortem, effacing whatever identity he managed to jury rig in his short life out of the nullity of oblivion. No witness of the virtuous ilk that we have come to expect; only a judicious one who performs his role mechanically because every eye taken must be redeemed by the taking of another eye or, if at all possible, with the whole mug.[4] This, as Rabelais predicted in the tragi-comical mode, is the world of the human turned on its head. This is the ethical ideal of a humanist world rendered mindless, heedless, headless. Not only is the witness adulterated or absent altogether, but what kind of subject is a dead martyr? What subjecthood the *ness* of humanity?

Religious, of course. The fundamentalist, who knows not what he does or why, has been programmed to believe that suicide or 24/7 praying constitutes martyrdom and thus bears witness to Allah, God, YHWH. But he's "only a pawn in their game."[5] In evangelical churches across the bluest parts of the US, photographs of young soldiers killed in roadside bombings in Iraq are presented as portraits of martyrs for democracy, the Christian world order, you name it. In cities across the Middle East photographs of young soldiers killed as human bombs are presented as portraits of martyrs for theocracy, for some Islamic new world order, for a crossless crusade. Islam, of course, inherited this crazy logic from Christianity where martyred believers like Stephen (Acts 22.20) were said to be bearing witness for the faith. The only *just* witness here is a dead witness. So what, in this case, I've been asking "true believers" of every stripe for years, is the point of life at all? Why not just cut it short as soon as you've convinced yourself that there's something better elsewhere, another place for the something we all dream of, and that everything's just hunky-dory there? Rather than pray, are we not meant to prey upon each other's forces to preserve life rather than take it?

> Preying since last worse said on foresaid remains. But what not on them preying? What seen? What said? What of all seen and said not on them preying? True. True! And yet say worst perhaps worst of all the old man and child. [11.5]

And why do we tolerate these travesties of the value of martyrdom when it's meant to survive as part of a living, breathing, responsible witness

---

4 This quip deforming the Talion Law, sometimes attributed to François Rabelais, is from French writer and activist, Paul Vaillant-Couturier (1892–1937).

5 I hope the reader will indulge my predilection for lines from Bob Dylan.

who is devoted to the preservation of life? Why does a martyr-witness have to be either saint or wretch? Something must have really got off track somewhere along the line leading to our wonderful world of today. This is twisted, sick, acephalous. At first there were only martyrs. And these martyrs were witnesses. Then came the Christians. Then, shortly before Islam, came Old Anglo-Saxon. Which begot Old English and, eventually, the English we speak worse and worse today. Let's take Beckett's suggestion and get back to the bare bones of our story. No matter what Pat Robertson "thinks" (i.e. believes), the early Christians, of course, didn't speak English. So, the early Christians couldn't avail themselves of all that the word "witness" harbors and whose dwelling's floor plan *Worstward Ho* is an attempt to build. "Witness" is the closest we had for translating μάϱτυϱ — the Hellenistic Greek word that the Christians borrowed for their wacky idea that there's something beyond *purgatorio*. Our denial must be overcome: in witnessness, witness and martyrdom must once again be seen, understood and lived as coextensive. The two valences of the same *ness* preserve the bearer in life through humble adjustments of oneself to the other called lessening and worsening. Jew and Arab are semite alike, as Fethi Benslama, Denis Guénoun, Gil Anidjar, and so many others remind us.[6]

Of course the quintessential martyr who dies bearing witness (albeit through his various evangelical spokesmen) is Christ. And Calvary was indeed a fair enough metaphor for the existential cards that we're all dealt. But why should that be an experience reserved for the Son of God? And why wouldn't we be even better than he if we stuck around to stick it out with our fellow sufferers? That was Beckett's wager, in any case, and why he kept his school copy of Dante's *Purgatorio* with him, close at hand, throughout his life and why the "shades" that populate his late texts so closely resemble those of Dante's middle kingdom.[7]

The system of justice that we have inherited in the transition from pagan to Christian Greek, through Paul of Tarsis translating the untranslatable of Jewish to Christian law, through Roman law before it . . . not only requires witnesses willing and able to testify: these must be objective. Of what consists this precious objectivity? The objective witness is the

---

6 In addition to the Anidjar and Guénoun books previously cited, see Fethi Benslama, "La Représentation et l'impossible."

7 [. . .] *"Martira, martira!"*
   E lui vedea chinarsi, per la morte
   che l'aggravava già, inver' la terra,
   ma de li occhi facea sempre al ciel porte,
   orando a l'alto Sire, in tanta guerra,
   che perdonasse a" suoi persecutori,

   Purgatorio XV, 108–13

dispassionate witness. Although he is reputed to be a man equipped with feelings and has perceived the perpetration of the crime right there — on the body of his newly acquired, then immediately lost brother — he's been trained to "be a man" and put all emotion aside. This is as much as to say that the ideal witness is a mere thing, a vessel, an object to be utilized by the justice machine. The agony suffered by the victim he might have been and whom he can now only help in the mode of "it is too late" — that agony, that passion remains foreign to him. The passion of the martyr remains the domain of the martyr. And those remains remain at an objectifying distance to be exploited by justice, serving no (greater) ethical purpose.

Meanwhile, the utter martyr — the paradigmatic victim — is one who without having uttered so much as a word is murdered by gas, reduced to ash and smoke, carried off as far into oblivion as the wind will cooperate with the executioners. Primo Levi calls him the complete witness, whereas I prefer to reintroduce the slightest of slippages between witness and martyr in order to further understand their shared witnessness. The victim's status as witness is complete, says Primo Levi, because his capacity to bear witness has, in conformity with the plan, been definitively arrested. Those whom the SS machine somehow missed — the survivors — retain, in their reprieve, the possibilities of anamnesis and speech or muteness and oblivion. Yet even if these exceptions, in turn, take what they saw and felt with them to the grave of their bodies' natural demise, distinctions between the ones who died and the ones who live on are not so clear-cut. Something happens between what Primo Levi called "touching bottom" and the reprieve. The thought that before the executioner I am indistinguishable from the complete martyr haunts me and transforms me. The dead live on in the survivor and the survivor must face the inexorability of taxes and a natural death. In the meantime, hand in hand, the complete martyr becomes witness through the survivor, and the witness-bearing survivor a martyr of this secular faith.

The witness is also, apparently, a surviving martyr of what he witnessed on condition that some infinitesimal modicum of the event affects not the body but "only" the mind/imagination. For the demand of the law, for the requirements of established justice, Beckett's witness is of no use whatsoever. Heeding the rallying cry of "worstward ho!" Beckett's *one* heads "first [to] the bones," straining to hear "what it is the words [their marrow] secretes say" [11.4]. Under the law, the event always already took place in the past. Beckett asks, has always asked: What if the event is forever present, always a *now*? And, if so, Beckett has always asked further, Doesn't the difference between witness and martyr become asymptotic? Doesn't it become one in which both maintain each other in life? For poetry and an ethics possible "after Auschwitz" (Adorno) and perhaps for a form of justice in accordance with such an ethics, Beckett's worstward bent witness is just what Primo Levi discovered he had become through his practice of testimony. In guiltily striving to maintain a radical differential from the *Muselmann*, this Jew had fused with the *other* Semite.

Beckett's characters appear and proceed in pairs. One is always apt to be beside oneself. *Worstward Ho* generalizes the rule that one is never just one: you are never left alone. One is always two, at the very least. One is always on the verge of the other — everyone, in general, Everyman, *l'on*. But is the relationship of one to the other one with me a relationship of perfect equality and reciprocity? No, of course not: one always preys on the other. The other is alive for me only to the extent that bones may yet have something nourishing in them.[8] This is the one in whom I have a stake, on whom I depend for my own life. He, in and on me as well. Those remains allow me to remain as witness: the martyr nourishes the witness causing him to cherish and preserve the gift of life everywhere.

In *Worstward Ho*, Beckett imagines a schema in which martyrdom ("worsening") is reunited with the capacity for witnessing without this reunion sounding the witness's death knell. Lessening the distance between me and you, *worrying* the differend,[9] heading worstward with the rallying cry "ho!" means directing ourselves "on back" to our origin as witness-martyrs, to the bare bones of what it means to be in relation to what we fear most: the vision of my own death as I decipher it on the body of my brother. This is a true one-on-one relationship — a martyr-on-witness and witness-on-martyr reciprocity. Primo Levi toiled his entire adult life to map out this schema in a pure, rational, dispassionate language — one that was, however, no less repetitive, in certain ways, than Beckett's idiosyncratic poetry that shuttles between French and English. Meanwhile, etymology — at which Beckett was wicked good — speculates that the Greek μάϱτυϱ may, just may, have come from a Sanskrit root meaning "to bear in mind." "Bear in mind" . . . What could be a more basic metaphor for what our wit does? Our wit or witness — older English words for consciousness itself, our "so-said seat of all." Let us bear witness.

---

8 My allusion, of course, is to Rabelais' famous parable in the Prologue to *Gargantua* about the dog encountering a marrow-bone (1534, 207).

9 I will use the term "differend" throughout in the sense lent it by Jean-François Lyotard: "I would like to call a *différend* the case where the plaintiff is divested of the means to argue and becomes for that reason a victim" (1996, 9). Bill Readings gave the following helpful expansion of Lyotard's definition: "A point of difference where the sides speak radically different or heterogeneous languages, where the dispute cannot be phrased in either language without, by its very phrasing, prejudging the issue for that side, being unjust" (1991, xxx).

1.3 "al fondo"

Ill till still.[1]

"Worstward ho!" is Beckett's rallying cry with which his 1982 text leads us "[i]nto the hell of all" [17.5]. We — no, *l'on*, everyone, including Beckett — make up this avant-garde. Taking command means expecting the worst, yet never dwelling in it — consciously, that is, "in" life. It is in endlessly striving that we are at our best. The unacceptable goal of the untranslatable rallying cry is that state beyond wretchedness whose name is death. To live on, *l'on* must hold on, maintain at the threshold, ever vigilant. Considered as a set of events, feelings, and circumstances whose metaphorical topography ranges from hillock to deepest abyss, life's endpoint in a worstward trajectory would be rock bottom. Events and circumstances for the poor soul appear as bad as bad can be; his feelings, so full of dread that life would hold no reason nor hope for living. The bottom is where brutality of badness pervades and madness takes over all sanity. But the touch is ever so brief. The one who strives worstward *touches* bottom, but musters the wherewithal to escape being flattened there. He knows virtual annihilation, but recovers just enough to remain before the threshold — Blanchot's *"pas au-delà."* "Half *no* but *on* the verge," writes Beckett in *Still* (240–41; my emphasis). Almost is all less all. Beckett's model man strides "into the hell of all" but always, immediately, emerges alive "out from the hell of all" [17.5].

Into, then out. Beckett proffers the two moves in immediate succession. But what an experiential gap there is *between* them! "Unknow better now. Know only no out of" [4.3] registers the incomprehensibility within knowing that one has touched or been touched, of sensing at the edge of knowledge that the event of death may occur in an instant, that the lowest of blows may fall, but that it may also blow over in a flash. For the witness who comes to know and to survive (in) martyrdom, there is no alternative than recovery, of consciousness, of the name, "one," of speech. "No choice but up if ever down" [7.4]. But just as the paintbrush leaves its trace on the canvas, the blow leaves its mark: having touched bottom leaves one forever between the witness, as we conventionally think it, and the martyr,

---

1 A "progression" of my own facture in the manner of the late works of Beckett.

as we have forgotten it. He who has touched bottom remains in the crux of the fold joining martyr to witness. It is never quite clear if the Beckett character who is "*crevé*" is dead or just dead tired.

An asymptotic approach to my limit (as other) is what Primo Levi, from one end to the other of his oeuvre names "reaching" or "touching bottom" — *toccare al fondo*. If "the bottom" be the other I might have been, then *Worstward Ho* doggedly advocates for just such an approach to my fellow man: I will be I *and* the other — "not I" — in a lifelong project of lessness. Levi names that other that I approach, yet cannot become if I am to survive, for now, for the sake of continued consciousness, so that I may keep my wits about me, the "complete" witness. There are other names, more disturbing still, for this altogether other who is nevertheless, somehow, "nohow" me. Contradiction, however, fundamentally disrupts Levi's consistent correlation of "touching bottom" and survival. The faculty that allows me to maintain my approach as an asymptotic differential is the faculty of cunning, knack or know-how — a kind of wit that is the product of the imagination's labor.

As early as an early passage in his very first book, *If This Be a Man*, Primo Levi evokes a category of *Häftling* (or prisoner) known in *Lager* lingo as *die Muselmänner* — disturbingly, "Muslims." The evocation is rather laconic. It is a particularly dramatic episode of this book of 1947 and the passage does not introduce any conceptual development of note. Nor is Levi the only writer of survivor narratives to mention *die Muselmänner*: Bruno Bettelheim, Filip Müller, others have as well. It is nevertheless notable, in passing, that this passage appears in the chapter of *If This Be a Man* entitled "The Drowned and the Saved" that Levi recycled some forty years later as the main title for one of his last and most important books.

After the publication, in 1998, of Giorgio Agamben's controversial *Remnants of Auschwitz*, discussions of *die Muselmänner* multiplied and inspired a groundswell of reactions ranging from the indignant to the sycophantic.[2] However one reads it, Levi's very first evocation of "Muslims" — almost in passing — is a fascinating mixture of repulsion and attraction. It is a phenomenological description of the feeling a Jew had at the instant he touched bottom — an instant in which he simultaneously cast a fleeting glance at and glanced away from a Jew altogether othered by the epithet "Muslim." "Altogether othered" in the special sense that the Muslim is the "other" Semite.[3] Yet, I think I can show that Levi comes to

---

2 Most of the bibliography and many of the elements contributing to this debate may be found in Mesnard and Kahan 2001. Although their study is exhaustive and their side in their differend with Agamben cogently argued, that book is not without its inaccuracies — one example being the imputation of the term "complete witness" to Agamben, when the expression is already to be found in *The Drowned and the Saved*.
3 Cf. again, Benslama, Anidjar, and Guénoun.

terms with his extreme ambivalence vis-à-vis another human being who is, in fact, *himself* in terms that allow us a theoretical preview of what the witnessness of all of us is.

> All the *Muselmänner* who finished in the gas chambers have the same story; *they followed the slope down to the bottom*, like streams that run down to the sea. [. . .] Their life is short, but their number is endless; they, the *Muselmänner*, the drowned, form the backbone [*nerbo*] of the camp, an anonymous mass, continually renewed and always identical, of *non-men* who march and labour in silence, *the divine spark dead* within them, already *too empty* to really suffer. *One hesitates to call them living: one hesitates to call their death death* [. . .] They crowd my memory with their faceless presences, and if I could enclose all the evil of our time in one image, I would choose this image which is familiar to me: *an emaciated man, with head dropped and shoulders curved, on whose face and in whose eyes not a trace of a thought is to be seen.* (1996, 90; 1989, 81–82; my emphasis)[4]

I have highlighted not only that which Levi borrows directly and explicitly from Dante's *Inferno*, but also the disturbing expressions by which the Jew "others" himself for survival by using "Muslim" as an epithet. This is not to deny that Levi indeed "saw" his own death once and forever at the moment of his glance away. He did so by means of a series of *mental* glances altogether more powerful than the aborted ocular one.[5]

The bottom, in any case, is the worst, not infinitesimally approached, but *reached*. So, of what bottom does Levi speak, here? Of what is this bottom the bottom? It is where the minimal overall conditions for an individual to sustain himself in life ebbs irremediably. If we think of our overcoming the hardest knocks that we suffer in life as bootstrapping ourselves, then at the bottom on which we have been crushed, the bootstrap is either broken or we no longer have the strength to pull it. Levi's image is clear: the drowned, the vast masses of non-survivors were precipitated to the bottom and were bootstrap-disabled there. Once having touched the bottom, there is nowhere else to go, no ascendance is possible. For these

---

4 Primo Levi, *Se questo e un uomo* [1947] (Torino: Giulio Einaudi, 1958). The work was first translated into English by Stuart Woolf as *If This Be a Man* (New York: Orion Press, 1959), then retitled — aberrantly or logically, according to the logic of the culture industry — as *Survival at Auschwitz* (New York: Touchstone, 1996). Page references are to this English edition, but the passages I read are so crucial to Levi's thinking that the reader may wish to refer to the original Italian.

5 For this point I am indebted to Edward S. Casey and an idea he developed in the 15 May 2002 session of my seminar at the Collège International de Philosophie. See also Casey's *The World at a Glance*.

emaciated men "in whose eyes not a trace of a thought is to be seen," who are definitively "down," there is no hope of "up."

More important still, would Primo Levi have agreed with Samuel Beckett? Can *he who goes on* accompany *he who touches bottom* — the "Muslim" — yet escape the death that is but a breath away? Going back to the series of images touched off by the metaphor of "being crushed against the bottom," What does it mean to touch this bottom? And what are the consequences of merely scraping it momentarily as opposed, for example, to remaining there? In touching bottom, does an individual still stand a chance to escape sinking beyond its level and drowning? It is urgent that we ask these questions because if there is any doubt in the text of 1947 as to what touching bottom means, in a much later Levi text, there is none. According to the logic of the phrase's context in *The Drowned and the Saved*, touching bottom is the definitive and absolute cessation of all life forces. It is not simply a minimum (which might, after all, be sustainable), but an irremissible zero point. The touch is not, more precisely, an approach, but an actual definitive contact and final resting place.

In *If This Be a Man*, Levi describes how minutes before being tattooed with the number 174 517, he and the hundreds of other *Häftlinge* with whom he had been freighted off to Auschwitz were disinfected and forced to run naked through "the icy blue snow of dawn" from showers to a barracks. There, after dressing and with some time to consider the new configuration of "reality" that had befallen them, Levi realizes that *"we* have reached the bottom" (1996, 26; 1989, 23; emphasis mine). In *The Drowned and the Saved*, however, a book published some forty years later, and where three pages of terse prose deliver a veritable theory of the witness, Levi blatantly asserts the precise contrary: the tiny minority of survivors to which he belongs goes on breathing life today precisely because "we did *not* touch the bottom" (1986, 83; emphasis mine). This later book (almost too late, as it turns out, if we think of it in terms of his impending apparent suicide) provides no indication that this assertion — that Levi and his cohorts "did *not* touch bottom" — is meant to rectify any erroneous previous one. No greater "play" — if we accept this word as a powerfully polysemic understatement for the "margin" we call "error" — can be imagined on such a fundamental issue. Imagination — precisely imagination — is, as I argue here, at the very heart of the stakes entailed in harnessing the power of play's excess. Witness and martyr find their asymptotic point of linkage at this instant at life's rock bottom. There and then is sparked the ethical intersubjectivity that we value so much in survival narratives. Substituting this very worst taking place in the real by its being imagined and retaining it as a force will be the project of *Witnessness*, Part 3. However close Levi's and Beckett's visions of human-ity may appear in some respects, the part of Dante's work that is nearest the soul of Beckett's oeuvre is *Purgatorio*, whereas for Levi it is decidedly and expressly *Inferno*. *Inferno* is real, unmitigated hell; in *purgatorio*, there is margin for error and the salutary work of the imagination.

Within those same three pages published in 1986, the wiggle room that proved just sufficient to allow 174 517 to recover human identity and eventually go back to calling himself Primo Levi is starkly expressed as follows: "I must repeat: *we*, the survivors, are not *the true witnesses*. [. . .] *Those* who saw the Gorgon [. . .] the drowned [are] *the complete witnesses* [*i testimoni integrali*]" (1986, 83–84; emphasis mine).[6] It is within this conceptual margin for error — between *complete* witnesses and, the implication would be, *partial* witnesses, between *them* and *us* — that Levi provides *us* with the most valuable theory of the witness, in my view, that is currently available to philosophy.

Forty years after surviving Auschwitz, and less than a year before his death, Primo Levi explains in *The Drowned and the Saved* — in the plainest, starkest of terms — how his existence as witness is a status both intimately related to *and* in necessary contradistinction with that specific category of *Häftling* known as the *Muselmann*. As readers familiar with Primo Levi expect, he theorizes all this cogently and cool-headedly. But this sangfroid and cogency are, as so many observed traits about everything, both true and misleading: *true*, thanks to Levi's characteristically limpid and dispassionately scientific style; *misleading*, because parataxis intervenes to add some unexpected undecidability. And *untrue*, especially, because of the blatant contradiction Levi inscribes in his descriptions of the descent to the bottom, to the depths of sustainable existence.

My religious friend had told me that I survived so that I could bear witness. I have done so, as best I could, and I also could not have not done so; and I am still doing so, whenever the opportunity presents itself; but the thought that this testifying of mine could by itself gain for me the privilege of surviving and living for many years without serious problems troubles me because I cannot see any proportion between the privilege and its outcome.

I must repeat: *we*, the survivors, are not the true witnesses. This is an uncomfortable notion of which I have become conscious little by little, reading the memoirs of others and reading mine at a distance

---

6 This bears comparison with one of Filip Müller's more poignant observations: "The occasional contact with prisoners outside the block — though, of course, strictly forbidden — but also the more humane attitude of our four *Kapos*, led me once more to think about my future, and to ponder on the amazing resilience of human nature: for the monstrous mass destruction had by no means ceased; our own deaths seemed certain and indeed imminent; and yet, even the slightest improvement in our living conditions was enough for all this to be pushed into the background" (Müller 1979, 53).

of years. *We survivors* are not only an exiguous but also an anomalous minority: *we* are those who by their prevarications or abilities or good luck *did not touch bottom*. *Those* who did so, *those* who saw the Gorgon, have not returned to tell about it or have returned mute. But *they* — the *Muselmänner*, the drowned, the complete witnesses — *they* are the ones whose deposition would have had a general significance. *They* are the rule, *we* are the exception. [. . .]

We who were favored by fate tried, with more or less wisdom, to recount not only our fate but also that of the others, indeed of the drowned; but this was a discourse "on behalf of third parties," the story of things seen at close hand, not experienced personally. The destruction brought to an end, the job completed, was not told by anyone, just as no one ever returned to describe his own death. Even if *they* had paper and pen, the drowned would not have testified because their death had begun before that of their body. Weeks and months before being snuffed out, *they* had already lost the ability to observe, to remember, to compare and express themselves. *We* speak in *their* stead, by proxy. (1989, 83–84; my emphasis; tr. modified)

This unabashedly insistent "we" resists the unity suggested in the preposition "one." An infinitesimally small detail in representation distinguishes the *Muselmann* from the altogether dead. They are called *Muselmänner* precisely because, having given up, no longer knowing or feeling anything — *apparently* — they teeter on the brink. But, again, precisely because they are as close to being dead as the living can imagine, they infinitely preoccupy the performing witness — infinitely more than the millions of altogether dead that Levi names *complete* witnesses. If any moment in Levi's *Urtext*, *If This Be a Man* can be said to exude shame, it is his brief account of how intolerable the sight of the *Muselmann* was. Reading that account, one vicariously feels the mortification felt by someone averting his gaze as if at the point of betraying his very self, replicated before him. We might contrast, in passing, Levi's ashamed denial of his semitic alter ego with that paradigmatic Beckettian couple formed by Mercier and Camier who collapse "simultaneously, as one man, without preconcertation and in perfect interindependency" (1974, 102).[7]

What motivates the contradiction inscribed, framed, and held out to us so blatantly with regard to "touching bottom?" Is touching bottom an asymptotic approach to a limit or is it indeed, as the metaphor of "touch" would imply, a contact? May "touching bottom" be — as contradictory

---

7 "Interindependency" is not only a "comic elevation of language" with respect to the original French "*dépendance*," as Steven Connor points out (1988, 180), its convoluted logic reinforces how these individuals conserve their autonomy despite the fusional nature of their intersubjectivity.

as the notion may appear — *both* a contact *and* an approach? If so, under what conditions may it be so? If we provisionally accept that "to touch bottom" concerns not only the body subjected to extreme conditions but also what we call consciousness (but with no specificity in regard to *whose* consciousness we are talking about), then we are compelled to reflect on manners variously deployed to differentiate forms and functions of consciousness — what early and pre-modern philosophy called "the five wits," to wit: common wit or common sense, imagination, fantasy, estimation, and memory. And we begin to ask ourselves if it is not possible that one can temporarily be deprived of whatever reason one has managed to amass in a brief life while preserving the imagination from being scathed. In the case of someone whose touch of the bottom was an approach of asymptotic degree, the reservoir of the imagination might turn out to be the preserved, unaltered retreat (*repaire, demeure*) for our capacity to witness under dire conditions. This line of thinking might also allow us to envision how witnessness functions both under conditions of extreme duress and constraint (being forced to touch bottom) or under voluntary or quasi-voluntary conditions of empathy.

The anomalous nature of the "we" to which Levi says he belongs is a function of having been protected by the presence in or around their being of three conditions — either singly or simultaneously — "we are those who by prevarications or abilities or good luck did not touch bottom." Good luck is simply the secular correlate of Providence for the believer. Prevarication is a somewhat cowardly variety of ruse and its evocation undoubtedly has much to do with the shame that colors much of *The Drowned and the Saved*. For a number of reasons, not the least of which is that as reader, one plies the path where the artifice of reading is one's only guide, it is the presence of multiple *nesses* despite all adversity that should focus one's attention for the sake of maintaining oneself in life.

Touching bottom, the precise criterion for differentiating the anomalous witness from the complete witness, flash pans us back to the very first existential summary Levi gave on the state the SS imposed on the newly arrived *Häftling* who was not immediately gassed. Levi's descriptive summary comes in the second chapter of *If This Be a Man*. After being disinfected, beaten, and compelled to run "barefoot and naked" through the snow before donning the *Lager* rags, "we became aware that our language lacks words to express this offence, the demolition of a man. In a moment, with almost prophetic intuition, the reality was revealed to us: *we had reached the bottom [siamo arrivati al fondo]*" (1996, 26; 1989, 23). But, as we have already seen, forty years later, in the book-length expansion of the chapter in *If This Be a Man* where the *Muselmann* first appeared, Levi writes: "We survivors are [. . .] those who [. . .] did *not* touch bottom." This "we" — the "we" reappearing after a forty-year interval — is constituted of the *same identities*. Either they did touch bottom or they didn't. Is this a flagrant contradiction? Forgetting? *Dichtung oder Wahrheit?* We are compelled to allow that in some fundamental way, Levi and the surviving cohort did not touch bottom and, further, that their consequential anomaly is in perfect harmony with the concomitant declaration that he (they) is (are) not (a) "true" witness(es).

"True" witnesses, then, are always others, others who cannot speak, others that are altogether other, "those who saw the Gorgon," those who are in permanent contradistinction to me and to you, those who sunk in the SS shit. And we who are reading this text so closely, we who are in no way among that other "we" to which Levi belonged, we are before the unveiled "true" witness that even surviving witnessing witnesses can only become by proxy. So that we understand, in spite of this non-coincidence as well — drastic, absolute, and vital ("They are the rule, we are the exception"), that Levi was able to produce testimony, to bear his witnessness forth as witness borne by his dead brethren. So that for one who reads, for one who as reader becomes imaginer and, as such, is albeit in a position of non-coincidence vis-à-vis Levi (though a less drastic non-coincidence than with the *Muselmann*), this is the promise of one's own witnessness.

We cannot, in all good conscience, count ourselves among that *other we* called "they" any more than Levi could. And yet the hypothesis of *Witnessness* is that an innate aptitude for operating as a complete witness must be measured in relationship to this non-coincidence. "Touching bottom" will be the standard of that measure. Beckett's project was to bring the other on home, shamelessly, poetically. "I want to bring poetry into drama, a poetry which has been through the void and makes a new start in a new room-space" (quoted in Knowlson, 477). Drama is history in all its hellishness and poetry, the saving grace. One can touch bottom and live to tell about it on condition that some infinitesimal part of the event is reserved for the imagination. The skull of another, occupied by me, is the room-space where witnessness operates.[8]

---

8 One of the most sympathetic faces among the witnesses who testify for Claude Lanzmann in the making of *Shoah* is Filip Müller. Müller was a Czech Jew who lived on even though he had served in the SS's *Sonderkommando* at Auschwitz. The *Sonderkommando*'s job was to drag gassed bodies out of the death chambers. They lived on literally at the threshold of annihilation, plumbing the depths of "all the last moments" (Didi-Huberman 2003, 13; 2008, 4).

1.4 error's margin

No choice but up if ever down. [7.4]

To ask what is at stake in your becoming a witness is really to ask what knack or knick of time comes between you and another whose fate might be or might have been yours. Wherever betweenness marks the essence of a relationship, there is always a margin of error. Wit is that sweet nothing where the witness expected naught. "Margin of error" names action's last recourse within minimal space and minimal time. Whoever can become a witness does so by assuming a state of liability to this particular play between self and other. When we follow Primo Levi's analysis of himself in his capacity of witness, we discover that a characteristic of that state is a discrepancy with respect to some lost wholeness. Play comes into play between two entities meant or thought to fit, two of a kind whose failure to coincide is simply due to their twoness. Yet discovery of this margin of error is fundamental to your coming and my coming to being in our shared witnessness. And precisely this sort of out-of-jointness with respect to some all-too-intangible complete and final totality is necessary for witnesses like Primo Levi to exist and speak. This inadequacy that is ours corresponds to the excess of play present between what becomes Levi's definitive portrait of the witness in *The Drowned and the Saved* (1986) and what he wrote in *If This Be a Man* (1947).

One kind of margin inherent in error and whose degree is "sufficient," as science puts it, is a *necessary* play, insofar as the witness who goes on to bear witness does so as survivor standing in vital distinction to "the just ones" or "complete" witnesses. But another of error's margins, of which there tends to be too much — too much, at least, to satisfy the demands of realist consistency, derives from the fact that if shortly after having returned to the tranquility of home in Turin, Levi could write eloquently about how he had "touched the bottom" in Auschwitz, it is precisely, he would explain forty years later, because he and other survivors had *not* touched the bottom that they were able to become witnessing witnesses. This *excess* of tolerance is "unreasonable" or "unimaginable," yet is apparently required for witnesses to be able to bear witness — necessary if we are to continue to deem desirable the bearing of testimony.

Tolerance is a tolerable measure of looseness in the relationship between (or among) parts, bodies, entities, monads, if you will. The very success of

Primo Levi's theorization of the witness is precisely the consequence of the fact that his assertions, descriptions, arguments, and other such discursive elements *fail* to satisfy demands for consistency, logical purity, and "good form." Survival or, in Beckett-speak, "going on," is a matter of such play, such collapse, such vagaries of tolerance. "Try again. Fail again. Fail better" [1.4]. As Primo Levi teaches, some loss in translation, a gap, void or "grot" might, perhaps, widen into an abyss or a differend. A differend appears inherent to situations that beg for a witness. Mindfulness of the gap or error's margin, of which Primo Levi has left us the most eloquent and striking illustrations, forms the basis for the concept of witnessness.

The margin of error that *is* the witness and that Primo Levi conceptualizes despite himself, in a state of *being beside himself*, is echoed in Jean-François Lyotard's, *The Differend*. Elsewhere, I have identified at least four guises for the witness as Lyotard presents them in that magisterial work of 1983.[1] Yet as myriad as Lyotard makes the position appear, the witness always returns to constituting a single platform for what he terms a "phrasing" that is salvageable from the disaster of names perpetrated in the name of a monolithic rendering of "reality" through acts of physical violence and acts of discourse — *Auschwitz* and other such crimes against humanity. Leaving a definitive and complete portrait of the witness in the suspense of quasi-impossibility, one of the witness's avatars that Lyotard suggests will be most helpful to us as we begin to trace the ways in which wit and witnessness form the generic, model witness according to Samuel Beckett is one that he might have enjoyed our calling the "wee 'we'." Here, again, is Primo Levi in 1986:

> I repeat: we survivors are not the true witnesses. [. . .] *We* survivors are a minority that is not only small but also abnormal: *we* are those who, through prevarication, knack or luck, did not touch the bottom. [. . .] They are the rule; *we* are the exception. (82; my emphasis)

In *The Differend*, the far more pessimistic Lyotard whispers terms under which a local, basic, primitive, weakly linked we-subject might be salvaged from the disaster. This "wee 'we'" appears at the eleventh hour, very much as the trio of motley characters that inhabits *Worstward Ho* does. This minimal, hesitant first person plural, a near degree zero of community, subsists at the outer limits of precariousness. Yet it hovered already at the threshold of the main body of Lyotard's text, already in the tongue-in-cheek "Reader's Guide" which plotted its coordinates in the form of "reader" and "author" (1988, xiv–xv). The introduction of the witness as third party — a *terstis* made up of a tenuously linked

---

1 Cf. Robert Harvey, "Témoinité" (2008).

"we" — calls for ploddingly careful reading: "[the third party] is the reflective movement of [an] impossibility, i.e., the dispersion that comes to self-knowledge and arises from the annihilation in the affirmation of nothingness. The *we* made up, at least, of *I* who writes and *you* who read" (1988, 103; my emphasis on "we").

Amplifying what Lyotard murmurs, here, seemingly despite himself, a few remarks . . . No hermeneutic excavation is necessary to determine that the impossibility *The Differend* is obsessed with is that of the "totalization of I's under the name 'Auschwitz'" (1983, §158). A grammatically affirmative expression for this absolute negation perpetrated at the heart of rational humanism would be this: Auschwitz definitively atomized the human subject, where "human subject" meant the possibility of unifying of all humans. With the death of the human community comes the death of humanism. But with minimal *ness* and know-how remaining, is "death" "definitive?" For the rare survivor recreating an exceptional and heretofore-thought-to-be-impossible "we," the experience of arising, Lazarus-like, from *Auschwitz* is an experience whose best descriptive approximation was given by Kant in describing the recovery of sense through the experience of the sublime. Eloquent pages in Lyotard's *Heidegger and "the jews"* convincingly draw this parallel (1990, 13, 31–32f.). Just as usefully, however, we could look again at Primo Levi who "skillfully" (his own word) avoided laying eyes on the Gorgon by arresting his gaze.

That skill (enhanced by luck), followed by guilt, precisely measures the felicitous margin of error between survivor and drowned. Facing the Gorgon's face is the experience of bald, irremediable terror: the all but fallible harbinger of annihilation.[2] Skillful avoidance in the presence of the Gorgon leads, on the other hand, directly into an experience of the sublime and the mental, ethical creations which that experience may instigate. Kant taught that with any experience of the sublime, the attendant and subsequent feeling — a *thought* — comes by intervention of the reflective judgment. An abyss — "the affirmation of nothingness" — a gap in which a tenuous "we" may form is open, already, between the gift of what has been written and the promise of reading. Error's margin, which at first seemed excessive, becomes manageable, then workable in the recovery of imaginative skills. Aided by imagination and bolstered by time for recovery, the mind can come to terms with having been beside itself without reduplicating the doomed "human" model.

---

2 A handful of the so-called *Muselmänner* survived the camps and even regained the capacity to speak of their experience. This is one of the fundamental contradictions of Agamben's *Remnants of Auschwitz* — one that he nonetheless willingly inscribes by adding the testimonials of surviving *Muselmänner* in the appendix of that book.

1.5   vicariousness

Say a body. [. . .] To be in. Move in. [. . .] Only in. Say in. On in. Still. [1.3]

Witnessness is an affective osmosis through which I might listen differently — you through me, me through you, in order to spare us both — that is sometimes referred to by the rather unfortunately deprecatory expression, "vicarious experience." With stoic directness and characteristic lucidity, Primo Levi declared this proximate approximation of the other thus: "We speak in their stead, by proxy."

The poverty of our usual understanding of vicariousness is that any feeling of pleasure the experience entails is turned exclusively back to benefit the subject of the experience, stroking and flattering the ego of the vicar. Whereas the stirrings of becoming-witness that are touched off by reading the other in a universal, all-encompassing sense, is akin to the responsibility to all others before me that Emmanuel Levinas describes as coming to me in the night before fully recovering myself.[1] This suggests that mundane, egocentric vicariousness must evolve toward empathy through the accumulation of additional qualities.

Given the body considered as the dwelling place (among organs and muscles and other paraphernalia) of consciousness and the soul, then imagine a body other than yours as a place toward which your mind is inexorably, despite all, attracted. That's Darl getting so far into Tull that Tull feels like he's looking at himself. That's also Faulkner in writing *As I Lay Dying* — lest we ever forget — creating Tull and Darl.[2]

The skid row bum who has *scraped* rock bottom. That touch, no other.

---

1 Dostoevsky writes the following in *The Brothers Karamazov*: "Each of us is guilty before everyone for anyone, and I more than the others." Marie-Anne Lescourret has called Levinas' repeated use of this quotation as "fetishistic" (1994, 46–47). See, *inter alia*, Levinas' *Otherwise Than Being*, Chapter V, p. 146. Toumayan 2004 provides a thoroughgoing analysis of Levinas' use of the Dostoevsky quote and of variant interpretations on what Dostoevsky might have meant.

2 Tull says of Darl, "He is looking at me. He dont say nothing; just looks at me with them queer eyes of hisn that makes folks talk. I always say it aint never been what he done so much or said or anything so much as how he looks at you. It's like he had got into the inside of you, someway. Like somehow you was looking at yourself and your doings outen his eyes. (1984 [1930], 81)

Go there. Move on in. Then think about how this vantage has changed
your perspective. Think about what it means to you, for you, to him, and
for him for you to see things his way. With respect to the dead and out of
respect for the dead, you have become a busy hermit crab apprehending
the world from the vantage point of what your still living soul mates could
become if you weren't there to protect them.[3]

George W. Bush hasn't said much of late, but he was once in the habit
of declaring his ability — not unlike that additional talent of his of seeing into the soul of other great leaders — to feel for the young men and
women fighting to protect US freedom in Iraq. By this we were supposed
to understand him to mean that he could experience feeling in their place,
that he could feel what they felt because he possessed such a highly
developed faculty of vicariousness. In repeating that declaration, I think
he would have liked the public to believe that this ability enabled him to
empathize with the soldiers and thereby somehow ease their experience
of war by their knowing that the man who had been elected to the highest office in the country on whose side they were fighting was somehow
there, with them. If being a witness gets one into the higher reaches of our
ethical possibilities and vicariousness is one of the functions that enables
the witness, then sincerity must somehow underpin empathy and real
protection must somehow be part of its effect.

If even the likes of George W. Bush could invoke it, then something
like an instinct for vicariousness must be absolutely fundamental to homo
sapiens. Consider, for a moment, the case of a very strange text by Maurice
Blanchot, entitled *The Instant of My Death*. The experience of asymptotic
approach to death in someone else's boots, followed by recovery of life
is a straightforward illustration of what Blanchot meant in another book
of his by "the step not beyond" (*le pas au-delà*). If you're ever so near to
a fellow human who dies that you feel that you too have died, but then
you recover from that horrific belief to the point of understanding what
actually happened, you have experienced that moment of equivalence
between "the young man" and Maurice Blanchot, who signed *The Instant
of My Death*. And it was then that Blanchot realized a capacity for vicariousness enabling him to see his own witnessness. It was this or something
quite close to it that led Blanchot to state unabashedly that the voice of
The Unnamable is the voice of literature itself (Hill 2004, 72).

To recover his self-authorization to say "I" after eluding death as the
other inside him, Maurice Blanchot had to restore a certain safe distance
— error's margin, let's say, *du jeu* — from "he" who had his scrape with
death. Primo Levi, Filip Müller, Bruno Bettelheim, other survivors, all

---

3 Citing Blanchot, *L'Entretien infini* 565–66: "The narrating voice that is inside only to
the extent that it is outside, at a distance without distance, cannot embody itself [. . .]
Let us (for amusement) call it spectral, ghostlike" (Hill 2004, 72).

found themselves haplessly tagging the hopeless *Muselmänner*; in order to write *The Instant of My Death*, Blanchot must have also preserved or recovered the ability to go back and visit a very similar empty shell that was left standing there, for all intents and purposes devoid of life. "Hence another. Another place where none," writes Beckett [4.3]. In beating around the bush as to what was really meant by *Muselmann*, the absurd etymology of "shell men" has even been speculated as a possibility. As absurd as that origin is, however, there is some poignant truth-value in the image of entering another as if he were hollow. If the witness who testifies may be said to be "on" when he performs, then the vicarious experience he has in relation to the victim might, in a wretched poetic echo of "on," be designated by the preposition, "in." "On in," Beckett beckons us.

And, at the same time, like Tull by Darl, I am inhabited by you. I feel your presence as a look, of course: not watching over me (you're not a god), but watching *for* me, through my eye sockets, substituting for my eyes. You're under my study, but I'm your understudy. No superiority, perfect reciprocity. The soul was said in medieval times, to be reached by a look penetrating me at my pupils, as if that gaze were a pair of arrows striking these targets. I'm your hostage and my soul is your dwelling place: you come and go at will. I am preserved in life under your watch, your wake, in me. And this fact of my life is that (or at least *could* be that) of every one of us: "As the soul once. The world once" [9.3]. Once this is good for one, it is good for *l'on*. And this only has to be good for one *once*. If this can happen only once to my soul, between our souls, then we will have regained the world for *ones* as it once was.

The life-preserving condition of some vital part of an event occurring through imagination is a function of one's capacity to live vicariously.

> Say a body. Where none. No mind. Where none. That at least. A place. Where none. For the body. To be in. Move in. Out of. Back into. No. No out. No back. Only in. Say in. On in. Still. [1.3]

Do I need to have a third party present in mind, memory or imagination in order to experience the other vicariously? How does proxy experience or vicariousness become generalized empathy? Or what, at least, is the relationship between them?

What if those who recount near-death experience all actually died? (This, after all, is what *Auschwitz* was designed to do. This is why even the ranks of the *Sonderkommando*, of which Filip Müller was a survivor, were radically replaced at regular intervals.) What if all that was left were their memoirs, their testimonials, their remnants? (This is what "Holocaust studies" ultimately tries to prepare us for.) What kind of witnesses might *readers of the witnessing* that those women and men bore become, in their turn, through their reading? (This is what the question, "What species of witness are we?" means.) Dare those readers remaining through the vicarious power of reading call themselves, in turn, witnesses? Dare we, if we count ourselves among that readership, call ourselves witnesses? The question is not so much that of knowing *of what* you and I may be a witness in this second-hand witnessing. The question has always been: How do I (and How may I) become a witness at all if I was only there (i.e. at the event, *in* the event) by the proxy of the text? Even Filip Müller, as one of the "witnesses of all the last moments" (Didi-Huberman 2003, 13; 2008, 4), was still only a hair's breadth from his own death. A further question will be, simply: Can I be a witness with no artifact whatsoever on which to rely?

There is no question of our ever being the absolute equal of those departed innocents. We are not their double: otherwise we too would be dead and thus unable any longer to resist death with anything, including our words. Rather, in learning how to substitute for their living presence, we can only hope to become the next best thing — no more than a little worse than a perfect surrogate. Of Malone and Sapo's mutual "slipping into" each other, Beckett first has the voice of *Malone Dies* say, "I shall try and make a little creature [. . .] And seeing what a poor thing I have made [. . .] I shall eat it" (1956, 226). Then, just a few lines on, we learn this: "I slip into him, I suppose in the hope of learning something." Not a phony or a fake supplanting the real thing (our sincerity is true because *we dwell* where *he was*), but a ghost, like the writer who brings forth the story of another.

There is a great tendency in us, despite endlessly repeated failures, to try to substitute for one another, to experience the world as we imagine the other experiences it. Whether or not this ness is impelled by innate virtue — as in the case of empathy — is contingent on other factors that take us beyond the witness into the realm of wit. If we share something, it is our vicarious bent, our vicariousness. Even though I may say to my friend, "Brother, I wouldn't want to be in *your* shoes," it is because I think I indeed *can* well imagine being in his shoes that I pay homage declaratively to the hombre's capacity for handling his dire situation. And since I pride myself in being his friend, I don't just proffer this admiration, only to walk away. We arrange to meet again, as soon as possible. I listen further and I at least *try* to make suggestions, based on a more or less vicarious assessment of his problems, for lines of flight, lines of fight.

Vicariousness actually begins in infancy, in our state of *infans*, when we are still quite dim vis-à-vis the adult — with all his chatter — that we will become (Lyotard 1988, 3–4). One may recall all the examples of sucking and substitution in Beckett's early trilogy. When mummy withdraws her breast, it's as hard on me as it is on her. But whereas she can rationalize the pain of her milk drying up with logos founded on language, all I've got is my scream. So to pacify me she gives me a dummy to suck on in

lieu of her nipple. This is undoubtedly my first lesson of vicariousness —
imposed from the outside world. And so I go on, as I must, for the first
of many times.

    Worstward Ho stages that of which Tull complains. Except that in
Beckett's late work consciousnesses are no longer named and dummies
are stones gathered at the seashore. This namelessness and aimlessness
turns out to be a legitimizing feature of the vicariousness that underpins
witnessness. It is very much like the situation of the viewer before photographs out of Auschwitz that Georges Didi-Huberman eloquently and
exhaustively describes in *Images in Spite of All*:

> Looking at them, we must neither dismiss them [. . .] nor "believe
> ourselves to be there" [. . .]. Imagination is not identification [. . .].
> To approach does not mean to appropriate. (Didi-Huberman 2003,
> 113; 2008, 88)

But instead of being wrought out of outrageous irresponsibility, out of the
chutzpah "to speak for the dead," which Claude Lanzmann has wrongly
accused Didi-Huberman of doing,[4] *Worstward Ho* provides a plan whereby
one can finally approach the living-who-will-be-dead-like-me without
appropriation. Or, as Dante put it at *Purgatorio* II, 76–78:

> *Io vidi una di lor trarresi avante*
> *per abbracciarmi, con si grande affetto,*
> *che mosse me a far lo somigliante.*[5]

---

4 Cf. Lanzmann, 2000.
5   I saw one of those spirits moving forward
     in order to embrace me — his affection
     so great that I was moved to mime his welcome.

1.6 talkativeness

Né 'l dir l'andar, né l'andar lui più lento
facea, ma ragionando andavam forte,
sì come nave pinta da buon vento;
e l'ombre, che parean cose rimorte,
per le fosse de li occhi ammirazione
traen di me, di mio vivere accorte.
E io, continüando al mio sermone,
disse: "Ella sen va sù forse più tarda
che non farebbe, per altrui cagione."

Purgatorio XXIV, 1–9[1]

Non lasciò, per l'andar che fosse ratto,
lo dolce padre mio, ma disse: "Scocca
l'arco del dir, che 'nfino al ferro hai tratto."

Purgatorio XXV, 16–18[2]

The chit-chattiness of Virgil and Dante as they worked their way up through *purgatorio*, ends up as dead silence on account of their separation and Dante's interlocutor's absence from the threshold of paradise. With his affable guide no longer at his side, Dante falls dumbfounded by beauty incarnate at the water's edge (XXVIII, 62). Letting oneself be transformed from talker into listener is one succinct and accurate way of understanding what Dante's pilgrimage between *inferno* and *paradiso* entails. Similarly,

---

1   Our talking did not slow our pace, our pace
not slow our talking; but conversing, we
moved quickly, like a boat a fair wind drives.
And recognizing that I was alive,
the shades — they seemed to be things twice dead — drew
amazement from the hollows of their eyes.
And I, continuing my telling, added:
"Perhaps he is more slow in his ascent
than he would be had he not met the other."
2   [. . .] But my dear father, though our steps
were hurrying, did not stop talking, for
he said: "The iron of the arrow's touched
the longbow; let the shaft of speech fly off."

Beckett's oeuvre may be understood in a nutshell as delimited by unfettered loquaciousness in its first two-thirds, and wizened quasi-silence or, to be quite precise, oozing at wit's end.[3] In the final prose works, critics even stand watch for the very word "word" . . .[4]

Yet whatever voice it is that speaks the words and the rudimentary sentences of *Worstward Ho*, it pronounces "say" some eighty-four times in the course of a forty-page text. A great many of those sentences begin with "say" — a syntax that usually indicates the use of the imperative mood. But does the voice of *Worstward Ho* command anyone to speak? — Yes and no. As with the voices of many other characters in Beckett's oeuvre, this one is prodding itself, spurring itself on. "Say" is the life-giving mantra of the weary and the damaged. Even if what is said will be "ill said," it will do. The goal is not perfect speech, emblematized by the elusive "killer word"; the point is not even to make do as if perfect expression might some day be attained. Error is as valuable as trial. The point is to keep on trying. Yet error matters not little, since without it the string of trials would come to an end. No systole without diastole.

Before the law, under the gaze of justice, the only witness of any use is one who can and does, eventually, testify. A witness unwilling to speak up is of no use whatsoever to civilized society. (But what has civilization ever cared about ethics?) Yet, during a trial in the middle of Werner Herzog's film, *Where the Green Ants Dream*, a man arises from the audience unsummoned and launches into an odd speech. His verbal gesture, his bodily demeanor, his proper dress and the sincerity of his voice all indicate that he is talkatively bearing witness. He's got lots to say and he says it. Perplexed, the judge queries the attorney for the plaintiff: "This man was presented to the court as a mute. He obviously can speak. Why was he not called as a witness?" "Your honor," the lawyer explains, "Mr. Balai-La is the last member of his group alive. He is called the mute because no one understands his language. He speaks, but no one hears him." A mute witness, however much we might sympathize with the story he wishes to tell, must be dismissed. For the law, the mute witness — a living, breathing oxymoron — is no witness at all.[5]

One talks before one can read. But you talk because prior to your own

---

3 "[O]oze is not equivalent to words," remarks Garin Dowd, "rather, ooze is the modality of words, their manner of being projected, expelled or shed" (2004, 333).
4 "From now on my words will fall short," Ruud Hisgen exclaims, "How inadequate are words, and how weak, to express the image in my head! And this image compares so poorly to what I saw, that even to call it poor is too much" (1998, 534).
5 *Wo die grünen Ameisen träumen* [*Where the Green Ants Dream*], dir. Werner Herzog, 1984. The definitive study of this film and its application to Lyotard's philosophy of the differend is Bill Reading's "Pagans, Perverts, or Primitives? Experimental Justice in the Empire of Capital" (1992).

effing, you were effed to.[6] You heard, then you listened, until you found
ways of matching audible coordinates on the grid by which you'd been
organizing your opening upon the world that began the day of parturi-
tion. You mastered the strange code of those giants that kept yapping at
you. Your readiness today — just about now — for becoming a conventional witness is a function of your talkativeness regardless of your ability
to read. To fill the role of conventional witness, all you need to do is see
(take "it" in), then say: nothing could appear easier. But when has bearing
witness ever delivered justice other than punctually, ephemerally?

If an accident occurs before your eyes and a third party is needed to
determine responsibility, you may be called upon to speak up. For the
occasion of a trial, in passing, you will be a witness. But what had you
done for justice up to that point? And what will you do for your fellow
Everyman (*l'on*) from now on, until you can no longer go on? That's,
after all, what being a permanent witness is. For your *ness* as witness to
come to the fore, you have to remember that you are readable before you
talk and that you must be readable for all. Loquaciousness characterizes
Beckett's classic stand-ins of the first manner, shall we say: Didi, Godo,
Hamm, Clov, Winnie, Krapp; taciturn legibility is the lot of the late shades
whose forerunners are the "I" and Bom of *How It Is* or even some of the
pairs barely perceptible in *Texts for Nothing*. Witnessness comes when we
master this liability of readerliness, when we recognize this passivity of
the other in me. Why be a part-time witness when you can get full-time
employment and make ends meet?

The sadistic Pozzo of *Waiting for Godot* barks the order "think, pig" to
his "lucky" partner/slave and logorrhea ensues. The incessant "say" of
Worstward Ho says so much and *does* even more. As imperative, it thrusts
its addressee up against the necessity of opening himself onto the world
by emitting approximations of his thought in the form of language. As
we perceive the world of events, we are forever making approximate
translations into prelinguistic formulations of what we read, in view of
producing maddeningly inaccurate words. The ethics of testimony allows
this trial by talking to include the error of merely plausible or evocative
utterances, as in the case Dori Laub has brought to our attention.[7] Whether
loquacious like Lucky or circumspect like the later anonymous ones, those
of Beckett's characters called upon to *say* do so either in inverse proportion
to the demand or unsatisfactorily with respect to the rules of realism.[8] In
this, again, Beckett's witnesses are much like the photographs studied

---

6 For my discussion of Beckett's bivalent use of the verb, "to eff," see pp. 134–8.

7 Dori Laub, "Bearing Witness or the Vicissitudes of Listening" (1992).

8 Rare descriptions of Beckett's own manner of speaking tempt us to consider the
   author as incarnating qualities of both Pozzo and Lucky's voices and speech pat-
   terns. Biographer John Knowlson reports this characterization by Clancy Sigal: "A

by Didi-Huberman whose "interplay of shadow and light [. . .] offers the equivalent of the way a witness might speak: the pauses, the silences, and the heaviness of the tone" (2003, 53–54; 2008, 36).

The voice of *Worstward Ho*, to the extent that one can still call it such, is altogether sparing. Its testimony (narrative) is almost not. It's as close to being mute as a literary informant dare be. That voice may be said to be surveying an imagination. But whose? It appears to test the limits of what imagination is capable of apprehending in and of the other, in a continual process of taking stock of its capacity as witness. Beckett offers this voice that speaks his errors and trials up as the voice of all, the voice of *l'on*. What can it mean, then, for the state of being witness that endless trials of approximation — failures, really, more or less — are favored over the ideal of certainty in a single monolithic truth, one view of one event? An answer might take the form of the relative truth that we find in Pirandello's *Così è si ve pare* or in Kurosawa's *Rashomon*. The answer is blowin' in the wind. Or the answer might be akin to the description, given with sudden intensity, of the Auschwitz prisoner revolt by one survivor who claims that she witnessed the destruction of four crematorium chimneys when only one, in fact, came down.[9] Though appearing in the usual position for the imperative, few occurrences of "say" in *Worstward Ho* convey the sense of a yacker's compulsion to yack. No, another compulsion drives *Worstward Ho*'s repetition of "say" — the compulsion to experiment without relent, to engage in the compulsion of the potent lifelong witness, to use the imagination. "Say," then, means "Let's try" or "Allow me to try" or "Bear with me a moment while I suggest that we might consider *x*" or "How about *y*?"

Is it not obvious to anyone who's had to listen to a gabber that what keeps his chatter-box going "on and on" is that his words — no matter how numerous, no matter how many are tried — can never do any better than to estimate in the most tentative and consciously inadequate way some perfect thought that we all know we have in our head? In *Texts for Nothing 2*, we read: "The words too, slow, slow, the subject dies before it comes to the verb, words are stopping too. Better off then than when life was babble? That's it, that's it, the bright side" (1995, 106). If you recognize yourself in that description, it's because the chatter-box is you, me, all of us. "No matter," though: just keep on saying — stating while introducing what you say with the second person imperative of what you're performing. Is it me or you who speaks when I introduce what I'm saying by "Say . . .?"

---

grainy, almost silent voice, a courteous Irish lilt and lisp, with a repressed, lean bark" (1996, 513).

9   Dori Laub comments extensively on the value as admissible testimony of this distorted memory (1992, 59).

Saying or essaying, trying is only half of an economy whose completeness defines *l'on*. One's wholeness, one's oneness is predicated on remembering that in infancy, one was once eminently sayable and, alas, far too often said. The reader of others will thus have to revert, at least partially, to this originary legibility. To make oneself legible as one's self is to allow the other to make one out. Or, more simply, as Blanchot famously put it in *The Infinite Conversation*, "to speak is not to see." Thus, Primo Levi's reading of his own death in a mental glance upon the body of the "Muslim" initiated a slow process of remembering his own legibility as witness-martyr. This is suggested by another sense of "say" when it introduces the sentence in *Worstward Ho*. Sometimes "Say!" is exclaimed as if to another whom the speaker is trying to revive or keep alive. Like splashing water on the face of a fellow who is down, fading — "Eh, Joe!" you say something like "Say something, man, anything!" to someone whose life, you fear, ebbs. As if saying were the last proof of life. Famous last words.

Authorization to speak as a conventional witness opens a vista of vicariousness similar to the experience of seeing oneself in mirrors facing each other in infinite regress. Recalling that the way we conceive of "witness" derives from the notion of a third party, we reassure ourselves of something much more important than the necessity of bearing witness, of baring, of blathering all: Primo Levi's writings were made "on behalf of third parties" (1986, 84), meaning that whosoever reads them becomes that third party. Whosoever reads what was witnessed — even by substitution — is drawn into the abyss *between* the martyr and the witness. Primo Levi was thus a talkative witness, much like early Beckett characters. In Beckett's case it is obvious that the talkativeness of his early surrogates gradually but inexorably gives way to taciturn availability for being deciphered "as if," Brian Finney observes, "the speaker were trying to bow out of his own performance" (1987, 66). By the same token, in a quite similar move, Primo Levi, by bestowing his writing on us as *his* third parties, his imaginative readers, moves all the talk of the early testimonials toward legibility and witnessness.

And so, when the vital core of an event has occurred in your mind/imagination, language fails you: you try and err but never quite succeed. Does the absence of others really count for so little? "Pah others, that's nothing, others never inconvenienced anyone," Beckett wrote, between dismissiveness and tolerance in the early 1950s, in *Texts for Nothing 2* (1995, 106). But, then again, he was swift to add that even in the absence of others "out there," they are always "in here," in the imagination: "there must be a few here too, other others, invisible, mute, what does it matter." Or, as he puts it in *Worstward Ho*, more cryptically, telegraphically, polysemically, "No matter."

1.7   betweenness

Since atwain. Two once so one. From now rift a vast. Vast of
void atween. [16.2]

Between the two fictions of hell and heaven, the netherworld best
describes the only life we're bound to know in actual, lived experience.
There is something terribly wrong with Giorgio Agamben's fundamental
definition of the "remnant of Auschwitz" as "neither the dead, nor the
survivors, neither the drowned, nor the saved, but what remains between
them" (2002, 164), for this evacuation of all living matter surrounding
the "limit" kills in the process the possibility for the remnant, as witness,
to ever speak to us. As possibility for any future humanity, Agamben's
remnant is truly void and mute — the opposite of the "light between
mind and truth" that Dante affirms always, imperturbably, as capable
of speech.[1]

Beckett's remnant, on the other hand, lives on in our shared *purgatorio*
and speaks possibilities for togetherness between martyr and witness.
Martyr and Witness, Man and Woman, Molloy and Watt, Mahood and
Worm . . . turn their initial letters on their sides and see them fit together
like hands interdigitating. They do not kiss in the mode of verticality: they
come together asymptotically, on a plane of horizontality, kept equal, on
a level playing field. "The photographic image," writes Didi-Huberman,
"arose in the fold between two impossibilities: the immanent death of
the witness and the certain unrepresentability of testimony" (2003, 15–16;
2008, 6). The position of third is that of the witness; the position, that is,
between next-to-nothingness and the wrongly supposed unrepresentability of testimony.

An Arabic proverb has it that if one possesses two languages one's

---

1   *Veramente a così alto sospetto*
     non ti fermar, se quella nol ti dice
     che lume fia tra 'l vero e lo 'intelletto.

                                        Purgatorio VI, 43–45

     But in a quandary so deep, do not
     conclude with me, but wait for word that she,
     the light between your mind and truth, will speak —

brainpower is doubled. If this is so, there are two types of men on this earth: bilingual and political. When we hear a man of politics claim that he can feel what the loved ones of lost soldiers feel, our senses immediately fathom the depth of his hypocrisy by his incapacity to range across the divide separating him from the idiom of death: monolingualism. Betweenness is beyond him. This man could never honestly and truly be beside himself. For Beckett, the vast reaches that separate me from you can never be collapsed, the divide gapes wider than either of us ever imagined. Yet the man doubled between two languages, unlike the man of politics, makes of that incommensurable void between you and me a dwelling place for all that pulsates in him, all that courses through his blood.

Between Beckett's two main languages, there is an adverb that he tried and tested early on, then quickly adopted definitively to illustrate in the *physical world* the relationship of symmetrical betweenness he envisioned for our *ethical world*. Toward the close of *Malone Dies*, the narrator implores his partner not to fret: "we must just accept ourselves as we are [. . .] Let us think of the hours when, spent, we lie twined together in the dark" (1956, 262). The precise position in which these two protect each other against the nocturnal onslaught of cold wind is named "tetty-beshy" — either an Anglicized "*tête-bêche*" or a Gallicization of "arsy-versy": whatever the case (and undoubtedly both), Beckett not only admits this interlingual invention to his lexicon, he employs "testy-beshy" (the later form) to describe chiasmatically twinned characters throughout the rest of his oeuvre. The most abstract illustration of this indivisible partnership is undoubtedly the geometric demonstration at the core of *Imagination Dead Imagine*: "Still on the ground, bent in three, the head against the wall at B, the arse against the wall at A, the knees against the wall between C and A, that is to say inscribed in the semicircle ACB," and so on (1995, 184). And always the idea that in this world, where the worst may always be expected, the chiasmatic betweenness I share with my fellow sufferer is the best there is: "No, life ends and no, there is nothing elsewhere" (1995, 185). Primo Levi had the misfortune to verify and corroborate Beckett's intuition by his experience (and luck) at remaining human in face of ultimate inhumanity: "I have two neighbors in the adjoining bunk. They lie down all day and all night, side by side, skin against skin, crossed like the Pisces of the zodiac, so that each has the feet of the other beside his head" (1996, 51). The witness and the martyr — your witnessness and, I dare say, your martyrdom — are such arsy-versy twins.

By the time Beckett gets around to writing *Worstward Ho*, he's jury rigged a dwelling place between two languages, a linguistic sweet spot. Interchangeably, French and English are the measures of his expressive soul. He wrote texts in one, then the other, shuttling back and forth by means of self-translation — for better or worse. He knew that the translator is one who is never quite here nor there and that in order for the sense of a word or the sense of a phrase to be borne across the interval between the two idioms, the translator must be able to ply the gap, mind the gap, show the gap, never quite closing the gap. *Worstward Ho* is untranslatable because it is *in itself* translated: it contains its own translation. *Worstward Ho* is written *between* French and English — even though the words on the page would be difficult for the monolingual Francophone or the monolingual Anglophone — the man of politics — to fathom. *Worstward Ho* was written for the forked of tongue, for the one who speaks the languages in the twain of witness and martyr, that language bridging the gap between the two. Thinking of *Worstward Ho* as being written between languages (though it looks like one) not only allows the reader to enjoy a fuller understanding of what the narrative offers, it also allows you to imagine yourself neither here nor there, two-in-oneself, incapable of writing one language without another. As Deleuze and Guattari (1975) described it in the case of Kafka, causing static, acting parasitical, infesting, infecting, running interference.

In 1971, in one of her very first articles, Elaine Scarry fixes our attention on an image found in Beckett's fifth *Text for Nothing*: "Between them where the hero stands a great gulf is fixed, while all about they flow together more and more, till they meet, so that he finds himself as it were under glass (92, 93)" (280). This image speaks of Beckett, first and foremost, and of his figments as well. No one in recent memory was quite so inextricably and complexly between two languages than the Irish-Frenchman who wrought those words. No one, in imagining a humane humanity through his own creations, more insistently envisioned us each as in a pair, flowing together.

Since before Aryximachus in Plato's *Symposium*, we have held to the quaint delusion of the possibility of fused beings. Between two individuals, however, there is always, necessarily, a gap. Two beings may also join. However, a third possibility — the only one worth pursuing — is that of a joint between us that preserves the gap pried open by "I." A hyphen between Judaism and Christianity — as Lyotard brilliantly positioned Paul of Tarsus,[2] a chiasmatic bridge, bodies incredibly joined apart as those of Tristan and Isolde, hazelnut and honeysuckle, "neither me without you, nor you without me." Already scintillating as a budding scholar at the University of Connecticut, Scarry observed that "the large structural outlines" of *The Expelled* may most usefully be described as "the act of union-division" (1971, 288). The shared somatic intimacy Beckett sought repeatedly to describe was neither grasp nor abandonment, neither penetration nor centrifugation. Thus the action of hands as described in *The Expelled*:

---

2 Jean-François Lyotard, *Un trait d'union*.

We advanced side by side hand in hand . . . Sometimes they let each other go. The clasp loosened and they fell apart. Whole minutes often passed before they clasped again. Before his clasped mine again." (1971, 154)[3]

Beckett is singularly preoccupied with how two bodies may best fit together, interlock, reduce the gap between them to the "leastmost," without either body losing its singularity.

Who knows? There may still be hope for this world if men of politics learn to situate themselves between two languages. The bilingual know that politics is an imperfect togetherness, forever subject to trial and error. Politics manages most of the time to maintain — at best — a status quo of unequal freedoms and wealth. At worst, it leads to the destruction of untold, untolled numbers ("We don't do body counts" was the sneering mantra of the Bush II Administration).[4] But politics thus practiced will always ultimately fail us because it focuses on the singularities that make up the *polis* and not on the potential *between* them, the potential that binds them. Politics and its men know nothing of the symbiotic potential of *bifrons ones*. They cannot, because our symbiosis belongs to us, here, and not over there, in Washington or in Beijing, in the hallways of power. Betweenness frightens men of politics. Betweenness is anarchy. Betweenness is anathema. Without politics, before politics (Aristotle and the *oikos*) and after (worstward ho!), each and every one of us is in the thick of our relationship to the other. No need for politics for this betweenness to be with us at every step not beyond.

So the third party, the witness incarnates duality and bilingualism. Primo Levi counsels us in vacillation between *inferno* and *purgatorio*, between "the hell of all" and "up if ever down," between integral and

---

3 In this context, we might also consider H. Porter Abbott's extremely thoughtful commentary of the following passage from *Ill Seen Ill Said*: "Spreading rise and in midair palms uppermost come to rest. Behold our hollows" (Beckett 1981, 32): "Reading *the gap between these two sentences*, we connect them with implicit words — 'as if they [the palms] were to say' — and in doing so *imagine* how her *hands* look held out in midair. Other things too: the ironic contract between the epic grandeur of 'Behold' and the modesty of the subject, *the sheer emptiness of these hands*, the act of lifting up and displaying *nothing*" (2004, 14; the emphasis is mine).

4 Often thought to have originated with former Secretary of Defense, Donald Rumsfeld, the formulation was first that of Tommy Franks, former Chief of the US Central Command and was supposedly only meant to refer to soldiers or "enemy combatants" and not civilian casualties. Rumsfeld used the expression on numerous occasions, of which this response to Tony Snow on *Fox News* Sunday 2 November 2003: "Well, we don't do body counts on other people. And we have certain rules on people we capture, in terms of exposing them to the public, Geneva Conventions and the like."

abnormal witness, between the martyr one might have been and the witness it is one's duty to be. Beckett teaches, further, that *one* is one only by having survived the test of two; "two once so one" means that one is the solution of two and that one becomes a *one* (*l'on*) on sole condition that one is *between* here and there, "since atwain." Neither here nor there, but between: half fig, half raisin, as it goes in French. Neither you nor me, no longer authorized to say "I" so blithely, never yet authorized to say "you" unequivocally: just "one" for me, for you, for every one.

As Beckett had himself learned and began as early as *Waiting for Godot* to teach us, one's life is a *temporal* betweenness as well. "My mother gave birth to me astride my grave." A feather and a stone will take the same time to fall from crotch to pit so long as the experiment is conducted in a vacuum. But life plays out in the air of lived experience, where drag and headwind delay the trajectory from point A to point B. A lifetime is akin to the ordinal betweenness of one in every three points on a mathematically straight line: the imagination can see it as horrifically foreshortened; it nonetheless has a life of its own. A life of consciousness is epistemologically dependent on the values we set for the two points between which it hovers, the only two events that it is impossible for me to know: my birth, my death. The only way I know my birth and my death is by experiencing your birth or your death vicariously. Betweenness is the only part I can know.

What one, by convention, calls "life" takes shape (or falls apart, depending on one's mood) neither here, where I delude myself into thinking that I am, nor there, where I think you are, but between us. And, so, one lives life with death at the doorstep: "Half no but on the verge" (*Still*, 21). The secret of being is no longer sought in oneself or on oneself but *between*. And, as Gilles Deleuze knew and Giordano Bruno knew before him and Democritus before that: being *between* is *to become*. Not to become oneself but to become two-self, three-self, and so *on*. Being toward the other is the very meaning of becoming. And this becoming requires forgetting oneself in favor of the link that gets you from now to there, where "there" is, of course (how could it be otherwise?) the future.

Betweenness begins the begetting of witnessness — the witness to come. But still, always already, the conventional witness foreshadows mastery of our witnessness as a hope now. Once happenstance brings me to be designated as a potential witness in the juridical sense, I really don't know quite what to do with this self-as-witness until I'm subpoenaed. In the meantime, the condition of witness shifts me into a limbo between my potential for future intelligent performance and my usual tendency for stupidity. Raymond Queneau treated this situation thoroughly in his first novel, *Le Chiendent* (*The Bark Tree*), where a rush of ethical concern lent the usually flat and nameless Étienne Marcel a full-blown three-dimensional body.[5] Once you're subpoenaed, you're on the verge of being confirmed as an actual witness — that potential for bearing witness is about to become actualized. You now step into that tertiary position — between the judge, the judicial instance, and the victim whose truth is to be spoken through you — for which the word "testimony" and the Latin for "witness" (*testimonium*) owe their beginnings.

Beckett takes that betweenness, constitutional of the witness, and radicalizes it until it's barely tenable in *Worstward Ho*. The speaker ordains: "Ooze on back not to unsay but say again the vasts apart" [13.7]. It's not that anything you say, in your role as witness, needs ever to be recused; it's just that however close you might feel to the fellow in whose stead you stand fast and testify, identification is impossible. To identify would be to *be* him: dead. Untenable, unimaginable. Impossible, in any case, if you are to testify. The chasm between you and that fellow is vast. And yet, beside yourself with responsibility, you transcend yourself and straddle it. Testimony is just talk; fellow-feeling bred of betweenness, and capable of protecting him from harm, derives from the stillness of imagination.

Perhaps betweenness encapsulates in one *ness*-noun the great story of twentieth-century thought. When Deleuze takes flight on inspiration taken from Henri Michaux's *La Vie dans les plis* to map baroque epistemology through Leibniz, he knows that the secret of the monad is in its interconnectedness with two others. After all, what is a fold but the line which, like the point, is no place at all even though it describes the juncture of two planes. When Derrida reconstructs friendship on the delicate foundations of Nietzsche's "perhaps" (*vielleicht*) and, more secretly, on the ruins of Jean Genet's "language of the enemy," it is because he knows that love is nothing if it does not accept everything from the loved one.[6] To my view no one has staged the story of one's betweenness more completely and succinctly than Beckett in *Worstward Ho*.

Our temporal trajectory — our little personal story that we think of as so very special —consists of this: first there's birth, then there's "life" (which itself is a story *en abyme* whose main attraction we think of as the development of a consciousness of which we become more or less conscious [of which we bear witness] depending on our wits and curiosity), then death puts an abrupt stop to it all. All "life" consists of subsisting in that mid position *between* forgotten "trauma" (birth, my past) and the oblivion of death (my future). We are necessarily witness by virtue of the midst; that is, our balancing act above the abyss.

---

5 Cf. Harvey, "Queneau/Dog/Man/Body," 1996.

6 This is indeed an old story — at least as old as Alcibiades's realization that Socrates (or Diotima), the subject of love, is both lover (*erastes*) and beloved (*eromenos*). Cf. Derrida, *Politics of Friendship*, 1997; Harvey, "Genet's Open Enemies: Sartre and Derrida," 1997.

My immemorial past is also my innocence, my purity with respect to events and what they do to me in their wake. The logic underlying Freud's underdeveloped theory of *Nachträglichkeit* consists of thinking this purity as affect before language.[7] In language we say that the tree makes no noise if it falls in a forest where no one is present. The infant is that one who hears it but cannot say. But since he yet has no speech, no *logos*, since the little one is witless, he is said to be no one. Yet who will deny that he heard the tree fall? Likewise, Freud will question our denial that what we call a trauma can nonetheless affect the speechless. Once I'm touched by the world of events, I am between that lost purity and the moment of my death. The perceptual anamnesis of the event that befell me before I knew the word "event" or any other word might occur or, then again, it might not. If it does, it will ooze out through the voice of someone I was not (yet) when it occurred. This betweenness is homologous to my relationship to the dead brother, the one who didn't manage to survive. And let us not forget that just managing to survive (*organisieren*) is what Primo Levi is all about.

All this betweenness is good and well, but without some sort of dynamic to ignite and tend it, it will remain just a pretty (or messy) picture. A contained space in which a condition of consciousness is acted out as illustration and model for the audience would be the stage of a philosophical theatre in which such a dynamic could emerge. At various moments in literary history, such a theatre has been attempted.[8] *Worstward Ho* is the epitome of such philosophical theatre. On its stage, in its space, within the allotted time of its action, an epic drama unfolds. The difficulty of accepting that I will one day die and the ease of ignorance at why and how it came to be that I possess something I call consciousness — a consciousness that decided one day to call itself "I" and dwell in my head: these are the temporal markers between which the action of *Worstward Ho* unfolds. And the stage is my skull, my noggin.

Your intrinsic betweenness that draws you closer to me than you think reserves some part of your experience for the imagination.

---

7 For two quite different perspectives on Freud's famous and famously undeveloped concept, see Lyotard's "Emma" and Laplanche's *Problématiques VI*.

8 Plato's *Symposium*, *The Farce of Master Pathelin*, Diderot's *Actor's Paradox*, and Stein's *Ada* are notable examples that I pause to plug.

1.8   afterwit

But but a shade so as when after nohow somehow on to dimmer still. [13.6]

In his *Ephemerides of Phialo and Short Apologie of the Schoole of Abuse* of 1579, the OED tells us, Stephen Gosson wrote that "Afterwittes are euer best, burnt Children dred the fire." This is not as abusive as it appears, for such youthful afterwits would most certainly have the wherewithal to elude Swift's solution of being "stewed, roasted, baked or boiled." A quaintly archaic way of signifying hindsight, the OED defines afterwit as wisdom after the event: the lightbulb illuminates, but too late. All of the authors chosen for the quoted examples of afterwit in the great reference work tinge the phenomenon with a sarcasm underscoring the utter pointlessness of pissing in a violin. All but one — Gosson. His maxim speaks volumes of the circumstances, shared by all, that make us witnesses even without having actually witnessed an event. We learn everything we know well by trial and error but, so often, "after the fact." Wit consists of both innate gift and acquired skill. And that which is acquired requires a lapse of time: distinctly after being touched, whether by fire or a hand.

For a universal ethics to be possible, one shouldn't have to wait for a lesson to befall one, whether that lesson is meeting the Gorgon head on or just reading Primo Levi. The *ness* that may (but is in no way obligated to) lead to some actual bearing of witness ought to be in one from the outset. The dimness of infancy harbors abilities and experiences that turn those hard knocks of later life into remembrances rather than realizations.

One's own life story — the life story of each one of us — is a series of recoveries. After each moment where I thought there was no way to go on, I found a way, somehow, to go on — even if I was not aware of having found it. Beckett's axiom. It may, stupidly, have been my liver or my heart that "found" the way. So, on I go toward my death, making do with what I've got, with what remains of "I am." "But," I say to myself, so as not to despair, "hold on, get a grip on yourself." What I thought was the end, the bottom, total darkness, was merely the momentary eclipse of my sun, the sun for me, "but a shade." Is there really life, still, after the season in hell, "after nohow?" Can the one I call "I" really go on? Yes, "somehow." In the wake of cyclical philosophies of history — Vico, and Nietzsche, after him — I must shake myself loose from the illusion of linear historical progress and know that the only good is that which I-one make, repeatedly, in partnership with you-one. Yes, "on to dimmer still" — I must embrace the eventuality that at least in imagination this stillness that is dim, dimness yet again will repeat itself time and time again.

The story of the life of one caring for someone else is a series of attempts to compensate, for always arriving too late even if with redoubled care. Primo Levi's oeuvre constitutes culture's most eloquent expressions of such attempts. Trying to figure out how to counter his religious friend's contention that providence saved him at Auschwitz, Levi was drawn back for the umpteenth time to proximity with his virtually dead fellow Jew — der Muselmann — via his mental glance at him-it. Forty years of meditation about arriving too late with that "ghost of an ancient smile," as Ill Seen Ill Said puts it (1996, 79) brought Levi to the conclusion that a stroke of luck, prevarication, and a glimmer of wit are the only things that come between the drowned and the saved. Better late than never. Belated, in any case. One could do worse.

The rarity of recovery through anamnesis of what we "experienced" before we "were" only confirms the quasi-universality of experience before the light of reason. Freud's concept of Nachträglichkeit — officially translated as "deferred action" in English — is famously underdeveloped, at least by Freud himself.[1] Drawn-back-ness — to deploy it literally — may trigger not so much "deferred action," but a delayed reaction. This is perhaps why, in French, Nachträglichkeit is called après coup. So, in deference to the belated wit of infancy, I'll dub Nachträglichkeit afterwit. However embryonic, Freud's concept of afterwit has enjoyed a rich afterlife. The father of psychoanalysis imagined traumatic experience that affected one (who might one day resort to becoming his patient) at an age before language, before consciousness and before humanity. A horrific accident would befall him or a crime be perpetrated on his body. But when we write "horrific accident" or "crime" or "traumatic experience," as we write "body," we are using constructs of logos, of language, of humanity. And since this "bad" would befall Freud's future patient between birth and initiation into the talkers' club, let's call it "event," to have it retract from reason. Freud imagines that without language to lend the event a story, it would be as if it had never taken place in the victim's mind, although a place to receive it — the inscribable body — is indeed ever there. Later, from within his fully developed humanity, the victim's inhumanity will go on resisting and something will trigger the immemorial. Or, as Shakespeare put it chiasmatically, with two clauses that hold to each other testy-beshy: "Too early seen unknown, and known too late!"[2]

---

1 Laplanche and Pontalis 1967, pp. 33–36.
2 Romeo and Juliet. Juliet to Nurse, end of Act I.

The witness is to the martyr as afterwit is to the event. To the extent that I knew nothing at the time of its occurrence, the event, says Freud, did not occur. This is how revisionists deploy their sophistry, reckoning that they can get a pry into *Auschwitz*. The event did not occur, so they reason, because for a crime to have occurred is for a victim to have been able to narrate it. Our afterwit assures us, nevertheless, that it befell one. We know it in our bones, yet we do not feel it on us as it was felt *on* that one who is (yet again) me. To the extent that the martyr can only speak on through me, I carry the guilt of his reality. And *that* reality, negationism cannot touch. I am beside myself. "Once lying" prone, touching bottom, as *he* did, *I* am "now standing" as if the event never took place. And yet, there is my imagination: denigrated yet fundamental to truth and true justice. When the event befalls you, your wits fail you. You are not at, but rather beyond, your wit's end. But when things calm down, you regain your composure and "from now" — one sense, of course, of the pervasive "on" of *Worstward Ho* — you work with the martyr within you, from now on perceiving the world through those jaded, haggard eyes.

Afterwit's celerity may render quasi-immediate action that more than compensates for the dumb paralysis at the moment of numbing trauma. The afterwit of great witnesses has been observed time and time again. Here, for example, is how Georges Didi-Huberman characterizes it in the cases of Filip Müller and David Olère, both of whom had recourse to images — not photographic, this time, but discursive and graphic — to carry out their witnesswork:

> One may no doubt speak of these images in terms of *afterwit*, but on condition that one stipulate that afterwit may form immediately, that it may be an integral part of the image's very moment of emergence. In an instant it transforms the *temporal monad* of the event into a complex *temporal montage*. (2003, 45–46; 2008, 30)

Theodor Adorno once wrote that "Thought waits to be woken one day by the memory of what has been missed, and to be transformed into teaching."[3] Even in the best of cases, it takes a very long time for the afterwit of our condition as witness to dawn on us. The fullest expression of this anamnesis came late in the work of Primo Levi, as it came late in the work of Samuel Beckett. To take it all in, "the hell of all," and then and only then to perform an act of bearing witness is to always be too late. But to be too late, as a witness, makes no sense and sounds like a lame excuse for reverting to adult inhumanity. Embracing eternal return means that

---

3 Theodor Adorno, *Minima moralia* § 50, p. 81.

"late" is always early for the next time. Certainly not too late for us who witness in turn by the proxy of reading.

To become the afterwit of the other, to serve as afterwit for the other, "in advance of the broken arm" (Duchamp), if already I may not come to speak of the blow that touched me unless I experience anamnesis, then at least this vicariousness intrinsic to one consciousness may be applied elsewhere. Recognition that some part of the event has occurred through imagination comes in an afterstroke. This is not mere "facile hindsight," which Levi discusses in his chapter on shame.[4] It behooves us to investigate this 20/20 afterwit at the heart — which is the mind — of the witness. Though forgotten before forgetting exists, the vision of myself as dead man remains as an after-image persisting in the nerves of the overstimulated retina. Maurice Blanchot writes repeatedly, obsessively, of the step not beyond, that "subreptitious friendship" of recognition that he maintained with the young man that he once was — the young man who brushed up against death and survived.[5]

Recognition is no particularly elevated form of intelligence at all. One can even be rather dim and still recognize someone or something. To recognize that I am, at bottom, no different from the martyr is to see well enough, all right, but no better than "all right." I don't see this indifference immediately, when I first see the martyr that I am a hair's breadth from being. Indifference of indifference. Seeing my indifference from his eyes, I might actually *be* him and perish. How otherwise to explain the Jew's seeing (a vision that is both sight and realization) his indifference (which is both non-difference or identity *and* betrayal) to the other Semite, *der Muselmann*? Yet the image inheres to me as the flash of light's afterglow to my awed noggin, on the edge of its nerves, still deciphering the stimulation at the retina. All I know, in recognition, is that something has shown forth.[6] And my retina — like the imagination in Kant's endlessly fruitful account of the experience of the sublime — begins to recover from the overstimulation. My understanding operates in this calculation after the event — this aftermath. No: in an afterthought — *eine Nachträgliche Idee*, I see myself as no different from him. In the experience of afterwit, I can never be there, where the martyr was, yet I have learned to be him. We are only ever becoming each other. This is a becoming the other for which a skill exists that we name "wit."

---

4 *The Drowned and the Saved*, 78.
5 Maurice Blanchot, *L'Instant de ma mort*, 1994, passim.
6 Whenever I use this verb, it is in homage to John Sallis' brilliant *Force of Imagination*.

2.0   wit

On. Say on. Be said on. Somehow on. Till nohow on. Said nohow on. [1.1]

Nohow worse. Nohow naught. Nohow on. [18.6]

Said nohow on. [18.7]

Between that initial "on" and this final "on" one reads the entirety of *Worstward Ho*. "On" is not only a predominant word in the text, as we have already amply shown, with it the text *tellingly* begins and ends. Standing alone, as its own sentence and exordium, at the end it is preceded and presumably modified by the adverb, "nohow."

Here, we must pause immediately and reconsider once and for all the terribly misguided reputation attributed to Samuel Beckett for being a depressive author of pure negation. Dr. No. Nothing could be more erroneous. With its worried insistence on *on*, Beckett's work is designed and fit to *inoculate* against annihilation and nihilist negationism. Beckett is steadfastly vivifying and his characters embody dogged resistance to nothingness and oblivion. But of course, he uses the poison of negativity to rectify negation. He who goes on can never escape the erosion of no. The on/no palindrome inhabits us and, therefore, the Beckettian corpus. As long as we're alive, *one* never cancels out the *other*.

If *Worstward Ho* is in any way a remnant of the traditional novel, what transformation in the existence of the main character — whoever or whatever he or it is — does the difference between "novel" and "remnant" signify? Primo Levi reinforces my strong disagreement with virtually every other reader of *Worstward Ho*, for whom its conclusion means — literally — a dead end. When the Turin chemist inspected himself after the descent into hell, all he knew was that he had not died: he could go on, he went on. The precise point in the *Lager* timeline at which things turned in this direction was when he averted his gaze from his fellow Jew, the *Muselmann*. The moribund, the dead, the ashes, the smoke are the result expected by the annihilators, the foot soldiers for the engineers of nothingness. They are nothing but no.

Forty years after *If This Be a Man*, Primo Levi returns, by means of memory's imaging, to the bottom (*al fondo*), finding the wherewithal to list the three factors that allowed him to go on all that time: luck, prevarication, and skill. The persistence of guilt suggests that although he survived further, by turning away from the *Muselmann* — his own image in the mirror of SS hell — his entire existence as survivor unfolded as though he were living life inside the shell left by the Semite who had perished. Luck, like God, is most likely a figment of our imagination: some may believe in it, but no one will ever know if it exists. "No knowing." Prevaricating, making oneself scarce, blending into the woodwork, holding back: everyone who lives on will play dead at some point. That's living by one's wits. It's the crafty subset of the knack for survival. Skill, knack or know-how is the most interesting and pragmatically promising possibility that Primo Levi held up as a secret for survival. Though moments of dulling there were, Levi's organizational[1] struggle at Auschwitz sharpened and maintained his wits. It is in know-how that we can locate the difference between "on" and "nohow on" — a world of difference, in epistemological and ethical terms, a difference that glides "nohow" toward *know-how*.

Back a millennium ago and at least up through the fifteenth century, *witness* was synonymous with *wit*. With Boethius and Beowulf as first examples, the OED informs us that wit denoted "the seat of consciousness or thought, the mind, the faculty of thinking," while witness went on meaning "knowledge, understanding, wisdom" all the way into the nineteenth century. Meanwhile, wit signifies "a superior degree of intelligence or understanding; good sense, wisdom, sagacity" even in a dimwit: "I am but a fool [. . .] and yet I have the wit to think my master is a kind of knave." A line of inspiration thus would appear to run from Launce, in *Two Gentlemen of Verona*, through Diderot's Jacques (*Jacques le fataliste*) to a whole host of Beckett knotheads whose knack to know that the knight is a knacker makes the man who uses his noodle a wit.

The coincidence of *witness* with what we know today under the term *wit* gets lost in the difference that *ness* makes in the spelling of the two words. Just as witness is one of the rare English words where *ness* does *not* add its usual sense of "capacity" to the noun modified, so wit and witness once actually meant more or less the same thing. Meanings of witness and wit overlap as the words do orthographically. Witness contains wit, wit fits into witness, as any Scrabble player knows. Thus a witness is coextensive with his wit: he is no less a witness than he is in possession of some whit of wit. One can be beside oneself but there is no more a way out of being a witness than there is reaching one's proverbial wits' end.

---

1 See Levi 1996, 75–76, 93ff. on what the deportees meant by "organization" or "*kombinacje*."

Wit — as its prominent, preeminent, recessional place in the word attests — is an integral component of the witness. Witness is the archaic form of wit, lest we forget. Living on means living by one's wits. A wit is still witness, the "seat of all." Living by one's wits is to live in full possession of know-how, to have a knack, to ken the cunning of Metis. Luck and prevarication aside (although dilly-dallying is a formidable ruse), it was Levi's cleverness that by his own account saved him from "drowning." If even in the direst of circumstances he hadn't kept his wits about him, he would have given himself over to Thanatos. Ruse at the limit of life, at the threshold beyond which all wit ends.

if of all of it too [8.3]

Just as the word witness contains wit, so the witness holds the martyr dear. If for Aristotle the seat of consciousness was the heart, we of today tend to agree with Beckett in locating it in the noggin. The wit lodges the dimwit for free in his loft. The cranium is an atrium open to the other. In his little book entitled *Être crâne* (*To Be Skull*), Georges Didi-Huberman reminds us that Thomas Aquinas invokes the authority of Saint Jerome while meditating on the relationship between the cranium and Calvary (2000, 34).[2] "Theirs all these voices," we read in *Text for Nothing 5*, "like a rattling of chains in my head, rattling to me that I have a head" (1995, 120).

Wit and witness are part and parcel of the same being. They belong together and, if they play their cards right, will be as inseparable as the two parts of being reunited at the conclusion of *Film* — Beckett's only work for the cinema, which can serve as visual dramatization of the imagination coming to terms with its witnessness.[3]

No knowing how know only no out of. [4.3]

We're in this for the count. Count the "no"s and the "know"s as Beckett turns the remnant bits and pieces of living on into prose that flows and thrills. There's no knowing how I know, but the fact of the matter is that I do know one thing and that is that there's no way out of holding that other within my wit. Witness as *with*-ness. Witness and martyr, just as pairs and couples throughout Beckett's theatre, play the game so deeply with each other that like dogs and their masters they come to resemble each other in their mutual protectiveness. To paraphrase Didi-Huberman, accurately countering Lanzmann's indictment (via Wajcman) of the image and its use in fueling the imagination: integration by use of imagination is not

---

2 Cf. Thomas Aquinas, *Summa theologiae* IIIa, 46, 10.
3 For my sense of what "happens" in *Film*'s dénouement, see pp. 93, 121–22.

identification (2003, 113; 2008, 88). Wit will consist of gathering the givens that these little chapters name, arranging them in the cerebral toolbox and deploying them as implements, weapons of mass construction. So, forget about home and the false comfort of the old rocking chair. Leave it! You're off in the world to fend for yourself. How so? Better have your wits about you and be fit. And with know-how and nohow vying for your attention, what more fitting a synonym for mother wit than knack? Knott, know, knock, gnaw, Watt, what-not, nohow on — the onomatopoeic epistemology of Samuel Beckett.

When an inkling that we know something comes to us, we think that the knowledge is of some event and that the fact takes up residence somewhere in our body. We believe there is a core where cognition and understanding occur. And if we think about all this enough, we convince ourselves that the wee atrium we carry around up there between our shoulders is the "seat of all" and the "germ of all" — that wit, in another word, is born and maintains itself inside the skull. If we've got any skill at all, it's because we've got a skull that's not altogether numb.

The simplistic language that Beckett deploys in *Worstward Ho* belies its complex algebra. So, if the head is said to be the be-all and end-all of what we think we are, Beckett is out to make it prove its reputation. If "the head [is] said seat of all," then it ought to be able to accommodate everything — even a whole world, even my dead twin brother. "Germ of all. All? If of all of it too" [8.3]. What "it?" Who "it?" Or is that "wit?"[4] The other Semite has either been othered or else made altogether indifferentiated — Jew made into *Muselmann*. I will go *on*, as witness, for and with him who is under threat of transformation into *no*. The martyr will dwell as part of me. Consciousness has room enough to lodge itself. "Where if not there it too?" [8.3]. I've got it in my skull, turning it back into he. "There in the sunken head the sunken head" [ibid.]. My self-consciousness will be transformed — using my noggin, my skill — into consciousness of the other within. He will from now on dwell there, in my own sunken head — the head sunken over this paper, as I write. His hands, I see. His eyes, my eyes. He was always there. We are both shades of the same intensity: not much brighter one than the other, a whit more wit at our darkest hour. Dimwits all and dimwits we remain, "hand in hand" [5.5]. I shall live for that witness.[5]

The art of Beckett's hero of consciousness, the wit that Primo Levi possessed and which — combined with sheer dumb luck — allowed him to survive Auschwitz is a rudimentary instinctual ruse. Such cunning is

---

4 Cf. Martin Heidegger, "How did it come about that with Being It really is nothing and that Nothing really is not?" (1956, 278)

5 "[T]he lowest grade of universe would be a world of mere withness." William James, *Pragmatism* Lecture IV, 156.

not terribly efficient in terms of time invested before results are obtained: just consider how long — with the self-same unflinching wits — it took Primo Levi to contradict himself on the issue of "touching bottom." The trial engaged by the wit of the eventual witness — even that of a pretty good chemist — is not the wit applicable to scientific experimentation, but rather the wit that we apply to mundane experience. Out of an indeterminate and random number of erroneous results to approaches to a problem, suddenly, one day, there emerges the correct life-giving response from existence. No high-flying and clairvoyant insight here: just good old trial and error. The human in hard times is, as Kafka knew, hardly more clever than a cockroach.

Wit is the minimal resource of he who goes on. It does the best it can in the worst of circumstances. "Mustn't we make do and struggle with the impurities and lacunae of the image as one does with silences in speech?" (Didi-Huberman 2003, 155; 2008, 124).[6] The makeshift struggle to which Didi-Huberman refers and to be performed, imperatively, by the vicarious image reader is of the precise order of the "organizing" to which *Auschwitz Häftlinge* were reduced: getting by in spite of all, in spite of being reduced to one's wits' end. Living by your wits is how you ensure that some part of the event will be attenuated by your imaginativeness. I don't know about you, but I'm knackered, as the Irish say.[7] No matter, let's go on.

---

6 Here, I have radically altered the translation offered in *Images in Spite of All*. Here is the original, admittedly very tough to translate, given the author's paratactic language: "*Ne faut-il pas faire avec les impuretés, les lacunes de l'image, ce qu'il faut faire — se débrouiller, se débattre — avec les silences de la parole?*" And here is Lillis' attempt: "Should we not treat the impurities, the lacunae of the image, as we have to treat the silences of speech, which is to unravel them, struggle with them?

7 Definition 2 in the OED is "a trickster, deceiver": obviously someone with a knack, while definition 1.3 tells us that in the plural, knackers are testicles — linking yet another word to the witness.

2.1 now

Someone who says "I" — everyone — is, consequently one, *l'on*. Beckett writes also, more and more, as his work wanes, of one moment — one moment — which is incongruously all but unique; one moment when one's experience of the other causes one to feel as though the inexorable march toward death is arrested. Playing on undecidable possibilities in French, Beckett's contemporary, Maurice Blanchot, described what happened at that moment as an *arrêt de mort* — at once suspension *of* and condemnation *to* death.[1] The fusion of two beings takes place in this instant, which is the main reason spectators of *Film* and other parables like it believe that the protagonist dies, in the end. With his later prose — and especially *Worstward Ho*, Beckett aims to generalize this fusional beginning into a "onceless" experience.

> When if not once. Onceless alone the void. By no stretch more. By none less. Onceless till no more. [15.2]

"Time moves and yet we do not notice it," wrote Dante of *now* experienced sublimely (*Purgatorio* IV, 9). All, in the moment we call now, is, in the repeated words of *Fizzle 7* or *Still*, "quite still." As that impeccable reader Christopher Ricks points out (1993, 129–35), a writer as cunningly punning as Beckett could not fail to see that when uttering "quite," we — but especially English speakers nearest the core of the onion — mean both *altogether* and *somewhat*.[2] In mathematics, such undecidability is intolerable: zero is neither a positive nor a negative integer. With death ever hovering in the vicinity, the character who is "quite still" sends a chill not so much of sublimity, but of unmitigated terror up the reader's spine. To complete a sort of conceptual chiasmus made of self-contained paradoxes, Beckett uses "quite" to qualify another adverb that incongruously signifies *immobile* as well as *yet*. "What," asks Ricks at this point, "is it to *go still*?

---

1 The title of Blanchot's 1948 text, *L'Arrêt de mort*, despite Lydia Davis' fine translation, is impossible to render without the awkwardness of unpacking its double meaning.

2 Ricks goes on, "whatever Beckett may be as a writer, he is never remiss. He is not likely to have failed to notice, or to have decided to ignore, the wrinkling of the flat statement which is introduced in the English by 'quite dead'" (Ricks 1993, 129–30).

To continue to move [. . .]? To cease to move?" These are already stirring questions that course through the mind of the reader of *Malone Dies*. They become pressing questions of my ethical relation to the other by the time we get to such late texts as *Ill Seen Ill Said*, as this question of Christopher Ricks' attests: "What is it, when contemplating someone who may be alive now in memory only, for that time of hers to be 'still current', where not only does 'still' have its own internal cross-currents but where one of the senses of *still*, the unmoving one, precipitates a further oxymoron as it moves on into 'still current'?" (1993, 136). *Stirrings Still* means both that whatever being referenced has still some life in him, yet stirs without stirring. Still water is not Perrier.

Dante, once again, describes the one's feeling at that fusional onceless moment thus:

> *Quando per dilettanze o ver per doglie,*
> *che alcuna virtù nostra comprenda,*
> *l'anima bene ad essa si raccoglie,*
> *par ch'a nulla potenza più intenda;*
> *e questo è contra quello error che crede*
> *ch'un'anima sovr' altra in noi s'accenda.*
> *E però, quando s'ode cosa o vede*
> *che tegna forte a sé l'anima volta,*
> *vassene 'l tempo e l'uom non se n'avvede*[3]

For all its scholasticism, this description of the soul in the "stringent grip" (*che tegna forte*) of a "strong impression of delight or pain" (*per dilettanze o per doglie*) strikes me as directly anticipating the experience of the sublime as the moderns have translated it for us — beginning in the Enlightenment with Addison (in *The Spectator*) then Burke (in 1757) then Kant, with his *Third Critique*. We must once and for all understand that altogether unlike the beautiful, the sublime is an experience of the sensible, feeling mind and *not* a quality of "things out there." Kant famously wrote of that experience that it is the product of a paradox, a "negative pleasure," one that

---

3   When any of our faculties retains
     a strong impression of delight or pain,
     the soul will wholly concentrate on that,
     neglecting any other power it has
     (and thus refutes the error that maintains
     that — one above the other — several souls
     can flame in us); and thus, when something seen
     or heard secures the soul in stringent grip,
     time moves and yet we do not notice it.
                                        Canto IV; 1–9

"arises only indirectly; viz. it is produced by the feeling of a momentary checking of the vital powers and a consequent stronger outflow of them" (1951, 83). The experience of the sublime is a "state of mind" where the mind takes stock of its own state. Incongruously, as the wit gathers his wits about him, between the "momentary checking" and the "stronger outflow," time, Dante tells us, moves and yet one (*l'uom*) does not notice the movement.[4]

What more precise empirical description of the experience of *now* could one imagine? In nowness, one is oblivious to the passage of time. Wit waits for nothing and our irrepressible striving for it transforms uniqueness into oncelessness — the time of generalized witnessness. The ethical instant, the nohow of wit, must become every moment that I live. Other manifestations of time occur as if I were not living. When I don't care, it's as if I were dead. In one of his early major self-translations, Beckett came to a near-perfect expression for the time of carelessness by improving his English, thinking through French. The temporal marker of *"par le passé"* — which Christopher Ricks taxes as "bleachedly impersonal" (1993, 117) — found at page 75 in *Malone meurt* becomes "when I was not" in the new, improved, *Malone Dies*, page 45. May we deduce that being only goes on in the "stringent grip" of *now*? of *maintenant*? I think so.

In reason there is beauty, but there is no now: nothing save the sublime defines how an extensible now works. Philosophers since Aristotle have been trying to pin it down with *logos*, but we know only that something like what we call "now" exists because of the sedimentation of nows known as "duration." Time (and my conviction that I am) works the way Bergson described it in order to bolster our conviction that it is. Despite the insistence of metaphysics that "now" be the constitutive opposite of duration, that it happen "in no time," not even "in a jiffy," it seems (like me, you) to be ethically extensible. One senses now *now*. In a sense, there is only now. Later is always too late. Didi-Huberman lends gravitas to the instant within which Walter Benjamin declares famously that we read the image or, indeed, anything. In a key passage of the *Arcades Project*, Benjamin provides the fundamental definition that "image is that wherein what has been comes together in a flash with the now to form a constellation" (1999, 463). Reading the image, Didi-Huberman underscores by holding Benjamin's capitalization of *Jetzt* over into the French *Maintenant*, is "the Now of its recognizability" (2003, 115; 2008, 89).

Yet now, again, is a time that happens in no time at all. Now has no duration. What is more, as instant that *maintains* in a mere instant, and at the threshold between "before" and "after," now is a temporal zero-point.

---

4 On this, one may profitably read the following pages in Lyotard's, *Leçons sur l'Analytique du Sublime*, pp. 75–76, 78, 86, 98–99.

Zero, a latecomer to western mathematics, still bears the stigma of having been considered the impossible integer. As mathematical symbol for nothing, zero nonetheless makes negative numbers possible as it does very large positive figures. Zero is naught, and yet despite its being the "instance of an iconographic hole" (Rotman 1987, 59), it is not exactly nothing: zero stands like an empty eggshell or an empty skull as that which increases other integers tenfold, hundredfold, etc. A now that multiplies out to infinite oncelessness.

Beckett filled *Worstward Ho* with words ill said meant to be ill read. What is ill said is also, necessarily, ill heard. But what is ill said to be ill read will be well understood because one always, inexorably, strains to hear the faint sound of the other within. If the witness be endowed with wit, then the time of this know-how is *now*.[5] *Now* is the time of one's know-how to counter absolute no, to bootstrap oneself, to take action in the form of *nohow*. And so, nohow is know-how ill-written, misspelled in order to show that wit is that moving forth (on! ho!) within the moment we call now. No-ho-w. No/ho/w. "Oho, noho" (quoted in Knowlson 1996, 230).

The indelible, inextricable, ineluctable interface that *Worstward Ho* (re) establishes between now and nohow means that the impossible is inevitable. "Nohow" minus "ho" equals "now," and is Beckett's shorthand for saying the other for whom one is responsible, and one's resistance to that responsibility is cancelled now. Now is one — one and one's other as one whole now, on the double, and witnessness is the tie that binds them one to the other.

Worstward ho "forms [. . .] the classically shaped Beckettian paradox, the aporia of 'how' framed by 'no' and its mirror image 'on'" (xv). Against the vast majority, S.E. Gontarski is absolutely right in his introduction to *Nohow on* to assert that "the final accent of the title falls on *continuation*" (xiv; my emphasis)[6]. In the context of wit, we may permute other Scrabble solutions to the enigma of "nohow on": *now — ho — on*. Ill said for ill

---

5 Here is a very precise accounting of the importance of "now" in terms of lexical frequency: "The entire text is riddled with direct time indicators, adverbs such as "on" (85 times), "now" (75 times) [. . .] "still" (37 times). [. . .] These direct time indicators make up as much as ten percent of the total of the text and more or less the same percentage of the number of words in *Worstward Ho*'s vocabulary. [. . .] extraordinary density of words referring to time" (Hisgen 1998, 457).

6 The vast majority of Beckett's critics spotlight "nohow" with tedious predictability, leaving "on" in the shade. Both belong together in the dimness of the Beckett skull. "Beckett's mind has taken him not only in the direction of the low level of discourse of American western colloquialism, but to a superlatively bad specific example of it. *Nohow* is also the worst word because as the final destination of this linguistic trek, it is a disastrous confirmation of the impossibility of ever reaching an end" (McMillan 1986, 209). I happen to disagree vehemently, unless McMillan means "disaster" ironically as some sort of boon. Hisgen writes "references to time in the text are in

reading: *Worstward Ho* was written in poor English in order to be read, if necessary, in a welter of tongues — French and perhaps even, occasionally, in Greek. If the latter, too, then *on* might also be "to be" with echoes of Aristotle's curious expression of "now" — *ho pote on* — reverberating in the vicinity. *Ho* or *hos*, meaning the or that, now for Aristotle is *what it is*, a zero point in the midst of time, uniting past and future.[7]

Wit — like a Freudian *Witz* — is sudden and immediate by definition. One's quick-wittedness is recognizable by one and all now, in a flash. It's only when afterwit is examined under a microscope that *now* seems slow. At the other end of the spectrum of stimuli, dim-wittedness may be slow, but impatience before it is instantaneous. One (*l'on*, *l'uom*, Everyman) needs to use nohow only once in order for it to be good for all occasions — forever. Once it has been determined that touching bottom happens as a glance of the bottom, a scrape with death — once — all other times are onceless. So one goes on oncelessly, until one is no more. Restlessly until finally still.

Now is the time of wit. Kant said of the transcendent, that it "is for the imagination like an abyss" (1951, 97). Engulfed *al fondo*, in hell, in a "strong impression of delight or pain," one survives by surfeit of wit — surwit. The event happens in a flash, and the capacity to witness is no slow, gradual gathering of wits but rather a now or never. Now, the present, absolute presence of consciousness to an event without duration — the concept of now has challenged philosophy since Heraclitus, since Aristotle. But all ordinary man knows is what comes after now, in the aftermath: how to go on and what one might expect, even as things get worse and the light of life grows inexorably dimmer. Ordinary man, one, the one who goes on, the one called *l'on* and who says "on" in response to "no" — this one knows no now, but "ho." "Ho" proffered alone, nowhere but in the title of Beckett's penultimate text, yet extractable, subtractable. "Ho" is the word that one may lift out from the midst of "nohow" to obtain the remainder, the remnant, "now." Expressed mathematically,

$$nohow - ho = now$$

Without knowing how, one creates now as an already past remainder by going on somehow from nohow. Now is intractable until it becomes part of *one*'s toolbox. Future nows are stills straining against the stillness of any present now. Nohow looks as ominous as a dead end, but it's merely now with ho injected into it.

Now, "now," when it all ends, is endlessly a new beginning. The first words of his first *Text for Nothing* are those from which all begin: "Suddenly, no, at last, long last, I couldn't any more, I couldn't go on"

---

fact equally many red herrings" (1998, 389). "Nohow" never goes alone: it always modifies "on."

7   Cf. Ursula Coope, *Time for Aristotle: Physics IV 10–14* (2005).

(1995, 100). Once is a one-time occurrence. Past is no longer. Future is not yet. Now awaits for no future and ignores the past: it is onceless, containing all time in the bolt of an instant. Now is the nick of time that allowed the young man of *The Instant of My Death* to become the "I" named Maurice Blanchot. Now is the nick of time, without "during," between Primo Levi's glance at his dying dimwit self — the so-called *Muselmann* — and his glance away, into a future imagined as remainder, or survivor. Now allows the knacker to know how to survive by saying "No!" to the negation that haunts you, me, one. The primordial primacy of ruse has the immediacy of now: it all happens at the speed of wit.

Though thought to happen in no time at all, *now* may feel endless if experienced *al fondo*. And it is prone to remanence. Now is how Primo Levi understood Coleridge's "uncertain hour": a now that incongruously goes on, a drama played out in the theatre of my skull, reminding me that my brush with death — seeing me as dying other — ineluctably renders me responsible. The now that was, then, renders an ever-renewable now (polysemically named "still") where my dead brother that will be me, at some uncertain now beyond now, conditions what I do with myself till then. The ceaseless unfurling of nows between birth and death, between first light and last dark, goes by the name "still," Beckett's adverbial alternate for "on." So, still I go on. Never content to lie still. Without permission to be still till stillness silences ill saying, ill seeing, ill reading.

> Since then, at an uncertain hour,
> That agony returns,
> And till my ghastly tale is told
> This heart within me burns.[8]

My responsibility in witnessness will consist of proceeding, doing something with the gnawing memory of that now, the way it returns *ad ora incerta*. The ill-heard knowing that goes on, must go on, gnaws at me, *Worstward Ho* tells us. The now of this gnawing agony, wit tells us, is "a time when try see" [4.3]. Agenbite of inwit. If, as in Blanchot's *The Instant of My Death*, I flinched when I thought the trigger was about to be pulled, if I, as in Levi's *If This Be a Man*, averted my gaze from the Gorgon in the mirror, from now on, in all the nows on, until I am stilled definitively,

---

8 Primo Levi places these lines (582–85) from Coleridge's *Rime of the Ancient Mariner* as epigraph to *The Drowned and the Saved* (1986; tr. 1989). *Ad ora incerta* [*At an Uncertain Hour*] is the title of a 1984 collection of Levi's poetry (Milano: Garzanti). *Ad ora incerta* is the title of four orchestral songs from Primo Levi, for mezzo-soprano, bassoon, and orchestra, composed in 1996 by Simon Bainbridge. Finally, *At an Uncertain Hour: Primo Levi's War Against Oblivion* is a title by Anthony Rudolf (London: Menard Press, 1990).

I must look after all the other ones who might similarly be repudiated by any shirking of responsibility. "No future in this. Alas yes" [3.5]. To welcome being beside oneself: the heart of *that* one burns within *this* one. Such is the lesson proffered by all of Beckett's near ill-twinned twins.

A blinking on and off of nows and not-nows in *Worstward Ho* suggests a number of additional temporal adverbial aspects of the algebra making up the witness presented as *l'on*, in all its glorious genericness. To begin with, now, juxtaposed with the once-upon-a-time that now is not, should remind us that a life is made up of momentous occasions as well as untimely and unexpected accidents. Not-now is the time of wit's slumber. To put this in terms of Beckett's own primordial lexicon of the theatre: one is sometimes on, but there are times, too, when one is off. In a future-oriented perspective, the dialectic of now and not-now recalls that one day, sooner or later, not just before one knows it, but with a knowing that comes impossibly late, one will go on no longer, evermore. Instead of still going on, one will finally be stilled. Till one is still, however, somehow ever, "till no more," one's life is still a seemingly endless chain of nows and not-nows.

Nows come and go in dim flashes to counter noes. We know now only by the emotional afterglow left in its extinction. If a now were ever to appear to possess some uniquely vivifying quality, as if it were distinct from all other nows, we might say, with Beckett, that it possessed onceness. All at once, I might become a witness actually bearing the gift of something to say. All at once, my latent potential as speaking witness might be awakened by a glancing blow that strikes me as my twin is ripped from my flesh, as the *Muselmann* is amputated from the complete Semite. I didn't know until we were parted that he who was there for my glance averted was there as part of me. Now he is gone, forever, and I bear the scar of the phantom twin. This is the onceness and uniqueness of a Primo Levi. Beckett is concerned only with the condition in which the vast majority of us find ourselves: oncelessness — mine, yours, ours. One cannot repeat the horrors of history at will. Thank Godot! One can and should, however, at all times, imagine actual, eventful nows.

Those of us whose lives are onceless nows must learn to rely on innate vicariousness to create onceness through the imagination. This is the imagination's power: the only power anyone actually ever has. Imagination is an economy of feeling that connects me across all cultural and experiential barriers, allowing me to know the onceness of a Primo Levi. Imagination is what allowed Spiegelman to draw and write *Maus*. Imagination is what allowed Kafka — in a much more complex relationship, still, to the onceless now — to write of the law, another phantom twin.

Already within my lifetime, in the time of my life, there is a beyond life — it occurs in my imagination — there is a beyond this "now" that I hope to see repeated again and again if only for a few days. I can never quite be there, at least as a witness, because I am here, now, as I — something other than a witness.

No trace anywhere of life, you say, pah, no difficulty there, imagination not dead yet, yes, dead, good, imagination dead imagine.

This is the incredibly positive opening argument of "Imagination Dead Imagine" (1995, 182). By the time we get to *Worstward Ho*, it would be more like: No? — On! No, you say? — On, I retort! Imagine, now, what raced through the mind of the dramatically bilingual Samuel Beckett, as he gazed at the word "now," and the functions with which he might entrust it in his one and only untranslatable text, *Worstward Ho*. After *How It Is*, now it was to be a question of *now it is*. After presenting us to so many pairs of characters who hit it off so well, yet who somehow always miss each other's ethical mark, now it's time to show us how one can go on, not alone, but with the other, hand in hand, until all is still, till no more stirring at all.[9]

To have know-how at one's disposal is to be able to think on one's feet, to possess knowledge even before reflection (before the time of reflection sets in — because reflection is too slow to help in a crisis situation): to have know-how is to know-in-the-now, before it takes on the duration that we know, deep down inside, it eventually has. Its eventual duration is what enables historians to do their work. But once it's got duration, it's already too late for the victims. "No once in pastless now" [15.2]. Assurance that some part of the event will necessarily occur through imaginativeness comes before you can bat an eye.

---

9 Shane Weller has remarked upon "the possibility [in Beckett] of one very specific kind of bond between solitudes [. . .] figured [. . .] as the 'hand in hand'" (2008, 104–05).

2.2 remains

Beside oneself, beside myself with dread, what part of me remains? — For Dante, as for those who avert their eyes from the *Muselmänner*, it is only a bit of flesh, a figure.

Là 've 'l vocabol suo diventa vano,/[. . .] rimase la mia carne sola.[1]

But for Beckett — ever resourceful, even at the limit of life, "Remains of mind where none for the sake of pain" [2.2]. The very materiality of our mind reminds us that no matter how much we might wish to care less (or *not* care less), some matter beyond us remains. As Christopher Ricks observes about that *aside* that Beckett utters frequently — "'no matter' [is] a casualness as well as a casualty, a mind imagining its final triumph over matter, while having to imagine that from one perspective mind *is* matter" (1993, 26). Let's thus consider agreeing to consider remains as a reminder of the other within. The other dwelling in my wit, my inwit bitten, smitten.

One may strive — *à la* Beckett — to free the mind of its incessant rumination, dim one's wit for a bit of relief, evacuate all words, empty one's skull. Yet however close the approach to nothingness, a *cipher* always remains with us. A *cipher* — the still imaginable. Let's agree once and for all to abandon the notion that remains — "the mind in ruins" — are nothing but ashy mush even after death.

The sweet nothing of living on when annihilation was planned, implemented, deemed inevitable: that's the mathematical value of error's margin. Wit is cognitive leeway, wiggle room for survival, the error of play when only precision was expected. Remains is the thinking substance that insists in subsisting in that tiny space. Remains are what one can go on with where no going on seemed remotely possible: there is still life in this still life. Reminder is the witnessing of that substance, the form that consciousness of and in that substance, in that consciousness, takes — the result of an arithmetic reduction we call the remainder. So, too, that which is indivisible by the divisor in division. The margin of error that is Primo

---

1 There, at the place where that stream's name is lost,/[. . .] my flesh alone remained. *Purgatorio* V, 97–102.

Levi's life saved by the transformation of his alter ego into remains —
becoming substitute for the complete witness — renders the remainder
he persists in calling the abnormal witness. When remains are definitively
separated off from the remainder, this residual wit becomes a witness. The
phenomenon of remanence, by which physics identifies certain objects by
their after-imagery and our inability to see them in the right time, is, in
a sense, a model for the logic of this wit. "What are these/So withered,
and so wild in their attire,/That look not like th'inhabitants o'th'earth,/
And yet are on't?" (*Macbeth* I.iii.39–42). When Banquo queries the reality
of the witches, he challenges not so much their existence — however evanescent — as their tacit claim to stand on the same earth that is his. *They*
remain at the place from which they should have vanished. *They* are like
the photographs taken by members of the *Sonderkommando* and slipped
out of *Auschwitz*: "Something remains that is not the thing but a remnant
[*lambeau*] of its resemblance" (Didi-Huberman 2003, 206; 2008, 167). *They*,
the inhuman, like the "witness" Lady Macbeth implores her husband to
wash from his hands (*Macbeth* II.ii.60).

One of the more foolproof and time-tested ruses for remembering
is poetry. Rhythmic, rimed, imaged, alliterative language was — if we
might follow Vico's *Scienza nuova* for a moment — the first way the
social animals that we are, kept stories alive. Allegedly primitive because
historically first, poetic language is actually the most sophisticated way
to speak (and eventually write). Its loss is why the world today is led by
mass destroyers who can hardly tie their shoes, let alone craft a proper
sentence. Then again, the foolproofness of poetry's mnemonic function
doesn't mean that fools, the dim of wit, cannot fiddle with words, fight
amnesia or eat a pretzel without putting their eye out. In fact, some of the
best poets have been rather soft of mind. Beckett sees the *Muselmänner*
who survived as just such poets: "Stare clamped to stare. [. . .] Out from
soft through skull. [. . .] That the flaw? [17.5].

Remnants of Auschwitz is the title Giorgio Agamben gave to his most
elaborate commentary on the *Muselmann* — that category of *Häftling* that
so destabilized Primo Levi as to introduce the vivifying flaw at the heart
of his theory of the witness. Before standing for defect or error, a flaw,
incidentally, was a fleck, a mote, a nothing. Reading Agamben's book
(at least until its appendix) leaves one — just as reading *If This Be a Man*
does — with the impression that no *Muselmann* remained in the wake
of *Auschwitz*. They joined the millions drowned. Levi and a few others
became the saved. No later work by Levi rectifies this conclusion. What
remains of Auschwitz for Agamben is Levi's afterwitty theory of the
Muselmann that Agamben assigned himself the task of drawing out from
the virtual into a pragmatics of witnessing. Both Levi's and Agamben's
arguments about the relationship of survivors to the dead are predicated
on the assumption that all *Muselmänner* died. However, the flaw begins

to be tantalizingly awkward when we remember that the *Muselmänner*, first of all, were not among the victims who were gassed on arrival at the death camp and, although we can assume that the vast majority of them did indeed perish, some, in fact, survived. And some of those who survived even regained their ability to think and form sentences. Then, remembering what they could, some even became speaking witnesses. It was as if they had retained "remains of mind where none for the sake of pain." The appendix of Agamben's book presents the surviving words of these remains, thus spectacularly nullifying the premise of their complete witnessness.

What remains of Auschwitz, then, is the remainder — not just a couple of survivors who speak, reminding us of the actual experience of their brush with death, but who retain the ability to imagine what life is in relationship to death. One's asymptotic approach to annihilation entails the survivor's going on, living on to render testimony, even if only as *Dasein*, of "being there," incarnating the indelible trace of he who was subtracted from him: the other Semite. "*Ich war ein Muselmann*."[2] Subtraction, but also addition: each survivor, each one, all of us is supernumerary. No testimony without the redundancy of remainder: lessness is not withoutness, as Beckett knew very well even though he let *Sans*, without remainder, pass as his own French title for *Lessness*. His later, intimately related text, *Worstward Ho*, makes room for this redundancy of remains and these errors of trial: *Worstward Ho*'s system, offered as one that can be everyone's, thrives on this accommodation. To see without precipitous insight how this works, it is enlightening to turn to Jacques Derrida's commentary on Maurice Blanchot's *The Instant of My Death*, which I dare say runs circles around Primo Levi on our relationship to remains.

The Instant of My Death, first of all, is a ten-page fascicule in which Blanchot recounts what we presume to have been his own having been spared execution before a Nazi firing squad. At the paradigmatic moment when the mind gives up the ghost before the body is forced to, Blanchot describes "a feeling of lightness that [he] cannot translate" (1998, 15). He says it was just like the undecidable "step beyond" or "step *not* beyond" of his notoriously difficult eponymous book. At that instant, the person

---

2 Giorgio Agamben concludes *Remnants of Auschwitz* thus: "Not only is the *Muselmann* the complete witness; he now speaks and bears witness in the first person. But now it should be clear that this extreme formulation — "I, who speak, was a *Muselmann*, that is, the one who cannot in any sense speak" — not only does not contradict Levi's paradox but, rather, verifies it. This is why we leave them — the *Muselmänner* — the last word" (2002, 165). He then reproduces ten of eighty-nine testimonial statements made by survivors in Zdzislaw Ryn and Stanislaw Klodzinski's 1987 *Auschwitz-Hefte* article, "At the Border Between Life and Death: A Study of the Phenomenon of the *Muselmann* in the Concentration Camp."

he was *then* addresses himself *now* for the first time in the first person, "I'm alive," to which death personified appears to answer from within, "No, you're dead." Notwithstanding that rebuttal, the man remains in life, going on being Blanchot, until he died for good in 2003. But that voice proved to him that, as Heidegger might have put it, death had taken up residence in him.

Residence indeed! The paragraph where Blanchot characterizes the untranslatable lightness he felt at the threshold of death begins with the impersonal verbal phrase, "*Demeurait cependant* [. . .]" or "There remained nonetheless [. . .]." *Demeure*, as noun, means abode or residence and became the title of Jacques Derrida's gloss of Blanchot's recounting of this scrape with death. That title, left untranslated in its English version, conjures enough meanings to amply foreshadow the exhaustiveness of Derrida's reading of the word's polysemy. Here is an inexhaustive preview: permanently (*à demeure*), a place of dwelling (*une demeure*), a final resting place (*dernière demeure*), the adjectival "live-in" (*à demeure*, again), to put on notice (*mettre en demeure*), to reside (*demeurer*), and, of course, to remain (*demeurer*). Oh and by the way (*au demeurant*), let it be noted how convenient it is for Blanchot and Derrida, for whom the neuter and pro-noun polymorphousness are paramount, that "there remains" (*demeure*) may (and more often than not does) legitimately begin a sentence with no subject pronoun at all and, further, not to be a child left behind, *un demeuré* is a half-wit.

The poetic constellation that Beckett puts into play with *Worstward Ho*, making that handbook the showcase of his ethics, extends in shorthand Derrida's observations. Not only is the redundancy of what remains alive and well in order to nourish the wit of the witness foregrounded with dunderheaded repetition, it is precisely such redundancy that maintains the witness in life, enabling him to go on. And yet, as I've said and shall continue never sated to say, this *reunion* of the witness with the martyr is for everyone to accommodate *within*. It is for *l'on*, which, as Beckett was acutely aware, is — albeit the apparent redundancy of its definite article — one form of the pronoun "one" and also the old word for "human." Folding the remains within, taking the remainder within our fold, is the task of one and all.

Ruud Hisgen, in his magisterial thesis on *Worstward Ho*, is right that Beckett's emphatic affirmation of consciousness as sole locus for whatever distinguishes us as human underscores the mind's remains, and that these remains consist of the imaginer imagining "itself" (1998, 396–97). "Mind — seat of all — germ of all," affirms Beckett. But *Worstward Ho* is emphatic that "Remains of mind [are] where none for the sake of pain." So, in order for the intended generalization to hold for all, the accrual of features that make of consciousness the capacity to be a witness must be the lowest common denominator of *any* functioning mind — even that of a *Muselmann*, a man bereft of the least spark of life. This is why, embedded in the word "remains," the reader of *Worstward Ho* must simultaneously read *"demeure"* with all of its meanings and even its defective, inflected forms, such as *"demeuré."* Otherwise, how else can one understand why Beckett is so intent on probing the "remains of mind?" More intent, in fact, on probing a mind's remains than he is a sound one? Otherwise, how else can one understand why *Worstward Ho* should remain an untranslatable because already translated text? One for all and all for one. If this *demeuré demeurant* be a man — a shell of a man — then I'm one too.[3] The wit of the witness must belong to the dimwit as well — a mind at the mind's limit (Améry). And it is at that limit that the survivor that I am must feel and think.

We must dispense with the injunction, shared by virtually every ideology, that the vicariousness inherent to empathy is, at bottom, an abhorrent invasive captivation by me of another consciousness. The other is with me as remainder, as reminder of what remains to be seen in the very life of consciousness. "Remains," understood the way Beckett helps us understand it, designates both the other in me and how the other functions in me. "Remains" is the me beside myself that cannot get beyond me and that I cannot get beyond, the step not beyond. It is by the same logic that recenters the peripheral, recovers the remainder, that the photographs Didi-Huberman analyzes refute, from the center, negationist denial. *"Ce reste d'images,"* that remnant of images, that imaginary dross (*scories imaginaires*), he writes, trumps the so-called "unimaginable" (2003, 37, 105; 2008, 25, 81). In Beckett's scenario of consciousness it constitutes one's potential for seeing to it that one other than me can never be reduced to absolute zero by any other means than the natural unworking of his own body. Although "merely" a remainder, the other (when) in me is in surplus — he goes over and above what I think I need to be.

The other remains with me not only in mind, but also in flesh. I go on, hand in hand, with him, as all Beckett characters do, with their sidekick. Contrary to what Primo Levi implies and Giorgio Agamben's book reinforces — notwithstanding the blatant contradiction illustrated by his appendix — the martyr is not the complete witness forced to take the step beyond the here and now. Accordingly, the body, in Beckett, is never quite a corpse. One's sidekick kicks one in the side to remind one that he remains. That's what company is for. Recovery is always just a remnant's breath away — a breath from within which words, once again, as always, however defective, take shape and are pronounced. Hence, *twixt* the yapping witness and the silenced martyr, there is nothing, really, except

---

3 Poignantly blind to the obvious connection of Muslim to Jew, Primo Levi offered "shell-man" as one of the first speculations on the meaning of *Muselmann*.

an *x* that can be deleted for a gap within which a discussion between one *twit* and another can take place in an economy of mutual caring. And, remember, poor dear reader, who in deciphering Beckett must imagine yourself interchangeably Franco- and Anglophone, that even if one lessens *twit* further — by a *t* — one is still left with the remaining *wit*, and that when lessening anything by *t*, in French, one makes the sound of witness, *témoin*.

Hand in hand, therefore, one twit maintains the other twit in life, in the now, in the *maintenant*, in the holding of hands. This is why all the politically correct warnings against vicariousness, and the condemnations of those who would dare to feel and speak emphatically in the name of the other, are unfounded and frivolous. Redundant, really, since if you think about it, even in the dimmest moments for our wit, we operate vicariously. Remind yourself of Levi's story of putting himself in the mind of at least two other people in line for the nourishment that would keep him from becoming a *Muselmann*. That one five places in front of me will get only insipid hot water; that one five places behind will get the dregs of potatoes drained of everything; I'll hold to my place and not in their stead and maybe, just maybe, get soup. A story of strategic prevarication (1996, 33; 1989, 28–29).

The witness is forever reminded, through the in-dwelling of guilt, of what he almost became, of what he could have been. Reminder maintains him in his betweenness, on the threshold between himself and his dead brother, between what he already could have been, once, and what he will be, one day. Beckett takes the guilt out and replaces it with witty responsibility. He knows a witness by its headstone and for the remains buried below. He apparently knew it early on in his writing career, when he had his *First Love* stand-in quip, "Personally I have no bone to pick with graveyards" (1974, 25).[4] Such is the attitude one must adopt toward the shades that haunt Beckett everywhere and that he inherited from Dante's *purgatorio*.

Wit is a lifesaver, a flotation device that remains when all else fails, when no more trying seems possible. Yet most of us treat our wit as if it were ridiculously redundant, as if we could do without it, as if it were really just an embarrassment. But it's neither nothing nor superfluous: it's the essence — an essence beyond what, like contented cows, we think of as our self-contained and replete selves. That part of the event that occurs by dint of imaginativeness is a remainder.

---

4 Christopher Ricks (1993) discusses this bit of wit in translation on pp. 83–85.

2.3 nothingness: the whit

No not none. [15.2]

Dante's silent yes

Notwithstanding their way of repeating "at all" when affirming nothingness — or, rather, in accordance with it if we think of "nothing at all at all" as pure denial — the Irish are ambivalent when it comes either to absolute affirmation or negation.[1] In adjusting English to their old language, as Gerard Manley Hopkins once noted, they tend to avoid "yes" and "no" altogether. As in Gaelic, so in Hibernian English: to answer in the negative to the question, "Did you read the book?" (*Ar léigh tú an leabhar?*), no "No": instead, the verb used in the question is repeated (negatively): "I did not (read)" (*Níor léight*).[2]

Minimal affirmation at the threshold of nothingness finds a correlate — and quite likely an inspiration — in yet another of those moments where Dante is overcome by an experience of the sublime. The moment is paradigmatic: as Canto XXXI opens, Beatrice commands Dante to confess. Her words, sword-like, "raise the energies of the soul" — as Kant says occurs in the first stage of the sublime (1951, 100). Yet Dante, situated "*di là dal fiume*" — on the opposite side of the river — is in that state of security required for the "negative pleasure" to eventually complete itself, according to the Kantian economy of the experience. Beatrice's terrible command results in the weakest of expressions of compliance imaginable:

> *Confusione e paura insieme miste*
> *mi pinsero un tal "sì" fuor de la bocca,*

---

1 For a further example of this all in proximity to none, this nothing at all that asserts, see *Finnegans Wake* 96.5–6: "and, ARRAH, sure there was never a marcus at all at all." (Such stutters also encourage me in my choice of "witnessness.") The yes of agreement with a negative proposition is another way the weak yes of no manifests itself: "Have you nothing at all at all?" "— I do."

2 In fact, the person not doing the reading — *mé*, or I — is not even usually expressed in Gaelic. Here is Hopkins: "Everyone in the country parts and most markedly the smallest children, if asked a question, answer it without yes or no. 'Were you at school on Friday?' — 'I was, sir.'" My source is Dolan's fascinating *Dictionary of Hiberno-English*.

al quale intender fuor mestier le viste.
Come balestro frange, quando scocca
da troppa tesa, la sua corda e l'arco,
e con men foga l'asta il segno tocca,
sì scoppia' io sottesso grave carco,
fuori sgorgando lagrime et sospiri,
e la voce allentò per lo suo varco.

Purgatorio XXXI, 13–21[3]

Thus too the Irish ambivalence about "no" (or "yes") gets transposed in Beckett as heightened care taken lest one exaggerate wholeness or emptiness, plenitude or void. When he describes writing texts such as *How It Is* as "struggling to struggle [. . .] with the next next to nothing," he not only cleverly characterizes his minimalist aesthetics and, perhaps, coyly denigrates his achievements, he declares his commitment to stay in intimate proximity with that which (and he who) barely exists (Knowlson 1996, 461). Let us rest assured that "nothing" can never quite do what we claim its name says it should: there's always something to nothing.[4] And let us recognize that Dante's mute acquiescence to fusion with the other is the way, as if to say "yes" with more than a dropped jaw might cause the other so near within to vanish forever.

Beckett's eloquent textual blanks

For the listener, who listens in the snow,
And, nothing himself, beholds
Nothing that is not there and the nothing that is
Wallace Stevens, "The Snow Man"

---

3 Confusion mixed with fear compelled a *Yes*
   out of my mouth, and yet that *Yes* was such —
   one needed eyes to make out what it was.
   Just as a crossbow that is drawn too taut
   snaps both its cord and bow when it is shot,
   and arrow meets its mark with feeble force,
   so, caught beneath that heavy weight, I burst;
   and I let tears and sighs pour forth; my voice
   had lost its life along its passage out.

4 Beckett's private formulations for scraps of work that he managed to get down on paper — "a most lamentable à peu près" (Knowlson 1996, 495) and "a long hank of near néant" (Knowlson 1996, 564) — are proof that he knew that failure is always less than utter. These expressions convey that sense of touching bottom asymptotically, not remaining there, and that a nothing is not no-thing.

In *Purgatorio,* Dante casts himself beside himself on the verge of union with the other. This prospect of shared being is Dante next to nothing. With words all but exhausted after *The Unnamable,* with lesser words his only recourse (*Texts for Nothing*), Beckett goes on at this same verge, in this place, at this time, and steps not beyond.[5] No, paradise is not of our world: only purgatory is.

So blanks between spurts of spare prose punctuate Beckett's post-*Unnamable* work. To read Beckett's blanks requires us to cast our gaze beyond the awed stupefaction that undoubtedly inspired them.[6] In *Worstward Ho,* the blanks are doubled by references to a vastness that separates what seem to be discreet characters populating the "story" if it can still be so called.

Blanks appear in text when words, temporarily, do not. Like anything silent but breathtaking, they are eloquent. This is precisely what Kant meant by the natural wonders whose viewing touches off the awe of the sublime. We are overcome by such gulfs, engulfed by these voids: they are unavoidably unvoidable. The nothing of a distance between martyr and witness is anything but insignificant. And what is not naught is "Naught best" [12.1]; cf. [15.1].

Steven Connor has offered the category he calls an "economics of nothing" to help us encapsulate the form and workings of virtually all Beckett's work from the mid-1950s onward (1992, 85). But rather than an expression of anxiety towards such an economics, as so many readers of *Worstward Ho* maintain, this manual boldly positions nothingness at the core of an ethics that must come (e.g. Dowd 2004, 327).

Having penned some theoretically captivating art criticism himself, as early as the 1940s, and with a similar penchant for what became known as minimalism, Beckett might very well have known, as Enoch Brater suggests, Marcel Duchamp's esthetic imperative, "Reduce, reduce, reduce!"[7] The result of putting such a call to practice might indeed render something resembling Brater's description of the reader's experience of Beckett's post-*Unnamable* prose: "Ideas collapse into words, contemplation backslides into sensation, and stories revert to color, texture, sensibility, and

---

5   I have already suggested the extent to which Beckett's stance parallels Blanchot's: "to encircle the point of its own pointlessness [. . .] reiterates itself to(wards) the point of near-nothingness [. . .] short of the point of intimate contact where *here*ness and *nothing*ness meet" (Krance 1990, 132). Asymptote. Place versus substance.

6   Awed stupefaction such as we find in the following example: "More than anything else in the text the void harbours paradoxes: it is at the same time everything and nothing, narrow and vast, boundless and bounded" (Hisgen 1998, 386).

7   I have demonstrated in "Droit de regard droit" that Beckett and Duchamp indeed meet at an intense theoretical node. Examples of Beckett's art criticism are "MacGreevy on Jack B. Yeats," "La peinture des van Velde ou le Monde et le Pantalon," and "Peintres de l'empêchement" in *Disjecta* (1984).

sensuality" (1980, 252). But just as with Duchamp, who believed staunchly that it is the observer who completes the painting, something must be done by the reader so that textual blanks become the colors, textures, and sensations that may come to have sense. As Charles Krance correctly puts it in a somewhat awkwardly exaggerated rhetorical question, "Could the pointlessness of the whole project lie in the very unnegativability of nega- tion itself?" (1990, 131). If "pointlessness" be — to paraphrase Parmenides — that the only thing we should do with nothing (or a blank, or a void, or an abyss) is to treat it as something, then "pointless" indeed is the project demanded of Beckett's reader.

Compelling the reader to work with blanks and to coax meaning from the nothingness between them with whatever there is in the "gentle skim- mer's" reading-fueled imagination seems to me Beckett's whole point, be it certainly, in some sense, pointless. Vistas for the reader's imagination open up in these wordless spaces. Against the order to "move along because there's nothing to be seen," the remains to be seen are infinitely more valuable than any vain attempt at verbal plenitude for them. The whit left for the wit in the blanks — mere nothings — nourish the conscience of the conscientious.

So, "Blanks for when words gone. When nohow on" is the metafor- mulation we find in *Worstward Ho* for what the text performs at those moments [16.1]. But of course, as we have amply seen, "nohow" is always also, necessarily, *knowhow* and declaring that words are *gone* from the whiteness between lines simply underscores what the reader sees beyond the vanishing: one and on. And just as with its ancestor, *Text for Nothing 6*, a "farrago of silence and words," each blank is a "silence that is not a silence" and the words are still, as always, "barely murmured" (1995, 125). As long as the imagination glimmers dimly, there is never nothing. What one deciphers as nothing out of what is gone is always something, however small. Never forget that to cipher is both to calculate and to cast into one's mind and that "nothing" in Latin is *res*, which gave the French *rien*, a sweet nothing is always something — *un rien*. To decipher is only to disentangle something from the zero that it appears to be and that zero in Arabic — *çifr* — gave us cipher and *chiffre* — something. To decipher is therefore creative going on when no resource seems possible, allowing *something* to be expressed, to show forth. As John Sallis puts it so well,

If all begins with a "there comes," then even bringing to presence in the most radical sense will have been submitted in advance to this coming. In these exorbitant senses, imagination will have come as if from nowhere to broach the circulation belonging to things that come to pass. (2000, 75)

Not only creative going on, but promise of a future. Yes, that reminder of the event that occurs in the imagination is a nothing and a nothing that reminds one of something is said *pense-bête* in Beckett's cherished French. Renascent eloquence out of textual blanks is to come from the reader.

The axiom that nothing is always something ensures that my approach to the other will never be an encroachment. The mathematical model for this axiom is the asymptote. From the Greek for that which does not "fall together," an asymptote graphed displays the characteristic of infinite approach to a limit without ever (at least in the observer's lifetime) touching that limit. It enacts an infinite lessening of distance that is, however, never without distance. Mercier and Camier's simultaneous falls might go hand in hand with Beckettian couples that come to resemble each other, like the proverbial master and dog, never do these twinnings entail a convergence of being. Nothing always stands between them — a nothing in which the work of ethics begins.

To approach, then, is not to encroach. In the economy of witnessness, autonomy is always preserved. When Beckett showcases characters joining hands in the air in celebration of the symmetricality of friendship, they preserve a nothingness of ownness. "Spreading rise and in midair palms uppermost come to rest. Behold our hollows," we read in *Ill Seen Ill Said*, preparing the way for *Worstward Ho* (1996, 67). The approach is not to zero — if zero be understood as death — it is an approach of one to another where the distance between approaches zero. This is the very illustration of an asymptote. There may well be sublime speechlessness before the apparent "nothingness" of oneness.[8] Opening upon the other is, after all, when (a) nothing separates us, a blank between words, a going blank, a speechlessness. Nevertheless, beside myself — Is it me or is it you? — there is the other whispering sweet nothings in my ear. It is but the asymptotic approach of utterance to muteness, uttered muteness, muted utterance.

Nothing, then separates me from you, *Muselmann* from Jew, witness from martyr . . . In one's weakening, as one's lessening goes on inexorably toward the zero of one's existence, which will never come so long as there is language, there will always be imagination. A numbskull that we all too brashly relegate to nothingness preserves a whit of imagination. This asymptote swaddles in sweet nothings the other otherwise in peril. Proof that model-wit is not so dimwitted as to be empty-headed.

---

8 "Face to face with this vision of the oneness of all, words fail him" (Hisgen 1998, 533).

2.4 lessness

So, a being who appears to be nothing is "no not none" — always, ever so slightly, vitally more than naught. Lessened being is never without life. "Mere-most minimum" [4.3] but always "for good" [10.15]. If wit is a minor form of intellect, it is more than enough to survive. For the state of mind open before witnessness and ripe for it, Beckett offers a term: *lessness*.

> Worse less. By no stretch more. Worse for want of better less. Less best. No. Naught best. Best worse. No. Not best worse. Naught not best worse. Less best worse. No. Least. Least best worse. Least never to be naught. Never to naught be brought. Never by naught be nulled. Unnullable least. Say that best worse. With leastening words say least best worse. For want of worser worst. Unlessenable least best worse. [12.1]

It takes quite a breathless number of little words to do it, but in the worst-ward calculus with which Beckett has graced us — the best words that can be found for the worst it can get without "losing it" — are words for tiny adjustments. The "best worse" is (or are) "unlessenable least." One's care for another worsens the first because it draws him away from caring only for himself. One can never become — in an absolute sense — the other. But one can approach the other until the void between is infinitesimally small. One lessens the gap in the dimmest of intimate lightings, with the faintest of movements of the soul. This is how Beckett expressed it in one of the texts that prepared the way for *Worstward Ho*:

> as the hours pass
> lesser contacts
> each more or less
> now more now less
> with the faint stirrings
> of the various parts
> as night wears on[1]

---

1 *Still*, 21. The cæsuræ are mine to show, at least, the 4/4/4/4/5/6/4 syllable *breathing* of these words.

This, apparently, is what he means by the capacity to lessen oneself for and before the other — the lessness with which one and all are equipped if they/we only knew. As the section of *Worstward Ho* quoted above attests, it takes far more words to define lessness than it does to say naught. *Naught* is a pretty good "worse," but *not* is an even better one. Why? Because to avoid "zero," that word for which there is no ordinary ordinal, *not* allows the ultimate approach to zero without touching it that we call "least" — "unnullable least." All this takes an inordinate number of words, and words that worsen and lessen at that.

Understatement, theology, and inequalities in mathematics are easier to express with a word for the quality of being less. No less than "the infinity of God's work" would be at stake without the concept of lessness.[2] For all its aptitude for abstraction, French has no word for lessness. You can say "I'm penniless" by combinatory use of the preposition "*sans*" — *je suis sans le sou* — but you can only go on with great awkwardness in French about the *pennilessness* of the multitudinous victims of Capital. Beckett needed a name for the resilience of one in his approach to the other one — the minimal fitness that he devoted his oeuvre to describing. That name was on its way to coming to him first in French with *Sans*, the title he gave to a "texticule" of 1969. Here is how he expressed to Lawrence Harvey the agonizing difficulty he had in grinding that gem: "Fear I've shot my bolt on me and the work both shadowier than ever. At least you'll have a long hank of near-néant fornenst you."[3]

A few months later, toiling in English, he called the text *Lessness* and wrote part of the blurb himself for the Calder & Boyars signature book cover in which he described it as having

> to do with the collapse of some such refuge as that last attempted in *Ping* and with the ensuing situation of the refugee. Ruin, exposure, wilderness, mindlessness, past and future denied and affirmed, are the categories, formally distinguishable, through which the writing winds, first in one disorder, then in another.

These few lines feature a key word in -ness and another in -lessness,

---

2   OED: 1635 Alexander Gill, *The sacred philosophie of the holy scripture laide down . . . in the apostles' creed.* Article 1, Chapter II, "The Father Almighty," p. 59. "[. . .] the working of God is infinite, with all the conditions of infinitie, as hath beene proved, for otherwise there should bee a greaternesse in being, and a lessenesse in working [. . .]" 1961 R.B. Long, *The Sentence and Its Parts* iv. 99. "Sometimes negation is semantically specialized to convey meanings of 'lessness,' as in *I don't have a dime*." 1970 S. Beckett, *Lessness*.

3   Reported by Knowlson 1996, 564. Samuel Beckett. *Lessness*. London: Calder & Boyars, 1970.

pointing us right back to the title whose translation (along with the text) back into his native mother tongue in the heady months between 1969 and 1970, brought Beckett to a rather simple but absolutely fundamental mathematical and logical corrective to the heading (direction, title, etc.) under which his late scenarios of solitary togetherness would be spun. *Sans* may be the preposition that French uses in front of nouns to convey what we mean when we add the suffix -less to mean without, it simply doesn't signify the condition thereby implied. Lessness *does* express precisely the state of that which or he who is in an asymptotic approach to zero, but — and this makes all the difference in the world — never *reaches* zero.

Again, simply put, *sans* means without — the absence of whatever substantive follows the preposition, whereas lessness means the *quality* of being less than something else.[4] Sure, zero is less than one, but that can be described in a trice (or, if you're Jean-Paul Sartre, in 660 much too verbose pages). The lessness of 0.000001 with respect to 0.00001 is much more intricate and implies a reversal of aspect that being and nothingness glosses over. It is the differential calculus that studies the infinitesimal approach of one (number) to another that apparently fascinated Beckett, though math was not his forte.[5] *Worstward Ho* is the description of that calculus, not in the realm of numbers or figures, but in that of consciousness. As for the realm of letters, it becomes understandable why "It" stands for "I": the martyr-witness with the other who is not quite himself. They are "vasts apart" and yet only the asymptote separates them.

Is it not fundamental to reinforcing the sense of innate witnessness that there be this asymptotic discrepancy between *sans* and *lessness* with which the man doing the reinforcing had to reckon? Taking the word "still" takes us further in this direction. Consider the ways in which Beckett's later work constitutes experimentation in stillness in terms both of this word and the undecidable state it designates. Observe that with the exception of Murphy, at the beginning, no Beckett being ever dies, *strictu sensu*. Whenever the absolute stillness of death is at hand, an impulse of words, a compulsion to speak, some talkativeness — if minimal — arrests the worsening and allows the figment to go on. Or, as in the case of *Film*, full integration of martyr and witness occurs. On the

---

4 Lessness, then, if I understand myself correctly, would be the quality that one could say adheres to the individual that Martin Crowley names *l'homme sans* in his powerfully convincing eponymous essay. I think we are, in fact, in agreement. By shifting from the state ("*l'homme sans*") to the quality, I am merely attempting to shift to the realm where quality (the other) and capacity (myself) become blurred enough for me to adopt — through empathy, vicariousness, etc. — a practice of permanent militant solidarity with the other.

5 "Extraordinary how mathematics help you to know yourself," Molloy observes (1955, 30).

verge of absolute stillness, being goes on, leastward still. *No* inverts to *on*. "Still," the adjective, metamorphoses into "still," the adverb. A whole, simple ontologico-poetic algebra that Beckett could elaborate, he realized, in English but not in French. *Encore* is no more the lexeme of immobility (fortunately!) than *sans* translates, precisely, lessness. And "*Cap au pire*," with all respect due to Edith Fournier, both does and does not translate *Worstward Ho*. For one of many things, "*Cap au pire*" can in no way reference the 1604 Jacobin play, *Westward Ho* by John Webster and Thomas Dekker, where words like "thitherless" and "lessness" and "worstward" had their place. For another, *Worstward Ho* calls for a hyper-translation along the order of Robert Coover's theories, if to be translated it must.

Samuel Beckett was bilingual to a tee.[6] He also had a pretty good grasp of mathematics. He knew, for example, that one can never be zero. What civilization has for quite some time been calling the human — and what I've been calling "one" — no matter how diminished physically or mentally, however lessened, is never naught unless the threshold of death has been crossed. (Much fruitless hand-wringing, demagoguery, and war in this early twenty-first century could be put to rest if we'd just agree that my death is mine and yours is yours. But that's for another venue.) Even annihilation cannot nullify one. Using words to have to say this is already bad enough; living on through it is worse. But what does "worse" really mean? In preferring English for his late hyperprecise works, Hibernian-English proved a special resource for Beckett. Thus the crucial word, "worse," about which the reader would otherwise no doubt worry needlessly, takes on a curiously paradoxical logic. If "better," in Irish vernacular, means more (e.g. "It's better than a week since she took ill"), then worse must mean less. Yet it doesn't necessarily follow that less is worse in the moral sense, for wherever lessening is of the distance between subjects, worse is indeed better.

There is one lessness-suffixed noun that bridges the infinitesimally small gap between *sans* and lessness: it's helplessness. Christopher Ricks quotes *Ill Seen Ill Said* — "She sits on erect and rigid in the deepening gloom. Such helplessness to move she cannot help" (1993, 49) — then comments, with thorough astuteness, as always: "In all of these, supremely in the last, it is not simply the 'syntax of weakness' but the incarnation of the human reality of it all, of piteous bodily weakness, and of the strength to

---

6 And T less the least equals naught. The OED team, admirable as usual, say this about "to a tee": "the original sense of T here has not been ascertained. Suggestions that it was the *tee* at Curling, or at Golf, or a T square, appear on investigation to be untenable; it has also been suggested that it referred to the proper completion of a *t* by crossing it (see b); or that it was the initial of a word; in reference to this it is notable that *to a tittle* (i.e. to a prick, dot, jot) was in use nearly a century before 'to a T', and in exactly the same constructions."

contemplate it, and to realize it, which is so moving" (1993, 148). And so it is "so moving" because for Beckett, so long as we can breathe, we can move to help another where self-help has long dried up.

As they experienced the *events* that altered their lives, Primo Levi in the midst of millions and Maurice Blanchot virtually alone learned witnessness by first being witness-bearing-witnesses-to-be. In that condition characterized by talkativeness, they were reduced to casting a type of glance — a mental glance, a glance of the imagination — upon themselves-as-other, the martyr, as he remained, for an instant, trembling awe-struck at the threshold of his death. Any more direct a glance and Primo Levi would never have been able to tell us so much about his *Muselmann* side; any more piercing a gaze and Maurice Blanchot would never have been able to tell us so much about the young man that he once was. Lessness spared them nullification by naught — a lessening out of which emerges the witness-martyr. A "*we* made up of an *I* who write and a *you* who read" is possible, at the very least, after Auschwitz, even the ever so pessimistic Lyotard writes in the wake of Adorno (1983, 153; 1988, 103). A lesson in lessening that the post-Auschwitz ones that we are have still not quite mastered. Nothing less than our ethical future is at stake. Who else but the eternal optimist uses the expression "at the very least" to convey a sense of his approach to life? It is ironically when wit outwardly appears leastmost, when it asymptotically approaches not a whit that "the dream image erupts from within that vital, if minimal, sleeping time of the prisoners" (Didi-Huberman 2003, 60; 2008, 44).[7]

So, in the stead of nothingness ("nothingness" itself, as in the last section, but also remains, wit/whit, "touching bottom"), not that it'll gain us much accuracy, but to alleviate much of the confusion, let's rather try to speak from now on in terms of lessness. The more one feels incomplete as *one* or (which amounts to the same thing) the less one feels oneself *possible* as one, the more one needs the other. While it is true that self-diminution is frightening and painful, the rewards are great. Lessward is the direction we head, anyhow, from the instant of birth. The countdown to the moment of one's death begins the moment the umbilical cord is severed. Lessness is hardwired to us.

Without anything or with nothing (but never without nothing [*sans rien*]), there is nothing, no movement, no breath on the mirror held to the lips of the fallen angel beside me. I must, braced by my love, be willing to go into the hell of all where she struggles still. In that lessness there is hope. Resilience returns. "Never sundered [by the] unstillable turmoil," we will go on, hand in hand, rebounding as we can.[8]

---

7 Cf. Levi on "the slave's way of sleeping" (1996, 70); *nostro dormire di schiavi* (1989, 62).

8 *All Strange Away*, 180; this text is a primitive version of *Imagination Dead Imagine*.

Striving lessward, worstward to our common denominator, "on," for the unnullable, unlessenable least is best from your point of view; it is only worse from mine, since I'm narcissistic through and through. Though *ness* may not function as a suffix in witness, lessness does so in witlessness. Becoming the living, caring reconciliation of martyr and witness, residing, remaining, dwelling on their betweenness, requires an endless process of lessness: the diminution — without elimination, in the last instance — of the distance between me and you.

All gnawing to be naught. [18.4]

Even if I am less intelligent than anyone else, even if my lights are mere faint glimmers of consciousness, I'm still not quite witless. Just as dimness is not darkness, lessness of wit is not witlessness. Lessness, inferiority, is always better than absence (*sans*). Standing as tribute to the mathematical precision of Beckett's title, the OED gives it as the most recent of five rare but extant uses of lessness. Indeed if standing in to stand up for my neighbor diminishes me, then lessness is indeed ethical moreness. There is a world of difference — all the difference in the world — between lessness, the noun, and -lessness, the suffix: -lessness is the zero limit that asymptotic *consciousness* never reaches.

2.5   fitness

Blood flows calmer in Harvey's town.[1]

> *Là ci traemmo; e ivi eran persone*
> *che si stavano a l'ombra dietro al sasso*
> *come l'uom per negghienza a star si pone.*[2]

To have the capacity to witness, one has to be able to retain a modicum of fitness. Survival narratives teach us that one nurtures witness fitness at the limit of wit, when wit is at its dimmest. "At the mind's limit," wrote Jean Améry, that is the bottom line. To be fit, one must exercise wit at the fullness of its resilience by practicing lessness. And this fitness can only come by never allowing oneself to lose sight of the other at the limit of one's oneness. Thus, the unavowed Zen Buddhist French Irishman, Samuel Beckett, advocated a fitness in lessness that absence cannot claim: "A little better worse than nothing so" [10.7].

The strength of the weak is a resilience most steady, already recognized by pre-Socratic philosophers, and brought back to the center of philosophy's attention — if only briefly — in the early 1970s by Gilles Deleuze, famously, and especially, by Jean-François Lyotard.[3] In Beckett, the power of minimal fitness is incarnated early on, already in the 1930s, by the indolent Belacqua, whom the author casts in an intertextual betweenness, not quite altogether outside *Purgatorio*'s Canto IV, where he first appears in literature, not altogether inside *More Pricks Than Kicks* or *Murphy* and even less so in *Molloy*. All of Beckett's misfits — but not, ironically, Miss Fitt in *All That Fall* — struggle weakly with what fitness they can muster.[4]

---

1 Knowlson reports that Avigdor Arikha in Paris received a postcard — signed simply "S" — from Beckett in Folkestone, the birthplace of William Harvey, that read: "*Sang coule plus calme dans la ville de Harvey*" (1996, 482).

2 We made our way toward it and toward the people
   who lounged behind that boulder in the shade,
   as men beset by listlessness will rest
   Paradiso IV; 103–05

3 Gilles Deleuze, *Nietzsche et la philosophie*, p. 69 inter alia; and Jean-François Lyotard "The Strength of the Weak."

4 Knowlson also recounts how Beckett told Lawrence Harvey that "writing was for

Left right left right on. Barefoot unreceding on. Better worse so. A little better worse than nothing so. [10.7]

In that "space of the slothful soul" (Caselli 2005, 36), with that strength of the weak, we are all like the Player in *Rosenkrantz and Guildenstern Are Dead*:

GUIL: Aren't you going to — come on?
PLAYER: I am on.
GUIL: But if you are on, you can't come on. Can you?
PLAYER: I start on.
GUIL: But it hasn't started. Go on. We'll look out for you.
PLAYER: I'll give you a wave.[5]

Stoppard's Player knows without knowledge — as Duras used to say — the givenness of life, according to that "x without x" logic that originates in and pervades the written thought of Maurice Blanchot.[6] In Guildenstern's scheme of things, on the other hand, a shift of venue and a shift in consciousness are required for one *to be on* and for others to know it. In Guildenstern's schematic diagram for formulating his directions to the Player, the stage is the privileged space for being on, "in the limelight" that is. But for the Player, as for any Beckett character, one is always already, inexorably *on*: no need to seek ways of acceding to the status of player to be on the world's stage with others — we're there as soon as we're thrown into it . . . Heidegger's *Gewörfenheit*. Playing the planks is a mere type of being-on within the holistic being-on that is "given." And *this* being on is one's fundamental fitness for oneness.

All the players in the infamous case of Terri Schiavo were as confused (or in bad faith) about *being on* as Stoppard's Guildenstern was. (This case, which unfolded in the US, concerned whether an individual in a persistent vegetative state should be disconnected from life support.) Terri Schiavo:[7] poor thing, poor *slave* to the delusion of others. Literally a thing, and a poor one at that: all that was left, by 2005, was the surname,

---

him a question of "getting down below the surface" towards what he described as "the authentic weakness of being" (Knowlson 1996, 492).

5 Tom Stoppard, *Rosenkrantz and Guildenstern Are Dead*, p. 34.

6 Just one example among many from Duras' work is this statement made by the young woman in *The Square*: "I am talking [. . .] not only of the things you know you want but also of the things you want without knowing" (1965, 44). Derrida mentions "death without death" in regard to *The Instant of My Death* (1998, 57) and Blanchot's "thinking of the 'x without x'" in *Demeure* (Derrida 2000, 89–90).

7 Incidentally, once and for all: it's not [shy-vo] as if it were some misspelled Ashkenazi name; it's [ski-ah-vo]. Remember that the Department of Homeland Security wants Americans to start learning "fern" languages.

imposed by filial law, and the family name, imposed by the patriarchal one. This, in and of itself, would be no different than the situation of any woman who ends up married and shedding her maiden name. But in Terri's case, nominal stultification was acutely poignant. Poor thing: no longer a "she," lessened well beyond worse, null and void, no longer even properly nameable — if she/it ever was.

The position and program of action adopted by the Schindlers, Terri's parents, combine to form a quintessential example of the transformation of a person who has already died into a martyr completely detached from the capacity to witness. This was cultural tradition not at its worst, but at its zero point: the only place where cultural *tradition* can really operate. Even by 2005, the Schindlers had still never admitted that Terri had been dead since 1990. They didn't have to in order for her dead state to be taken for minimal life: they are practicing Catholics and being dead means being alive (elsewhere) for Christians. This is what fed their delusional thinking that there was a live communication line open between the dead martyrs they select and themselves, whom they consider to be witnesses of the faith.

The players in the Terri reality show were myriad: a whole nation got into the act. Television — the postmodern avatar of the Chorus — adopted a position that turned Terri into the greatest perversion of the "complete witness" witnessed to date. The *irony* in Television's role is that to be the witness they just *knew* she was, Terri had to be brain dead, which Television was "tantalizingly" putting into doubt. One sees the problem in confusing nohow and know-how. Even the dimmest wit would resist, somehow, being suckered into this false integral witnessness. According to Levi, such a witness is an absolute paradox: dead and therefore forever beyond the capacity to speak or communicate in any way; uniquely qualified to describe what death is, yet incapable of doing so.

As for the US Congress, democracy's answer to TV as Chorus, it proved once again its desperate will to try anything to distract the public from its withering and dithering before the White House and its henchmen on the egregious war on the Iraqi people and the lies and deception that prop it up. Just as it had done during the impeachment of Bill Clinton for having put the Homeland's safety in jeopardy by "not" having sex in the Oval Office, the legislative branch of the world's sole superpower again proved its ability to tetanize and anesthetize its empire's subjects.

Parroting the grandstanding of our venerable elected representatives, Everyman (instead of studying *Worstward Ho*) improvised himself as expert of the Terri case. They hunted and pecked like mindless chickens, mesmerized by the image of the witless mouth twitch Television insisted on calling a smile — the bearing of witness from a non-existent beyond. Throngs of hysterical evangelicals shed crocodile tears for the martyr of their zealotry that passes for religious faith. But what was this demonstration, really? Are these robots to be dismissed? Perhaps. First, however, it must be recognized that they cried not for Terri, but because they were afraid of their *own* death and foresaw their demise on her still palpitating body. The bodies of the brain-dead, on the other hand, recognize brain death when it happens. Pagan wordcrafts were no dummies when they made the association between Christian and cretin.

Did the case that swelled around the poor thing called Terri raise important questions? Might it have taught us something useful? And, getting back on track, can the model of wit that holds forth in *Worstward Ho* help understand how the collective mind of the entire population on which rests the sole superpower could be held ransom to an hallucination? It should at least make us suspicious about two aspects of the traditional witness: mandatory testimony and speaking for the other without the most extreme caution.

The Schiavo case (like the O.J. and the Lewinsky cases before it and the Michael Jackson and the Anna Nicole Smith cases after it) was nothing but talkativeness on the part of jury-rigged witnesses. Non-stop commentary. Everyman was sure he knew what Terri was trying to say or what Terri would have said if she only could or what Terri was saying with the putative expressiveness of her eyes or what Terri was actually thinking but couldn't verbalize. Everyman got his fifteen seconds of fame on Terri's fitnessless hide. Of the thousands of hours of reprieve for the body where the brain had given up the ghost, six seconds of involuntary muscle contraction around the mouth and eyes was fed and refed to the witnesses no one subpoenaed. Everyone was shocked because nice conforming puritans hate the messiness of death, the presence of a corpse. Instead of glancing away from the *Muselmann* to be haunted forever by the mental glance, Everyman ("We, the people") stared with obsessive insistence at the face from which no life could radiate. And we yacked and we yacked because Everyman claimed he could feel what Terri was feeling and was authorized by this vicarious aptitude to speak in Terri's place. Vicariousness was every bit as much what motivated the Schindlers to lionize her Leninized corpse as it was Schiavo's motivation for getting the poor thing buried.

So what is the difference, at bottom, between what *Witnessness* claims everyone has the capacity to do with respect to his neighbor in order to protect him and what Everyman USA actually did when Terri's case came to a head? The difference lies in whose fitness we're talking about. The problem in Terri's case is not a problem of Terri's fitness — long gone along with the least whit of wit: it's a problem residing with the survivors. "Something not wrong with all." Terri's wit was beyond dim: oxygen deprivation to her brain had nullified it better than a decade before her "case" came to its endlessly spectacular head.

No nourishment can ever render fitness to one who is now, and for every conceivable future now, absolutely witless. Another tribute to post-modern stupidity is the politically correct term "disabled." In Hibernian English "able" means adequate, fit to cope with. "He wasn't able for the job," says the hapless worker. The old woman laments, "I'm not able for the stairs any more." Victims of life's enoughness. How can anyone ignore that the ones we are now, with demure correctness, supposed to call "disabled" are in some way or another "unnullably" fit? Wake up, people! Calling them "disabled" is even worse than saying that they can only earn their keep with cap in hand!

Yet the brain does not regenerate like a liver does.[8] The brain cannot be transplanted like hearts have been since 1967. One's only got one brain, so it's not ever going to be like kidneys either. Terri was not murdered: she was definitively — "terminally," if one insists — shown to have died and become a thing in 1990. These suspicions and modest proposals should lead to further investigations into the part played by the imagination in the wit of the witness.

Let us return to asymptotic survival to show its diametrical opposition to the absolute thingness of Terri Schiavo. We may hold up the story Primo Levi tells in *La Tregua* (*The Truce*) of the case of Hurbinek. "*Hurbinek era un nulla, un figlio della morte*" — a zero, well not quite, as it turns out (1989, 166; 1965, 21).[9] At fitness's limit, the tiny deformed three-year-old Hurbinek kept his wits about him. Every reader of Primo Levi is familiar with the portrait of Hurbinek, the "child of death."[10] The pathos of Levi's description and the exaggeration of equating him to zero should not distract us from what is essential in Hurbinek: the stare from those eyes of his is the *near* diametrical opposite of the empty look of the *Muselmann* and it is the *absolute* opposite of Schiavo's stare. From that stare is kindled Levi's guilt.

---

8   Cf. Will Self, *Liver* (2009).
9   "Hurbinek was a nobody, a child of death, a child of Auschwitz. He looked about three years old, no one knew anything of him, he could not speak and he had no name; that curious name, Hurbinek had been given to him by us, perhaps by one of the women who had interpreted with those syllables one of the inarticulate sounds that the baby let out now and again. He was paralysed from the waist down, with atrophied legs, as thin as sticks; but his eyes, lost in his triangular and wasted face, flashed terribly alive, full of demand, assertion, of the will to break loose, to shatter the tomb of his dumbness. The speech he lacked, which no one had bothered to teach him, the need of speech charged his stare with explosive urgency: it was a stare both savage and human, even mature, a judgement, which none of us could support, so heavy was it with force and anguish" (1965, 21–22).
10 §1.14 in Agamben's *Remnants of Auschwitz* links the obscurity of Paul Celan's poetry — one that Levi admired despite his misgivings about difficult poets — to Hurbinek, whose fitness lesson Levi immortalized in *La Tregua* [*The Truce*] (1989, 165–67; 1965, 21–22).

More important still than the stare is "*mass-klo*" — Hurbinek's word of indeterminate significance that he repeats incessantly. "*Mass-klo*" is a vocable comparable to the "*dodesukaden*" of the little dimwit in Kurosawa's film, who spent his days incarnating tram and conductor. What strikes us as the sign of Hurbinek's asymptotic difference from zero (*nulla*) is his "need of speech" that explodes from his look and from "*mass-klo*" with "urgency." Without making it explicit, Levi draws a crucial distinction between Hurbinek and the *Muselmann* based on a fitness measured by an infinitesimal gap. The one speaks one word and one word alone; the other speaks none. Even Hurbinek manages to enunciate what Lyotard called "something like communication," even "Jean-Do" Bauby "enunciated" with one eye; these asymptotes were long gone for Schiavo.[11] Hurbinek's "endlessly repeated" incomprehensible word (Agamben 2002, 46), this one utterance that no one ever understands is nevertheless every bit as much a model-word of witness fitness as the disquisition of the Mute in Herzog's film.[12] Hurbinek embodies and comes to emblematize, among characters in survival narratives, the strength of the weak (Lyotard 1999).

This said, the model-word, the uniqueness of this ultimate fit of fitness, its destiny magnified beyond all logic would mean nothing whatsoever if the listeners that we readers of Levi are were not meant to *do something with it*, in our turn. What significance could what Beckett calls "legless plodding on" [17.4] have if not to pass on the relay baton of witnessness? Readers, in reading, incur obligations. By inscribing the model-word, made by Hurbinek at the limits of fitness, at the core of his work as witness-bearing witness, Levi demands work from us, work to come, witnesswork that must come: "Barefoot unreceding on" [10.7].

Where there is a body (however unconfirmed) and a wit (however dim), there is *ness* for the wit of the witness. The diminished body — Hurbinek or the "shade" of *Worstward Ho* — is all but a corpse. It may look like a "black hole" merely "agape on all," still it transforms perceptual data into a "somehow" of survival by means of a simple binary economy of "inletting all [/] outletting all" [18.2]. Perception, even in the most dimwitted deformed body, managed to get transformed into a caring-for-the-other as tribute paid to the debt of survival. The brief saga of Hurbinek demonstrates that fitness remains not with the one about to give up the ghost, but with the one whose *ness* needs to go on caring and protecting wherever possible.

Beckett's final text — the one immediately following *Worstward Ho* — pays ironic tribute to the fitness of the weakest among us. (Please don't

---

11   Cf. Jean-François Lyotard, *The Inhuman; Le Scaphandre et le papillon* [*The Diving Bell and the Butterfly*], dir. Julian Schnabel, 2007.

12   Cf. p. 36.

call them disabled.[13]) The wit of the character portrayed in *Stirrings Still* is far from having switched off, been brought to naught, no matter how close to extinction the receptacle might appear. It goes on transmitting messages, however faint and difficult to reconstitute, as decipherable phrasing. Not yet stilled, not yet altogether a cipher or a zero with a flat EEG, the one still stirs. "Legless plodding on." As Deleuze so aptly pointed out, in "*L'Epuisé*," there is a world of difference — a nothing — between being exhausted (*épuisé*) and exhaustion itself (*épuisement*) just as there is a world of difference between lessness and *sans*, between an infinitesimally small something (*un rien*) and nothing (*rien*), between smoke or ash and obliterated oblivion . . .

---

13 Rather, read Eve Kosovsky Sedgwick's moving description of Judith Scott and her artwork, then be inspired to speak differently (*Touching, Feeling*, 2003, p. 22).

2.6   dimness

So leastward on. So long as dim still. Dim undimmed. Or dimmed to dimmer still. To dimmost dim. Leastmost in dimmost dim. Utmost dim. Leastmost in utmost dim. Unworsenable worst. [13.1]

At Beckett's use of the rare English verb, to dimmen, in *Ill Seen Ill Said*, Christopher Ricks frets, justifiably I think, about Anglo-Saxon denial of or resistance to the darker side of ourselves: "Why is it that in English there is no difficulty about bright/brighter/brighten, but more than a difficulty about dim/dimmer/dimmen? What does this tell us about a language's giving body to a people's hopes and fears?" (1993, 125). These are great questions, to which one would like an answer, if only a provisional one. But Beckett did not hold such cultural concerns. He was bent, rather, on describing to us what *happens*, what might happen, and what should happen in the dimness, in that grey zone that we carry around with us between our shoulders. Let us follow, as always, Beckett.

Dimness is the application of lessness to the realm of light. I imagine that Beckett saw with clarity that "dimness," every bit as much as "lessness," is untranslatable, or only awkwardly so, into his beloved French.[1] One can say or write *"obscurité,"* but this would take us completely outside the poetic constellation of *nesses* twinkling dimly about *witness*. The dimwit's mental dimness might kindle one's memory of *"dément,"* but is the moron who inhabits me by my practice of lessening ever altogether out of his mind? Not really. He's rather altogether *with* it, in all of "its" potential dullness. No, just as there can be no light without shade and dimness, so no life is worth living without lessness. *Worstward Ho* is Samuel Beckett's *magnum corollarum* to Enlightenment and the horrific consequences to which its advocates were singularly blind. Just as Sade's project was to relentlessly warn the optimists during Enlightenment's

---

1 As Edith Fournier's unimprovable effort shows, "dim" and its derivatives and declensions (let alone their unique, almost onomatopoeic effect) are largely lost in French: *"Ainsi cap au moindre encore. Tant que la pénombre perdure encore. Pénombre inobscurcie. Ou obscurcie à plus obscur encore. À l'obscurissime pénombre. Le moindrissime dans l'obscurissime pénombre. Le moindrissime dans l'ultime pénombre. Pire inempirable."* (Beckett [1983] 1991, 42–43).

heyday and in the parodic vein of impeccably rational logic, so Beckett picks up the pieces and suggests a formula for escape. Just as there can be no integer without the idea of zero and its limit, so there can be no light without darkness and its approach that we may now call dimness.

Metaphorically, of course, light or "lights" turn our attention to one's relative mental capabilities, hence reason and its apotheosis, the beloved Enlightenment. Beckett adored using this tool of language, as when *Molloy*'s narrator remarks that "every butcher has his slaughter-house and the right to slaughter, according to his lights" (1955, 37).[2] It is not the brighter bulbs that interested Beckett, however, but the slighter lights — those that are burned out, but not quite. Beckett's language outside English may have been more French than Irish[3], he nevertheless knew very well the value in the overstatement of "failed" in a comment like, "I saw poor old Paddy the other day and he's *horrid* failed — gone down in the neck." Paddy's health — physical and/or mental — may have declined: he's not yet gone anywhere else. The approach to nothing that lessness is is the only truly viable approach to the *not I*.

In a 1956 interview with Israel Shenker, Beckett famously explained how very different from Joyce's his own artistic enterprise was: "the more Joyce knew, the more he could. He is tending towards omniscience and omnipotence as an artist. I'm working with impotence, ignorance."[4] There could be no firmer proof of this trajectory than the witlessness involved in the wit's approach to the other: ignorance is not *absence* of wit but its dimming to facilitate osmosis. When your mind fades to the dimness of the dimmest dimwit yet you still manage to think, then it happens. As children whose eyes remember the vague vision of our first infant weeks, we all know the experiment: let go the habitual parallactic ocular focus and an inner vision commences. The language Beckett deployed in *Worstward Ho* creates such a diminished poetry. We've seen how "nohow" works as know-how and "ho" as how; "gnaw" rimes with or evokes nah, not, knot, and naught; and wit approximates whit; "on" is palindromic for no and it is *l'on* from Beckett's French. As Beckett does with language, so he suggests we do with our mind — our "lights" — in order to approach the other. In doing so, he extends the work of so many other thinkers of the night — Descartes, Hegel, Mallarmé, Nietzsche, Blanchot, Levinas.[5]

If *Finnegans Wake* is Joyce's book of the dark, as John Bishop argues

---

2 Cf. Ricks 1993, 91.
3 He had learned Italian, principally in order to be able to read Dante in the original, and his German was quite proficient.
4 *New York Times*, 5 May 1956.
5 I am thinking, of course, of Hegel's owl of Minerva, Mallarmé's *Igitur*, Descartes' ball of wax, Zarathustra's longest shadow, as well as Blanchot (in *Thomas the Obscure* and elsewhere) and Levinas and their *il y a* (as response to Heidegger's *es gibt*).

with force and thoroughness, *Worstward Ho* would be Beckett's book of betweenness, where shades reside within shades, one within I, the martyr within the witness. Dimness is the quality of light one would encounter if one came to dwell inside a skull — the skull of another, someone dead before one's own death. In such a situation, entering into such an abode, from such a vantage, it would be more advisable to rely on *touch* to figure out what's happening rather than sight. "Beckett's language," Enoch Brater writes of *Worstward Ho*, "demands of us that we say [. . .] words meant to be spoken and words meant to be heard, preferably in the dark" (Brater 1990b, 168). So, one feels one's way around. This will not seem such an absurd scenario if one considers for a moment that it's about the best way to describe life in the now, in the ever-present present that hovers, suspended between oneself and one's fellow self. It's the lighting at the core of what Beckett proposes for his model-wit.

To begin his essay for a catalogue to accompany an exhibition of paintings and sculptures by Italian *arte povera* artist, Giuseppe Penone, Georges Didi-Huberman speculates that early anatomists were disturbed by the dark and cavernous eye sockets appearing to stare out at them from the human skull that they nonetheless habitually kept on their desks. Otherwise, argues Didi-Huberman, why would they have forged evasive, inhuman metaphors for the cranium, like "the box?" Repressing and denying their affinity and consanguinity with these definitive numb-skulls, they nevertheless ventured "to open that box, taking the plunge, risking the loss of their own mind by letting themselves be devoured as if from inside" (2000, 11). Since the brain does not feel in the same manner that a finger does, we can only imagine its tactile perusal in a manner of touch prosthetic to the brain itself. This operation would take place similarly to the way an amputee might begin to imagine feeling through the plastic fingers attached to his artificial arm.[6] It is consciousness taking its own pulse after terror to complete the experience of the sublime.

True enough that feeble light will penetrate the pupils, peeping in through the eye sockets: stars will light a moonless night, but you'll still need to feel your way around. The dimness will be just enough to prevent you from falling while you explore the inner world of the other, your Virgil. While you still possess this dimmest of lights, you can still go on. Even if you're virtually blind — your lenses obscured by the thick, inoperable cataracts, you see by the dimmest light that you are still here. And your mind instantaneously translates that "here" into a "still now" that you can talk about with anyone who will listen, even if they don't understand. Remember the Mute who rose to bear witness at the trial staged by

---

6 The Greek Australian performance artist, Stelarc, has carried out many investigations into this phantom realm of the imagination at the service of life.

Herzog? — He was "mute" only because he was the last surviving speaker of his language on the face of the earth. Remember the cop who brushed you off, moving you along, saying "Nothing to be seen"? — Using your imagination you saw, all right: you knew, like the best eyewitness, what happened to Amadou Diallo and you knew, without having had to see, what happened to those people corralled into that cement chamber.[7]

> Still dim still on. So long as still dim still somehow on. Anyway on. With worsening words. Worsening stare. For the nothing to be seen. At the nothing to be seen. Dimly seen. [10.16]

What can wit (or a wit) do in the dimmest of all possible environments? Cognition, so touted by the Enlightenment, would shed light on all objects of knowledge and the mental training of *logos* would bring light on demand. None, following the advent of Reason, we were promised, would ever again live in obscurity, in poverty, under threat to life and limb, live life on a shoestring — that living death. No shadow would ever again be cast. But wait: all seen, everywhere? Instinct tells you that light has got to be mitigated by darkness, night must follow day or else one is blinded. Too late. All able to spy on all and denounce their deviation. Sleep deprivation from the ceaseless light. No more dreaming. Total security. Welcome to One State. All autonomous "I"s have become one univocal We.[8] In Enlightenment triumphant, all environments "dimmest" that allow movement to be sensed or imagined, are obliterated by the glare. In dreams, the scenes seen are lighted only enough for the contours to form and the displacements to be detected. Gone. Only Sade's scenes.

This is why the dimmest dimwit must be ours to cherish. He too, he perhaps better than any, will have borne witness to one of those faintest of sparks that keeps all of us "ones" ticking. The brighter the mind, the more cluttered the head, the more addled the wit. Better dim. No light without dimness. Instinctually, though, one has recourse to the imagination for counsel when all else fails. Minimal fitness means a whit of wit at the darkest hour. Kant knew this when he positioned the imagination as bridge between sensation and understanding. Such a bridge over an analogous gap on the outer surface of an edifice is called a tell-tale. Without imagination and its power, no enlightenment. Kant's Enlightenment (*Einbildungskraft*) came not under the blinding light of noon, when all

---

7   Among the thousands of sources on the murder of Amadou Diallo and the trial that ensued, one may read "Kadi Diallo's Trial" by Ted Conover, *New York Magazine*, 9 January 2000; online at <http://www.tedconover.com/2010/01/kadi-diallos-trial/>

8   These sentences mimic the plot of the great dystopic novel, *Мы* [*We*] (1925), by Evgenii Zamiatin.

shadows and figments retreat to their points of origin, but in dimly lit Königsburg, emerging from the threat of pain, from obscurity and extreme uncertainty. Beckett, reportedly, felt miserable when deprived of light (Knowlson 1996, 289). How does the Kantian subject know he's living and still learning? — he comes upon terrifying scenes of darkness where mortal danger looms and lurks at every turn. Not knowing what or whence, a moment later he realizes that it was all a sublime figment of his imagination. So, before the imagination runs amok altogether, it checks itself. No need to check itself in, just check itself *over* — the mind playing doctor with itself — creating the knowledge that consciousness lives on, witness to its own quasi-martyrdom. Only in the dim.

The French word for a telltale — that little instrument placed on a wall crack so that further movement may be detected — is *un témoin*, a noun better known to signify the same as "witness." Curiously, the same word designates the baton that relay runners pass as they race around the track. In taking up Adorno's challenge to go on, somehow, after *Auschwitz* in face of creeping negationism, Lyotard introduces the relay race baton as an example of how we link, weakly (1983, 56). By means of this altogether non-human "witness," Lyotard manages to entertain the notion of an inherently silent witness (silent in objective permanency) that nevertheless contributes to taking some measure of an event having occurred although it may not be to the satisfaction of the demand of realism. Although the baton (or "witness") is literally "the tie that binds," thus establishing the reality of the relay, it witnesses nothing, it cannot think, it is an utter dimwit. Yet if a speaker, by means of imagination, were to (dis)place himself as relay race baton ("Imagine yourself, for a moment, as a baton"), he would "become," by proxy, witness to the reality established. Such an imaginative speaker — precisely because he is working by means of imagination and betweenness — would thus be simultaneously (or alternately) inside and outside reality. A constellation of witnesses, situated at different registers on some scale of subjectivity-objectivity, begins to lend enriching complexity to the duo conceived by Levi as a "partnership" between complete witness and witnessing witness. Phenomena of sentiment — feeling, hope, future, fantasy — that are anathema to realism's demands, because they originate outside discourse, may also be considered fundamental to the emergence of the witness. The imaginative phenomena of consciousness that are abhorrent to realism because they originate outside the confines of reason are fundamental to our innate witnessness.

As the plethora of words it takes to say lessness, so dimness. Let's turn down the brightness as we turn down the volume. Yet "so long as dim still," there is light — just enough. As faintness of fitness, so light. Why strive for ever more complexity, asks Beckett with his puppet stand-ins, when more can be done with less? The primitive accumulation of capital has long ago turned into the cancerous reproduction of abstract value. In the dimness of the postmodern global cloaca, the skin supplants the eye as privileged organ for witnessing. The eyes feel their way around the inside of the eyelids and what do they see? Their future. Michel Deguy once referred, somewhere, to having "a child beneath the eyelid." Just look at the children of this world: Aren't they already showing us the future in dimness? They get older and older: thirty years old and still living at home, only twenty more years to go before retirement and they are still couch potatoes playing video games. Between the glimmer of the wit and the dimmer of the dimwit, there ain't all that much difference now is there? Wit diminished before the dilemma of touching or not touching bottom?

By means of his sculptures, Giuseppe Penone shows that the skull "is a place that teaches us what '*aître*' means" (Didi-Huberman 2000, 83). *Aître* is an old French word for dwelling. It derives from the Latin, *atrium*, designating for the Romans the large entry hall of a dwelling. For medieval French Christians, *aître* or *atrium* was an open space next to a church that might accommodate a cemetery. All this leads to what modern French would mean by the word *demeure*. The almost equivalent noun, *demeuré*, is a dimwit. And *demeure* should remind you of Derrida's extended commentary on the "instant of [Blanchot's] death." *Aître*, on the other hand, homonymically echoing *être* — to be — and suggesting a dwelling place for being complete, is the type of word Beckett could have definitely used in any translation of *Worstward Ho* . . . were it translatable. In his only work in the cinematic medium, Beckett shows us the completion of a being split not so much by the Cartesian subject-object rift as by the divorce of perceiver and perceived. The relentless prying eye of a camera pursues a one-eyed character, played by Buster Keaton in *Film*. The parable's dénouement comes when the camera is revealed to be the mirror image of the pursued, whose skull — a box camera, a *camera obscura* — pries itself open to accommodate the long-lost other that completes its being. *Film* was Beckett's effort to visualize the *cranium* as *atrium* — a *demeure* for the *demeuré*.

Worstward Ho elaborates that vision. As Primo Levi amply shows, being both oneself and the other who saw his own death — as in the mental glance at the *Muselmann* — is a stage in the process of becoming a *witnessing* witness — that altogether other, the self-authorized third party. The basis for such a paradox might well be the witness simultaneously within and without reality, if such a witness could make itself available to reading followed by writing in the same way that Levi's mental glance was transformed into a reading of his own death on the fading body of the complete witness. Georges Didi-Huberman goes on to elaborate on what Penone teaches him about the special kind of dwelling that *aître* is and that cannot altogether be said by *demeure*: *aître* is not a dwelling "that we inhabit, but one that inhabits and incorporates us at the same time" (2000, 83). As the body of the other in me is evanescent, so my mental grasp of his *aître*. His what? Oh, his *être*, his *atrium*.

In the penumbra of the yard, in the camp mud, Primo Levi, at rock bottom, caught a glimpse of a golem and averted his eyes. Run-of-the-mill witnesses need bright to moderate light to see what's admissible in court. But what if the old existential dimmer gets dimmed to its dimmest dimness? That's what it's like if you're ever so near to a fellow human who dies that you believe that you've died yourself. Ah! Here, now, you need to rely on your wits, brother. And there may be precious little of it left. If the *Muselmann* transfixes the post-*Auschwitz* imagination so, it is because he is that remnant of the other within us who maintains as long as a glimmer of life endures. In the *Lager*, he was also known as the dunderhead, the lamebrain, the nitwit. Your instinct was to glance away — Yes, I averted my eyes from the *Muselmann* that I still am, at bottom, the *Muselmann* that I will necessarily become. I refused to allow myself to see the other state of myself.

> failing light impression dead
> still even the hands clearly trembling
> and the breast faint rise and fall[9]

And now he — whom I treated as an *it* — haunts me. I palpate it, run my fingers over it, it kisses my soul. It inhabits me. It, or he, is me. He is the model that opens me to caring for all others in the world. I can see him clearly in others, now, but only dimly in me. I just need to feel around and touch in the dim of the dimmest dimness. My fitness in future will be measured by my receptivity to dimwittedness. Your instinctive reaction is to stare forth with the means at hand, as it were. The imagination — Yes, I may have glanced away, deluding myself into thinking I'd eluded the look of the Gorgon. But once I got a sense of the dimness beyond, it became my dimness here.

---

9 *Still*, 20. The cæsuræ to create a 7/9/7 syllabic scheme are mine, to undimmen the light on Beckett's poetic precision.

2.7 witlessness

By introducing the irrationality concomitant with the sublime into his critique of all things human, Kant dared to go where no rationalist had gone before. Hints that from the inception of his critical philosophy he was unafraid of domains where reason is lost were already present in the role he attributed to the imagination in the *Critique of Pure Reason*.[1] The seat of wit cannot take on the work of ethics, he reasoned imaginatively, without losing itself to witlessness from time to time. So, in the *Critique of Judgement*, we learn that the experience of the sublime is not all clarity and spiritual pleasure, but involves "a momentary checking of the vital powers" in order for their "stronger outflow" to occur (§26, 83).[2]

For that moment, in that vital moment when one touches bottom, when one is beside oneself with awe, in a state of witlessness one wondrously gathers the wherewithal to go on. All of Beckett's witless surrogates — with the exception of Murphy — are models of strength in the weak, of that strength of the weak that fascinated Deleuze and Lyotard in the thinking of certain pre-Socratics: Corax, Hipparchia, Protagoras, Eubulides, Kunika, Poros . . .

Say a body. Where none. No mind. Where none. That at least. [1.3]

How all but uninane. [13.2]

Beckett's "uninanity" is as untranslatable as "witlessness," where "untranslatable" means already translated, shared by all, owned by *l'on*. Now, if inanity is witlessness, then uninanity returns us to wit. This Beckett modifies, in turn, by the adverb "all but," signifying in discursive language the same idea as the mathematical operator for all not included in the set S. Uninanity, in other words, says the asymptotic approach to inanity necessary for openness to the ethical. You don't have to learn it or borrow it. Nor does it need to be contagious, because it is in one, two, three . . . all.

---

1 See, inter alia, (1998, 236–39) and this definition Kant gives in §24, on the application of the categories to objects of the senses in general (A151): "Imagination is the faculty for representing an object even without its presence in intuition" (1998, 256).

2 Tr. Guyer and Matthews (p. 128) suggests "inhibition."

What subsists, at the very least, if there's no mind and no body save one posited by another one who says "Let's say x" or "Let's say y?" What minimum mental existence can possibly subsist without mind or body? And in what time? What's the mind (my mind) like inside this body (your body) that we enter together to experience events in chiasmatic vicariousness? This is when the mind at the limit most resembles the entelechy at the crux of Leibnitz's *Monadologie* — an infinitesimally small, virtually witless state of consciousness.[3] It is then — now — that it matters least that we are just about as full of wit as we are in our dullest moments. When my wit, almost gone, beside itself, is lessened to the verge of virtual inanity, when I think without thinking that I've touched bottom, then I've achieved a state of witlessness where the betweenness that separates me from you asymptotically approaches zero.

Witlessness is the wit's skill at the leastmost limit of skill. If I am to act for and in the place of the other nobly, without depriving him of one whit of his autonomy, I must be ready to be deprived of my own wit — if only momentarily, asymptotically. In that moment, I will be virtually without my own wit, at my wit's end, in order to invest his. I will be *on* his case because *off* mine, in an altogether altruistic sense. In order to witness the world from his perspective and help him get on, I must be willing to allow my wit to be dimmed as far as possible. Witlessness is the ascesis of consciousness when complete, unegoistic empathy occurs between you and the martyr. You have allowed the dynamic 'tween you and the other to invert your positions. To follow Didi-Huberman on what the four photographs spirited out of *Auschwitz* do to the viewer, i.e. "faced with the photographs from August 1944," one is "stunned, stupefied," something *does* occur when one is all but uninane. Yet it is precisely in this state of witlessness that the image meets remnants of a mind "at a standstill" to mean something (2003, 46; 2008, 31).

Popular wisdom has it that Primo Levi's death in 1987 by probable suicide can be explained by a decline in his powers as a writer and as a thinker of survival. Accordingly, if *If This Be a Man* is the *Urtext* of our (post)modern sense of the witness and if its status as belated best-seller is justified by the fact that it tells the *only* story of "survival at Auschwitz" and its aftermath, it is because it is the story that sits comfortably with readers who never really want to be compelled to *be there*, if "only" via their imagination. To these readers, *If This Be a Man* and *The Truce* are Primo Levi in his prime, the "true" Primo Levi, Primo Levi before depression, before the misgivings expressed in, and self-contradiction introduced by, *The Drowned and the Saved* — a late and inferior work that must be glossed over to keep our neat little psyches undisturbed by what

---

3 Cf. Jacques Rivelaygue (Leibniz 1991, 31) and Leibniz (1991, 42).

threatens to haunt us. Unwittingly, the way afterwit always works, and most valuably for us, Primo Levi went on delving into the depths of wit to come to terms with his witless moment beyond which he would be forever sewn to the complete witness.

Primo Levi's witnesswork would never have left itself partially unworked, available for our work in order to envision anew our interpersonal subjectivity, without his daring knack for going back forty years to revisit the *Muselmann* and revise his relationship to the one he had forsaken. So too, true wit requires lessness: a humbling of consciousness before the other. Wit has the elasticity to lessen itself imaginatively in order to recover and use the experience of self-recreation as remainder in order, perhaps, to save others again and again. The practice of lessening one's own wit to rejoin the other whom one might otherwise lose develops a protective shell by the eradication of neglect by contamination. Primo Levi's work — if one takes the time to read all of it, complete with its contradictions — is an inoculating virus.

Wit's power may be suspended so long as to render visible upon the very faces of the witless their belonging, in spite of all, to the human species.

> *Ne li occhi era ciascuna oscura e cava,*
> *palida ne la faccia, e tanto scema*
> *che da l'ossa la pelle s'informava.*
> [. . .]
> *Parean l'occhiaie anella sanza gemme:*
> *chi nel miso de li uomini legge "omo"*
> *ben avria quivi conosciuta l'emme.*[4]

It is of this mark that the yet witful must be mindful. Recovery there can be. Recovery is our responsibility. We know that even a few *Muselmänner* survived to tell, as Robert Antelme did, of how they remained human, in spite of all. Dante reads the M between the two Os of their hollow eye: this spells man.

This is what Jean Améry meant by "the mind's limit." This is what Pierre Klossowski shows us Friedrich Nietzsche discovering right at

---

4   Each shade had dark and hollow eyes, their faces
     were pale and so emaciated that
     their taut skin took its shape from bones beneath.
     [. . .]
     their eyes seemed like a ring that's lost its gems;
     and he who, in the face of man, would read
     OMO would here have recognized the *M*.
                              Purgatorio XXIII; 22–24

his wit's end. When reason relieves itself of itself, when it abandons its project — if only temporarily — and gives itself over to the free-ranging force of the imagination, the witless mind finally becomes receptive to the other. Sure, the *Muselmann*'s eye shows no sign of life or will to live, but what do I know of his sleeping minutes and his capacity to produce dream-images? If a Primo Levi could go on even after having "*toccato al fondo*," then why not a dimwit? An example of how you might exercise your witlessness, then, would be to attempt to imagine what it might be like for a *Muselmann* to dream. From dimness to witlessness there's only one step — from outside in. Art Spiegelmann with *Maus*.

Without witlessness we would remain utterly clueless. So, fear not: witlessness is not permanent dimwittedness; it is not the consequence of virtual or actual lobotomizations. Witlessness is, rather, the ephemeral and necessary state of wit at the bottom, *al fondo*. Witlessness is like nothing else, that most modest something, experimental dimming of wit, "making a world of difference" by placing oneself beside oneself. Each one possesses wit, no matter how dim. Possessing wit means to ruse. One ruse would be to lessen wit so as to imagine oneself as the other with almost no wit left at all. In a manuscript found buried at Birkenau, Zalmen Gradowski has this recommendation for his future readers in order that they might "withstand the 'vision' of the things he relates: [we] must 'take leave' of everything. Take leave of our forefathers [*pères*], of our points of reference [*repères*], of our world, of our thought" (quoted in Didi-Huberman 2003, 47; 2008, 32). And, as we see, he gives this recommendation in the first person plural because he too had to do the same thing — take leave of wit — in order to stand it and live on. We all have to be willing to be as if we were not. If grief or trauma can force one beside oneself, one ought to be able to train oneself to go there. The importance of *als ob* for Kant is not far off.[5] To possess wit is to be gifted with ruse that can take advantage of lessness in existence, finding resource for resilience in deprivation. This lessening strategy, inherent to wit, is the know-how to go on when it appears that there is "nohow on." Beckett's mode of expression mimics this savvy. Obviously, one has to be quite fit to have such resistance as to be *as if* the other left in one's bones. But what good would wit be if it couldn't lessen itself? It's like the development of a striated muscle: it must contract and recover in order to grow. Without the contraction of lessening, no one would know how to go on.

If you plunk the monosyllable "less" smack dab in the middle of "witness" — between the witness's wit and the witness's *ness* — you come

---

5 Kant doesn't use "as if" logic very often, but when he does, it's important, as in the *Logic*, where he writes about "the reality of the idea of God [*die Realität der Idee von Gott*]" as being provable only by acting "as if there is a God [*als ob ein Gott sei*]" (§3, Anmerk. 2, AA IV, 99ff.). Cf. also Hans Vaihinger, *Philosophy of As If* (1911).

up with witlessness. Or, to look at this is as an arithmetic proof: if you perform the addition "wit" plus "ness," you obtain the sum witness. Of course, as we've already reminded ourselves, there's really no difference in meaning between "wit" and "witness." "Add a —. Add? Never" [10.2]. No matter. Now, to test your math, subtract "ness" from "witness" ("witness" "less" "ness") with the result of "wit." This is probably so simple-minded as to cause your eyes to converge as if you were about to swoon into the arms of Morpheus. Before you slip into slumber, be patient for Part 3, where we will reflect on means for increasing the witness's capacity for what he's named for without, for all that, compelling him to bear witness. It will be a question not of "less," but once again of "ness."

To do something reasonable and vivifying when reason has vanished is to put to work the will, as Didi-Huberman puts it:

> to wrest an external thinking from thought in general, something imaginable in place of that for which none before foresaw the possibility. [. . .] What is most troubling is that such a desire to wrest an image should occur at the most indescribable moment, [. . .] when there was no longer any room for thought or imagination for those dazed and dumbfounded ones who witnessed this. (2003, 16; 2008, 7)

Such witless behavior is notwithstanding the pinnacle of ethical action. Yet how often is it stamped with an adjective (or an epithet) applied to Beckett's enterprise: absurd. At root is the adjective or noun, "surd," from the Latin *surdus*, to give to phoneticians that which is uttered without vibration of the vocal cords, voiceless, "breathed" — something like sound heard in a soundproof room (or a model-wit). Too, it is from the Arabic, *açamm*, also meaning deaf, to give mathematics the notion of "surd root" — an irrational number like the square root of -1, one that cannot be expressed in finite terms of ordinary numbers and, from this, senseless or stupid, *i*. Arabic, which also transmitted zero to us — a nothing that is far from nothing.

In the concluding pages of "The Quest for Being," in perhaps the clearest expression of his entire original contribution to philosophy — Heidegger moves the age-old question of Parmenides — Why is there any being at all and not rather Nothing? — to the question with which we should be preoccupied today: "How did it come about that with Being[,] It really is nothing and that the Nothing really is not?" (1956, 278). The absurdly witless action of the responsible subject, bringing sweet nothing to the disorder of the world in order to protect his fellow dimwit is described by Dante as one might describe momentum:

> [. . .] *come fa l'uom che non s'affigge*
> *ma vassi a la via sua, che che li appaia,*
> *se di bisogno stimolo il trafigge,*
>
> Purgatorio XXV, 4–6[6]

All of the capacities — the *nesses* — that are suggested by *Worstward Ho* culminate in witlessness. It is just a letter shy of witnessness — the mode of consciousness uniting us before the obligation to speak: the babble of Babel. Witlessness makes all the other *nesses* attached to wit possible and puts one on the threshold of witnessness — the forgotten model for wit of which *Worstward Ho* is the anamnetic catalyst.

---

6   [. . .] like one who will not stop but moves
       along his path, no matter what he sees,
       if he is goaded by necessity,

3.0   witnessness

We now have seen wit bursting forth in a flash, the mind expressing itself as a potent nowness. Before that, we were confined to seeing ourselves as the more or less conventional witness, our mind being called forth for specific and limited futurity. What capacity, what *ness*, however, conditions every now and transcends juridical utility, joining us testy-beshy to our other? Before this moment — now, arriving with the celerity of wit or *Witz* — before tomorrow and my scheduled court appearance as witness, there must be some capacity that underpins both. How are we to now, finally, name this assembled nest of *nesses*? Neither "wit" nor "witness" will do, since although what they signify can be made to diverge, their meanings converge when they are used to describe phenomena of the mind. Either one or the other is redundant, or else the "ness" tagged onto "wit" in "witness" is superfluous. Neither word for consciousness — whose "seat" is the theatre for Beckett's allegory — evokes the predisposition shared by all that makes them possible.

No future in this. Alas yes. [3.5][1]

By dint of lessening the witness's gab, in dimming his lights just enough so he can see the other so near, and closing the asymptotic gap as between two languages mastered yet untranslatable, we have reunited the witness with his lost other. We are onto something: the witness has agreed to move on into the martyr without encroachment, because the martyr, as witness, has done the same with the first. Mutuality of caring awareness has been established. Let's now take the liberty of formally adding another -ness to witness in order to forge the word to stand for a state or condition (like something congenitally present), susceptibility or intrinsic tendency, a perennial potential to being a witness, to "witnessdom," to "witnessability." *Witnessness* is even closer to witlessness than wit is to the witness, despite their ancient twinning. They are about as close as the witness is to the martyr — inseparable, for goodness sake.

---

1 Here is a perfect example (and perfectly minimal) example of Beckett's French bleeding through his English. This "yes" carries the value of "*si*," which means "yes, to the contrary." There's nothing particularly thrilling about there being no future in "this."

To be a witness in the restricted juridical sense, I must first see, but then, especially, be compelled to say. First I am said, picked out in the process of selection, identified as having seen, designated by another to be an eyewitness. I am then asked to bear witness.

Dimly seen. Nothing ever unseen. Of the nothing to be seen. Simply seen. Worsen that? [10.10]

But what *Worstward Ho* asserts is that there is everything about a witness in every one of us before the required sight of the eyewitness and before the required discourse of the witness-bearer. It says that there is no need for an active society-bent finality in order for a *ness* to condition our existence with and for others. Everything potential about a witness remains in everyone well after sight and sound forsake us. Yet even this understates *Worstward Ho's* tacit claim. Beckett affirms the ironic yet dead serious notion that we are more apt for the qualities we attribute to the conventional witness when we are *disqualified* for being one on account of our overweening imagination than when we are admissible to a court of law. What's so earth shattering about this irony? Well, for one, it marshals the means to bury forever the negationist argument about *Auschwitz*. With my predisposition for relying on imagination, I know better and more about the harm that the perpetrators can do to my twin than when I conform to *logos*. *Logos*, and its daughter, the Enlightenment, would of course call our knowledge based on the imagination poppycock, inanity, dimwittedness, but we *no* better. We are predisposed to being legible to ourselves as the other in one. Witnessness.

With our witnessness adjusted to our advantage, we no longer have to wait to learn to read an event in order to be qualified to offer our interpretation and act accordingly ethically. Nor does it matter if we're blind or deaf or mute or dim: the event writes *us*, as the harrow of Kafka's tale wrote its victim, and we are thus readable to any who would care to read us with eyes or fingertips. Filip Müller eloquently, innocently affirms the power of aural witnessing to render one present at crimes unseen.[2] Imaginably worse than murdering millions, *Auschwitz* was the most

---

2 He evokes "the particular noise of the silenced small-bore rifles [that made him and his fellow *Sonderkommando*] present, so to speak, at the execution acoustically (Müller 1979, 30). And how, "from behind the door. I was unable to make out individual words, for the shouts were drowned by knocking and banging against the door, intermingled with sobbing and crying. After some time the noise grew weaker, the screams stopped. [. . .] They put down oblong boxes which looked like food tins; each tin was labeled with a death's head and marked *Poison!* What had been just a terrible notion, a suspicion, was now a certainty: the people inside the crematorium had been killed with poison gas" (1979, 34).

massive and rationalized attempt ever made to eradicate all witnesses, even those who only heard or smelled or touched.

As for us, we can only hope with our witnessness to maintain ourselves in a state of vigilance with respect to *Auschwitz*. We were not there, we will have never been where witnessness turns to complete witnessing of the event. We cannot imagine our death and die in the same now. We can only imagine as another. In this limited capacity we get on, we make do. We are here with a book by Filip Müller in our hand: we can only feel and know *as if* we had been in the gas chamber. Or we are here with the four photographs wrested from the Nazi program to create absolute oblivion: we can witness by proxy, by means of our imagination. This susceptibility to the image, this use of imagination to mount the vigil of the future and its eventuality is what I call witnessness. The mind whose mental processes are transcribed as worst, as Beckett could in *Worstward Ho*, sees all there is to see in the atrium of my fellow's cranium without acting upon it otherwise than to hold hands with that yet more vulnerable fellow. What enables a mind to hold hands? What enables a mind to care as much as a body can? Witness potential putting consciousness at the ready for going one step beyond.

It has been the wish of both Claude Lanzmann and Georges Didi-Huberman to train such responsible individuals without their having to ever endure an *Auschwitz*. Following the film, *Shoah* (and no doubt to protect it as hapax), no image could ever be deemed capable of approaching what happened. So, in the polemic that instigated *Images in Spite of All*,[3] stands accused of having "nullified thought" by having presented the four photographic images wrested from Auschwitz. But if the indictment against Didi-Huberman were not frivolous or, simply, insane, then witnesses — even those, including Filip Müller, whom Claude Lanzmann assembled for *Shoah* — were mere machines for testimony or, worse, their testimony would have held no ethical sway over those of us who have received it. Testimony would be an eminently disposable thing and the *ness* of the witness would die with him, forever precluded from being passed on to witnesses who *read*. In effect, Gérard Wajcman's argument is that of Auschwitz, there is nothing to be seen, nothing to be learned. The axiom driving Didi-Huberman's reading of the four photographs, on the other hand, is that even in the worst of circumstances for making an image and the promise of future perception — extreme dimness, ageusia, blindness, dumbfoundedness, and so on — there is *always* something to be seen.

---

3 The vehement attacks on Georges Didi-Huberman were made principally by Gérard Wajcman, under the banner of *Les Temps modernes* — for the sake, that is, of the increasingly megalomaniacal Claude Lanzmann. The references may all be found in *Images in Spite of All* (Didi-Huberman 2003; 2008).

I began with a different and no doubt more pessimistic presupposition: there were things to see, and in all kinds of ways. There were things to see, and to hear, and to feel, and to deduce from what one saw or from what one did not see [. . .]. (Didi-Huberman 2003, 81; 2008, 62)

Didi-Huberman's justification for lending credence to *these* images would be perfectly banal except for the very last element he mentions. To affirm ethical value from invisible and mute data is to recover the imagination for the sake of witnessness.

Just as most of Lyotard's readers have misread the postmodern as anything and everything other than the *dynamic will-have-been* (future perfect) within the modern,[4] so it is commonly held that the differend is a beautiful demonstration, but ultimately unworkable, leading to the impasse of insolubility and futility. Contrary to that popular belief, however, the differend and our willingness to engage it are what might just make going on for a while longer possible. The most concise and familiar example of a working differend is love — boundless, borderless, witless. Though experientially rare, some of us are lucky enough to know, in our flesh, the chiasmatic binding between two disparate yearnings. André Malraux illustrated this knowledge by reminding his readers of *La Condition humaine* (*Man's Fate*) of the phenomenon of hearing one's own voice resonating through the neck and head, rather than through the ears.[5] Ears are for hearing everyone else. So, the day you hear the voice of another implausibly sounding through the holes in your skull is the day love has befallen you. Love is the distance from me to you lessened asymptotically to the point that we live on as one: *as if* one's voice were that of the other. Lyotard worked this image of a vivifying differend where lover and beloved dialogue in the same skull, calling it the "soundproof room."

Ethics is born in such a radical state of susceptibility — total liability to the other. The mind dimly speaking in *Worstward Ho* is just such a liable witness: one who lives on by the pain he endures in proximity with his own remains. Witnessness would be our common predisposition to this liability — a debt to the law of the other that results from leaving one's mental ears open to the differend between the muted complete witness that I might have been and the witnessing survivor that I may never be asked to be. Always prior to any sign of wit and before conventional

---

4 A good deal of the confusion may be imputed to Lyotard who defined the postmodern inconsistently, over-emphasized putative unrepresentability, and sometimes provided perplexing examples.

5 In the chapter of *Soundproof Room* entitled "Throat" (2001 [1998], 82–91), Lyotard offers an arresting analysis of the passage in *Man's Fate* (1961, 47).

witnessing and testimony, with my witnessness, I have already come to occupy the differend, I have already made it the dwelling place from which all decisions — social, political, ethical — are proffered. The differend is thus a special type of betweenness where witnessness goes to work, unbothered even if the differend is yet unresolved. "No matter": it is the work and not the resolution that enables and ensures our mutual protection of each other. Witnessness is a wellspring of ever-renewable energy. From simply hearing, the subject who is liable to witnessness decides by means of the senses awakened when he has become the "soundproof room" for a differend. When tethered with a creative imagination at work, witnessness may come to deliver some unforgetting (anamnesis) of otherwise forgotten events. Such unforgetting is the only true source of justice — social or otherwise. With consciousness preconditioned by witnessness, the subject just may activate himself as agent whose principal project is to protect the other from harm of events now and for the future.

Is the differend between Primo Levi and Paul Celan of the nature of a soundproof room? Can the hermetic poetry of the one (Celan) be heard in the skull styled by limpid prose (Levi)? *"Niemand zeugt für dem Zeuge."* We must try to imagine Primo Levi's consternation before Paul Celan's vexing injunction — "No one bears witness for the witness": the seemingly irremissible final words of *Aschenglorie*. To the ears of the chemist who, having survived *Auschwitz*, retooled himself as a walking, talking testimonial to the dead's living on through his voice, *"Niemand zeugt für dem Zeuge"* might well translate as, "Shut up! You have no right! You have no business!" or, at least, as "Nothing you've ever said or can say may substitute for voices forever muted." An insuperable gulf lies between the living and the dead, between witness and witnessness, Paul Celan seems to assert. An image, however, can ignite the imagination of what death is. And no one may be the one who says "no" by going on "nohow" against and with death. The oneness of witnessness opens a soundproof room for *agreement* between the prolix project of a Primo Levi and the peremptory poetry of a Paul Celan. Witnessness provides an ethically reliable adequacy between knowledge and referent, opening onto the possibility for each to imagine fully the experience of the integral witness. Both Levi and Celan know that the living's liability to death puts the living "at bounds of boundless void" [18.6]. Living on is, therefore, not on this side of the Styx, but *in* the gulf itself. Being alive is to dwell in witnessness — the potential or the practice of bearing witness.

There is really nothing so very novel in what I am trying to describe as if it were announced as an age (yet) to come. Since the dawn of consciousness, as we think we know it, we have always already been witnesses in the absence of event. To witness without event is simply another way of saying that — whether empathically or not — ceaselessly, from the time we think even the slightest thoughts and begin only to mimic language, we put ourselves in the place of the other. That age where one begins to think even the slightest thought was known, in another age of language, as "the age of wit." There is nothing novel, then, to witnessness (except the word) and nothing novel to the by-product it makes possible: artificial witnessing, witnessing by artifice, a mode of consciousness available to every one of us wherein one is witness *as if* one had been there. In the work of Primo Levi, where the faculty to witness without the complete experience of event receives its clearest (if virtual) theorization, it would have simply been necessary for us to read more carefully. Levi's inscription of the lesson affirming that even in extraordinary cases where the subject was witness to an event, each and every being of a witness is an artificial construct — a state predicated, that is, on a temporal delay and a spatial displacement — afterwit is an unambiguous inscription. The reader — Levi teaches us despite himself sometimes — must be cautious and canny, for his witnessness is an intimate relationship of non-coincidence with an inert, hypostasized, definitively dimwitted witness whose Auschwitz name was *Muselmann*. The cunning witness in all of us must imaginatively approach the altogether-other to the point of embrace, while eluding his fate.

But, as I had Beckett remind us at the very top of this work, "Why people have to complicate a thing so simple I can't make out."

3.1 readerliness

As someone who made himself into an abiding self-translator, Samuel Beckett knew more than most about what it means to ready oneself for maximum legibility, to make one's thought as self as decipherable as possible. One's thought, like a painting, "With losses greater or lesser, paintings translate absurd and mysterious strivings toward the image. They are adequations — more or less — of obscure internal tensions."[1]

> See for be seen. Misseen. From now see for be misseen. [5.1]

Don't read just my lips, read the whole of me. Do as Darl did. Take me in. Give me shelter from the storm. If nowness is the temporal condition out of which our witnessness works, it is because it has the characteristics of the moment from which we gauge the future. Everything that we can do from now on is what counts. *Now* cumulates past nows and moments of lull in between to feed the from-now-on. Only the from-now-on has the power (with a little luck) to undo the wrong done in the past: it unties the useless regretfulness of "I should have" revising it to "I can and shall."

To be a conventional witness is the piecework of jury duty, whereas witnessness is fulltime attentiveness. Energy to attend to that additional *ness* entails one's being as potentially decipherable, as apt to being deciphered, as ready to be read as one might be good at deciphering the other. The harm that has befallen no one yet (not in my lifetime, not in my neighborhood, not on my watch, etc.), but that we all know *could very well* occur: this, it is my mission to prevent. Yours too! You can hope that others are already, in advance, reading the possibility of that event imaginatively on your body. But since those others are *you*, you too can read it. So, get to work!

With Lyotard's introduction of the notion that a fault line necessarily conditions two instances and challenges them to join without fusion, we readers of *The Differend* begin to see that witnessness is the positioning of oneself as a readable third party on a duality whose two components

---

1 My translation of, "[*les*] *tableaux* [. . .] *traduisent, avec plus ou moins de pertes, d'absurdes et mystérieuses poussées vers l'image, ils sont plus ou moins adéquats vis-à-vis d'obscures tensions internes*" ("La peinture des van Velde ou le Monde et le Pantalon" in Beckett 1984, 123).

engage wit, within oneself ("opening" and "demand"), rather than as a third party (witness) attempting vainly to report a monolithic unity ultimately and necessarily extrinsic to his lived experience. Lyotard continues: "[Writing] is the witness of the cleft in the 'I,' of its aptitude for hearing an appeal. The other, in the reader, demands not that the ego of the writer die but that it assume its liability" (1983, 168; 1996, 113–14). By amplifying all this with the notion of liability, Lyotard draws the work of imagination into the margin of error between writing and reading close to the sign-as-not-yet-phrased. Liability to the other means readiness to be read. It may be true that you talk before you can read, but aren't you readable before you talk? Isn't that how you get read and said before you can say? Taking control of that passive liability would be to place oneself in a state of readiness. Read on. Read *on*. Reading "on" silently allows it to be read interchangeably as *on*.

The cleft left by disaster and that Lyotard considers in *The Differend* appears altogether less hopeless than the *fêlure* at the heart of being, according to Lacan. Lyotard's cleft serves to join a family of conceptual images found in Kant — abyss, passage, archipelago — that point to the establishment of responsible intersubjectivity.[2] An intersubjective cleft [*fêlure*] over which subjects cleave to each other is an intersubjectivity determined and conditioned by an attentiveness that we usually associate with attitudes — hardly habitual in Beckett's century — with names like "empathy" and "caring." How to make oneself legible to oneself as other? One imagines oneself as architectural telltale applied to the cleft separating "I" from figment. The foreign tongue is in oneself but no longer babble of Babel.[3]

To put one's readerliness to work, one must be able to imagine oneself with the eyes of another. This has been the guiding structure in Beckett's narrative enterprise since the Unnamable trilogy and its drift in *Texts for Nothing*. In *Worstward Ho*, Beckett, as he has before, avails himself to "on" in yet another usage:

> On. Stare on. Say on. Be on. Somehow on. Anyhow on. Till dim gone. At long last gone. All at long last gone. For bad and all. For poor best worse and all. [10.9]

The larval predisposition that may lead to becoming witnesses is common

---

2 I have attempted such a reading in "Passages" (2001) and "Telltale at the Passage" (2001).

3 This is one of the explanations for what Brian Finney astutely identifies, in commenting on *Still*, as "the division of the 'I' into both passive listener and far-from-omniscient narrator undercuts the deceptive simplicity of the use of that pronoun" (1987, 68).

to all beings equipped with wit. I have termed this predisposition witness-ness. It is a function of empathy, which neurobiologists and linguists today often agree is an ethical consequence of our primal metaphor-producing abilities. Reading in the broadest sense of the term — reading a film or a look — is the paradigmatic post-symbolic means by which our capacity to witness — our witnessness — awakens. A feeling of anxiousness, a concern that was not ours to begin with becomes ours ineluctably, irresist-ibly. A predicament that we are not in, something that has not touched us directly, a situation in which criminal injustice has been perpetrated on the body and mind of another becomes ours in a surge of empathy through the act of reading. We can say that we have actually read a text when this occurs. This, already, is so many things. A text read may be almost anything: the look in the eye of another — I read it, I will have read it. The rubble remaining after the demolition of a house is testimony to its having been there — I read it, I will have read it. No right to read others until one allows and enables others to read one. What better other to start with, the parable named *Film* shows us, than oneself as other?

Lyotard affirms, against Adorno's dogged pessimism, an algebra most intimate for reuniting a "me" and a "you" into *one* after the shock of disas-ter: "*I* who writes and *you* who read." However tangentially, contingently, temporarily (and temporally) these constitutive units of minimal solidar-ity fuse, they open a creative margin for error that is the very essence of the economy constituted of writing and reading. But is this tenuously "wee 'we'" formed of "*I* who writes and *you* who read" the same relationship as that fragile and uncertain pact between author and reader that Lyotard seemed to mock in the "Reader's Notes" introducing *The Differend*? When that pairing occurs, it is one between discreet individuals dwelling within a common culturally determined space: a writer having already finished his task and a reader who may or, as is more often the case, may not take the time to acquaint himself fully with it. Yet if we read the "wee 'we'" as a "reflective movement," as Lyotard admonishes us to, in terms of Kant's description of esthetic judgment at work, we are compelled to conclude that the two instances of "*I* who writes and *you* who read" operate not in that commonality between discreet subjects, but *within the same mind*.[4]

---

4 There is also a necessary non-simultaneity involved in the emergence of a "wee 'we'" predicated on a relationship between "*I* who writes and *you* who read." Reading follows writing if we assume that what is read has already been written. The effect of reading may therefore be likened to the effect of what psychoanalysis calls "deferred action" (*Nachträglichkeit*, or *après-coup* in French). This subject, that would have to draw carefully and necessarily on several important discussions by Lyotard on anamnesis and the affect-phrase, cannot be broached here. I want to point it out with emphasis, however, as it is as important as "play" (mainly a category of

As Virgil showed Dante the way through *purgatorio*, so Dante showed Beckett the way from logorrheic writing to serene readability. At the summit of *purgatorio*, Dante finally stops chattering to let himself be deciphered — ultimately by Beatrice, but first by Matelda — with what must be the most suavely loving words in the *Divina Commedia*:

> *Tosto che fu là dove l'erbe sono*
> *bagnate già da l'onde del bel fiume,*
> *di levar li occhi suoi mi fece dono.*[5]

Thus the late learner receives the gift of the look of the reader.

Samuel Beckett taught himself to go on living as a writer while going increasingly silent. Already in the "pell-mell babel" of his writing in the early 1950s, he wrote with a "silence that is not silence and barely murmured words." He taught himself that gabbing on and on held not the key to one man's survival. To breathe, as we read in *Text for Nothing* 6, was proof enough (1995, 125). In §3 of *The Differend*'s Levinas Notice (the chapter is "Obligation"), Lyotard meditates the possibilities for an "atheistic" interpretation for Levinas's assertion that "Writing is not sacrificial, it is saintly":

> Perhaps writing needs to be understood, or rather presented, otherwise. Instead of the description of an experience carried out by an "I" seeking self-knowledge, maybe writing for Levinas is witnessing of the cleft, opening toward that other which addresses, within his reader, a demand. Perhaps it is responsibility before the messenger that the reader is. (1988, 113; tr. modified)

To follow Lyotard, one consciousness understands and accepts the existence of another only by working through contradictions that already reside within the one. Struggle and strife in the agora merely reflect the cleft being that dwells in the atrium. In order to cleave to the other, we must recognize the gulf within us, first. In the vocabulary of *Worstward Ho*, the "grot" within us corresponds to my being "vast[ly] apart" from the other.

Clearly the writing-reading shuttle of imagination as "witness of the cleft in the 'I'" is witness to an event whose unforgetting is demanded

---

space — both physical and conceptual) in elaborating a new paradigm of the witness after Lyotard.

5   No sooner had she reached the point where that
     fair river's waves could barely bathe the grass,
     than she gave me this gift: lifting her eyes.
                                        Purgatorio XXVIII; 61–63

even of the "wee 'we'" — the inner remnant of a much greater, "collective" subject — that may evolve from the I/thou differend.[6] As Enoch Brater writes of the experience of reading, at long last, *Worstward Ho*, "Before long we find ourselves reading the formerly unreadable, imagining the unimaginable, naming, and with considerable accuracy, the unnamable. [. . .] We have survived one more rite of passage, the *passage* of this text, and we are ready once more to resume the struggle, 'worstward ho'" (1990b, 161). Neither "complete witness" nor "witness-bearing witness," this witness of the cleft, this witness located *at* the cleft, intimately touches both. Its (his/her/one's) "witnessness" consists of keeping watch with its (his/her/one's) imaginative knack at ready, ensuring, if possible, that the cleft does not widen to become an incommensurable abyss. The discourse of witnessness is neither permanent muteness nor unabated prolixity. Rather, it is the patience of aposiopesis, the trueness of ice and fire, love minus zero over no limit.[7] Witnessness, with its margin for error, prevents the short-circuit of an all-too-quick, conciliatory, flattening passage that would necessarily wrong one side or the other. This witness's "witnessness" knows too (because it has always felt) that fiction and the figural contribute determinately to "real" truth — a truth whose presentation need never be present.

Although the conceptual ingredient of liability (susceptibility to, vulnerability) allows us to begin to perceive what energetics would be involved in the witness's relation to a psycho-ethical future that, in fact, inheres to its clefted[8] self, liability also marks the unfixed limit of what Lyotard was able to do with the witness in *The Differend*. After *The Differend* — little more than a decade that would prove to be the final phase of his oeuvre — Lyotard would fashion a number of tools or retool old tools that might, with more time, have allowed him to fully explain the integration of liability into his nascent notion of the "new" witness. From the mid-1980s until his death he would reopen the older mines of *Nachträglichkeit* and *anamnesis*. And among the new sites for exploitation would be infancy and the inhuman. It will remain to philosophers "after Lyotard,"[9] however, to assemble these elements into something like the "witnessness" of the witness.

---

6 Martin Buber is a minor but intriguing "discussant" that Lyotard briefly engages in the penultimate moves of *The Differend*.

7 Regarding *aposiopesis*, or "unexplained break[s] into silence," in Beckett, see Abbott in Oppenheim, 2004, 15. Bob Dylan's, as my reader will have already noticed, is a voice that has kept me company for over forty years.

8 Ever so slightly different from cleft, clefted means "having clefts, divisions, or fissures" (OED).

9 See Robert Harvey, ed. *Afterwords: Essays in Memory of Jean-François Lyotard*, 2000 and Geoffrey Bennington, *Late Lyotard*, 2005.

One of the most striking enigmas in Sartre's long series of them is how, as a young boy, with aspirations of fame fed by omnivorous reading, he came to see himself as absent from a throng of adults (cf. *The Words*). Seeing himself as missing, which is a reworking of Proust's observation of the same phenomenon, would seem to lead to that relentless writing of his that is so very obviously a rendering readable of the self through others. "But to be witness to [*assister à*] one's own absence is not so simple. It requires that the gaze perform a gnoseological, esthetic and ethical elaboration which determines the readability of the image" (Didi-Huberman 2003, 113; 2008, 88). The alternative that Beckett suggests that we adopt, after learning *Worstward Ho*'s lesson well, is to read the other as if he were inscribed inside our skull. Giuseppe Penone's mural cranial rubbings are massively blown-up exteriorized illustrations of those hieroglyphs.

One of the things that makes ethics so hard to imagine, one of its main paradoxes is this: On the one hand, all of its benefits would have to be legible in the empirical world of things, people, events; on the other hand, its foundations are religious, psychological, or imaginary. The western tradition of thinking holds those two worlds as incommensurable. *Worstward Ho* brings the imaginary and the empirical into a relation of proximate tension in whose magnetic field ethics maintains.

3.2 witnesswork in the witnessworks

With talkativeness tempered and readerliness readied, imagine your mind as your own little factory, a personal plant in which knowledge and judgment are manufactured out of wonder or awe or terror before the raw material of images you perceive. If Kant had expressed the "productive synthesis of the imagination" at the heart of his *First Critique* (1998, 238ff.) with an overtly industrial metaphor, we might have called that plant for consciousness a witnessworks. Playing on meanings of labor and work, Didi-Huberman writes that "an image without imagination is an image that one has simply not taken the time to work. For imagination is work, the *work-time of images* ceaselessly acting upon each other by collision, fusion, breaks or metamorphoses" (2003, 149; 2008, 116–19). We who think of ourselves as eternally at the cusp of a post-industrial world, tend to envision virtual factories as dreamworks. We thus make the legitimate leap to film, for the schemata are the same: no knowledge without the work of the imagination.

With images before its attendant eye, the mind rolls up its sleeves and gets down to work. Taking inspiration from Jean-Luc Godard's life devoted not only to showing us that "editing" is incremental rather than subtractive, but proving to us that *montage* alone is capable of showing a feeling, Didi-Huberman argues that witnesswork is essentially the same procedure. The collisions, fusions, breaks, and transformations act, "in turn, upon our own activities of thinking and knowing. To know, one must imagine [*s'imaginer*]: the speculative *workbench* is always there, in tandem, with the *editing table* of the imagination" (2003, 149; 2008, 119). In asserting that short of exercising the skill to go where the experience of the other once brought him, the filmmaker can make no montage, we are also saying that without that mad courage, there is no humanity in the being we say we are. It is thus that the seemingly endless controversy over proxy experience and its role in responsibility, while preserving the integrity of the other, is laid to rest forever.

Enough still not to know. Not to know what they say. Not to know what it is the words it says say. Says? Secretes. Say better worse secretes. What it is the words it secretes say. What the so-said void. The so-said dim. The so-said shades. The so-said seat and germ of all. Enough to know no knowing. No knowing what it is the words

it secretes say. No saying. No saying what it all is they somehow
say. [11.4]

The labor solicited from the witful body when anamnesis raises
consciousness up out of oblivion reveals the vastness between an untrace-
able yet irrevocable first whit of a strike and starkly evident afterwit
(*Nachträglichkeit*). As the effortless labor of falling water may be harnessed
into electrical current, so this move is apt to transform wit into witnessness
through the dynamic of witnesswork. Realities do indeed exist that are
beyond the capacities of discursive realism to grasp — witness *Auschwitz*.
Such realities are, however, well within the capacities of imagination. The
witness capable of establishing such levels of reality would (and should)
do so by means of creative imagination — that eternal tension among
representation, presentation, and other yet unexplored manifestations.
Imagination is a tensor between present feeling (perception) and future
understanding (justice). It is the *ness* with which the witness harnesses
the goodness between ones.

Now, right now, is the time of this witnessness, its "when-ness" as
memory of a remanence. Impossible to halt the march of time, yet witnessness suspends what is happening in a now that can be transmitted,
communicated from one to another in the form of an image. The man
who captures a crime from within that crime creates a suspension of time
necessary for him to have become a witness, even if he dies before he can
speak what he's seen with his own eyes. "By hiding in order to see, the
man interrupted and spirited away for his own purposes the task whose
iconography he was about to establish." The task to which Georges
Didi-Huberman refers is the man's own (forced) part in the industrial
demolition of a part of humanity defined by religion and ethnicity. A time
and a place — thought by so many to have been impossible — of an image
of *that* was created. "The image was possible because an ever so relative
zone of calm had been contrived for this deed of looking" (2003, 56; 2008,
40). Room was also made for the later imagining by others, survivors by
proxy. That time was witnesswork. That place was a witnessworks — an
example of which is *Images in Spite of All*.

This dynamic function has its little factory: witnesswork takes place
in a witnessworks. We always knew that "Where all always to be seen"
meant the wit of the witness. We now learn something of the whereness
of this faculty. Beckett asks us to imagine the survival of the mind as the
feebly sputtering manifestations of a factory in throes within the skull
of the other you might have been and will inexorably be. A skull is the
scene within which everything Beckett describes in *Worstward Ho* works
in a working-through that transcends psychoanalysis. To the extent that
everything that occurs between the first and last pages of *Worstward Ho*
is held within the brain's box, the little case we carry about between our

shoulders, the text/poem/prose is an exemplum of classical unity of space. The action of the "play" can (and should) be described as the workings of a minimally functioning consciousness — that of a *Muselmann*, for example. This consciousness strives ever further to reach new depths of minimalism. But unlike in traditional fiction, where the reader observes the protagonist at an irresponsibly safe distance, *Worstward Ho* elicits the reader's vicariousness, causing him to replace his own astute mind with the dim wit that is staged inside out, as it were.

What a piece of work! Everyone outside the dimwit's witnessworks, the *Muselmann*'s noggin, says there's nothing inside — nothing but death, naught but zero, dullness to the point of nullity, everything that's not human. Even Primo Levi, who came as close to being a *Muselmann* as anyone could, said so. To call *Worstward Ho*'s philosophical scene a cranial stage ("lumber") would yet not be too deviant to be meaningful if we could imagine miniature actors moving around within that cavity we all carry. Beckett returns us to the fundamentals of what has always been thought concerning the imagination. We create homunculi or figments to occupy the space of our portable stage. What was once plump, plentiful grey matter filling the cavity behind eyes that could actually see through vitreous humor — matter preventing wind from blowing through ears — is now a puddle of mush ("ooze") stagnating at the bottom of the cavity behind sockets long emptied of their expressively lively pupils. "No matter": instead of shunning him, let's shunt ourselves to him. Let's go inside the nearest *Muselmann*'s head, murmurs Sam Beckett. His noggin is dim — shady to the point of appearing vastly void, like the *aven* that Armand thought he'd discovered before he lit his lamp.[1] Words will reform in vague shapes in the shade; they will begin, once again, to fledge in preparation for flight. They are yet primitive and will remain so beyond now, they cannot and will not be spoken, they will not be understood. The grey matter has lost too much consistency and the words come out as mere secretions. From the cavity you will ooze the ever-penultimate byproduct of a tryworks, defunct dying factory (cf. [11.4]). Even in the most degenerative of conditions, something like words can still be extruded from the nearly desiccated cerebellum. Something still works when "your one" looks to be a complete lost cause. And the mute witness must have some addressee.

A moral refinery, your witnessworks lends definition and ethical substance to the *shuttle* of consciousness between the care that you take for yourself and the care that you extend to the other within you. Your

---

1 Aven Armand is a deep limestone grotto located in the Cévennes National Park in France. It was discovered by a curious blacksmith, Louis Armand, in 1897. Its over 400 stalagmites, some of which are nearly 30 meters high, are spectacularly beautiful.

witnessworks is no waterwork: no time for weeping over spilt milk, now's not the time for your tears. Didi-Huberman could not be clearer or simpler on and about Godard: "montage creates a third image out of the assemblage of two" (2003, 173; 2008, 138). It comes about in precisely the same way that a witness — coming between a victim and perpetrator — does. The labor performed in the witnessworks is far more than a simple remainder: it has the power to raise to 3 the sum of 1 + 1 (*testis, terstis*). Primo Levi has already shown us this dynamics of the shuttle in the margin of error that makes us human in spite of all, "if this be a man." "Ah yes," says the voice in *Text for Nothing 1*, "we seem to be more than one, all deaf, not even, gathered together for life" (1995, 100–01). As the shuttling accelerates to the speed of twenty-four frames per second, persistence of vision resists no more and three, then two become one — quintessence of dust.

3.3 imagination

The impulse to talk in lieu of action retreats into mute readerliness and the dim wits are soon available to the appeal of others. The mutual call is answered and the two nestle testy-beshy in each other's minds — "seat of all." The life-preserving shuttle of empathy may begin. The mental activity lending its impulse to the to-and-fro is the imagination. Preluding Beckett, singing it much as his Irish-French twentieth-century offspring would say it in the final prose pieces, stirring still, here is how the imagination behaves in Dante's words:

> Ricorditi, lettor, se mai ne l'alpe
> ti colse nebbia per la qual vedessi
> non altrimenti che par pelle talpe,
> come, quando i vapori umidi e spessi
> a diradar cominciansi, la spera
> del sol debilemente entra per essi;
> e fia la tua imagine leggera
> in giugnere a veder com' io rividi
> lo sole in pria, che già nel concar era.
> [. . .]
> O imaginativa che ne rube
> talvolta sì di fuor, ch'om non s'accorge
> perchè dintorno suonin mille tube,
> chi move te, se 'l senso non ti porge?
> [. . .]
> e qui fu la mia mente sì ristretta
> dentro da sé, che di fuor non venìa
>   Purgatorio XVII, 1–9, 13–16, 22–24[1]

---

1   Remember, reader, if you've ever been
     caught in the mountains by a mist through which
     you only saw as moles see through their skin,
     how, when the thick, damp vapors once begin
     to thin, the sun's sphere passes feebly through them,
     then your imagination will be quick
     to reach the point where it can see how I
     first came to see the sun again — when it

The canto begins near day's end, with the dawn of consciousness. Here is a paean to the extreme force of our mind's weakest resource. Dante calls upon each and every reader to recall the experience of being able to see with eyes wide shut (*vedessi per pelle*) because all — *l'uom, l'on* — have the *ness* to experience this. And *ness* is named imagination.

Philosophy too is about beginnings. Beginning again, always. And beginning is necessarily to imagine beginning. Imaginativeness names our capacity to give ourselves over to the imagination and to thereby begin. Witnessness is a function of imaginativeness. Here, though, we come to the heart of an enigma. If the imagination is a mere figment of the imagination, we imagine that it exists as generator of figments. The main streams of western metaphysics have relegated the imagination to a minor position, far below the awesome rigor of reason. Even if the imagination exerts, as John Sallis relentlessly argues, "a kind of oblique force on philosophy" (2000, 43), can this be enough to redeem the imagination in the eyes of the philosophical tradition? Or, does redemption of the imagination even matter? Imagination, after all, goes on doing quite well without it.

In the face of the historical denigration of fantasy, in the face of philosophy's abiding resistance to according any importance to "flights of fancy," no more powerful affirmation of its resilience and reliability can be found than in the incipit of *Imagination Dead Imagine*, Beckett's short prose piece of 1965:

> No trace anywhere of life, you say, pah, no difficulty there, imagination not dead yet, yes, good, imagination dead imagine.[2]

Even with odd punctuation, minus most logical operators, the message coming out of the impasse of too much talk (*How It Is*) is patent. The message is a motto, a mantra. You say your imagination has died? That there's nothing left? — Never! Not on your life! So, pull yourself together, man, and imagine still, imagine on. Your life depends on it.

---

was almost at the point at which it sets.
[. . .]
O fantasy, you that at times would snatch
us so from outward things — we notice nothing
although a thousand trumpets sound around us —
who moves you when the senses do not spur you?
[. . .]
at this, my mind withdrew to the within,
to what imagining might bring; no thing
that came from the without could enter in.

2 "After [Antelme], Beckett would say: 'Imagination dead' — but to bring us back *in spite of all* to the injunction: 'Imagine'." (Didi-Huberman 2003, 224; 2008, 181)

Your life and the life of all like you — all — your fellows. What you imagine, a figment, is and always will be yourself in the place of the other. That place, inside your own head. Acts of the imagination, not of reason, harbor the power to bind you to the other every bit as the imagination binds the sensate to the rational in Kant's critical philosophy. Though waves of thinkers with few exceptions have denigrated the imagination, trying to kill it, it will survive to keep us human, all too human to the end of humanity.

If we agree with contemporary medicine that the limit of life is the life of the mind, then imaginativeness is the residual *living on* even when imagination is deemed dead. This is the sense of the text's movement to begin again, to go on. *Imagination Dead Imagine* echoes the incipit of *Company*: "A voice comes to one in the dark. Imagine" (1980, 3).[3] Imaginativeness at the limit names the force at work in the witnessworks.[4]

That force subsists within us even when reason escapes us and vital forces ebb and lead us to the brink of the unlivable.

On back better worse to fail the head said seat of all. Germ of all. All? If of all of it too. [8.3]

But Beckett is certain that the dimwit always gets his grip back. Against reason, he knows this is all about the imagination. The "head said seat of all," the mind, the understanding, reason, judgment — each in succession or simultaneously were Kant's prime preoccupations. They're all nothing without the imagination. Without this "instrument of reason," the mind could never judge (1951, 109). Imagination is the necessary supplement. In rereading Robert Antelme's *L'espèce humaine* in light of the four photographs smuggled out of Auschwitz, Georges Didi-Huberman boldly equates the work of the imagination to the kernel of ethics. For ethics to be, the individual must recognize all that is similar to him. This, of course, includes all other individuals. But, most importantly, this recognition is the product of the imagination which, in turn, we all have at our disposal.[5] The imagination is thus superfluous or redundant only for

---

3 That the "late" Beckett became increasingly preoccupied with the imagination, which already had primacy in his early work is a truism. Witness this platitude from his London publisher, John Calder, in 1983: "After *Company* and *Ill Seen Ill Said*, *Worstward Ho* moves even further into the world of pure imagination" (cited in van der Weel 1998, 32). Well, fair enough, as my late colleague Michael Sprinker used to say.

4 Cf. "ageless imagination labouring on" (Krance 1990, 133).

5 Cf. Didi-Huberman 2003, 200; 2008, 161: "it is a question of engaging a 'process of recognition of the similar,' which grounds the very *ethics* of our relation to the experience of the camps. This is the process of *imagination*, about which Robert Antelme alerted us from the very opening of his book."

the most obtuse skeptic or cynic. For the rest, it is our inhumanly human remainder. It is a bridge. It does not just aid reason, it is *of* reason. Or, it can do without reason altogether.[6]

Worstward Ho is structured around dozens of typographical blanks — lines missing between blocks of opaque text. Beckett's textual gaps, like the absent stares of his characters, their gaping mouths, their dimmed wits have troubled so many of his readers. H. Porter Abbott, who has explored what he calls Beckett's "egregious gaps" comes as close as anyone can to articulating their importance in terms of an imagination restored to a status on par with or surpassing hegemonic reason:

> In arguing that, with regard to the egregious gaps in the work of these eight years, interpretive priority should always go to the experience of ignorance, I am not calling for a reductive or impoverished criticism. Quite the reverse. Beckett's crafting of the texture and feel of ignorance is richly representational, not of the absence but of the feelings it engenders and the schemata that vie to fill it. After all, egregious gaps make the greatest appeal to the schematizing imagination [. . .]. (2004, 22)

Along these lines, we must understand Beckett's whiteouts and silences in the way Dante asked his readers to behold the lightning quickness of their own imagination. Primo Levi recognized recovery in those moments as the miracle of knowhow, knack, *astuzia*. Right into those gaps, imaginitiveness is drawn as to that which fires it when the embers are nearly grey with "the sun's disk dimly glimmering through."

John Sallis indulges in no undue melodrama when he lends the title "Imagination at the Limit" to a section of the most comprehensive and, perhaps, most important book on the imagination written.[7] Imaginitiveness is

---

6 At this conjuncture, I would invite the reader to hold this: "W? But W too is creature of his powers of artistic invention. 'What kind of imagination is this so reason-ridden?' he asks" (Finney 1987, 73), against this: "*Le propos du texte est de faire de l'imagination la faculté mentale souveraine, réunissant aussi bien les prérogatives de l'intelligence et de la raison que celles de l'imagination et du cœur; il se déclare prêt d'ailleurs à lui donner le statut qui lui fait défaut. 'Quelle est cette espèce d'imagination si entichée de raison? Une espèce à part'*" (Clément 1994, 65), and let Beckett be the judge as to who is right.

7 The importance of Sallis' *Force of Imagination* can be measured in the book's expressed stakes: "it is a question of whether the imagined is no more than a flat surface incapable of reflecting anything not already explicit to the imagining consciousness or whether through imagining, through engagement with the imagined, something other can come to light, whether, from the play of the imagined, something can be disclosed that would otherwise have escaped consciousness, something that in a sense will have escaped consciousness by coming from elsewhere, by

the ultimate resource of consciousness, but it is also an irresistible impulse that consciousness shares with what it is not or, better, what is not it. The imagination is the capacity to greet the world beyond the confines of the skull *at* the image. The autonomy of the image from the function of the imagination is compromised irresistibly by the witnesswork's will to host the image. Human, I cannot but reach out beside myself and render intimate to me what I perceive yet cannot make captive. In doing so, I forget a bit of myself, moving emotionally, psychologically beside myself for the sake of that which and he who resembles me.

So, before Claude Lanzmann's camera, in phrases very nearly halting before the impossibility of going on, the otherwise almost effusive Filip Müller, manages just barely to give halting voice to what is so often left blank on Beckett's pages:

One never got used to that.
    It was impossible.

"Impossible" yet lived (or survived) by the likes of Müller and imaginable by us who enter those words. "Yes. One must imagine," adds Müller before Georges Didi-Huberman returns, after quoting him, to effect a convergence with the categorical imperative of *Imagination Dead Imagine* (2003, 55; 2008, 39). Any aesthetics of the unimaginable thus nullified, Müller's testimony resonates nevertheless with Kant's description of the mind's experience of the sublime.

A perfect example of a beginning with the mind withdrawing to itself (*la mente sì ristretta dentro da sé*) resides also in the *dénouement* of Beckett's only cinematographic work, *Film*. Whereas Deleuze contended that the protagonist of *Film* ends up "slipping into the void," the sense and logic of the filmed parable can only lead to the conclusion that *Film*'s conclusion is, paradoxically, a beginning.[8] The protagonist — played reluctantly by Buster Keaton with no concern for the film save its ability to furnish his ration of beer — in the throes of a drama of split being ends up, predictably, "going on." Stares at the culminating moment of the filmed drama are anything but blank. O has been pursued relentlessly by E. Beckett directs Keaton (O) to enter that room in shambles with no source of perception other than Buster (E) to have him play out the drama of the belated discovery of the imagination for complete being. O's eye expresses terror as E, who has finally managed to swing around in front of O, looks on with imperiousness or pity. E, for eye, has finally cornered object O, who

---

arising otherwise than through the explicit intention operative in the imagining" (2000, 11).
8 For Deleuze's discussion of *Film*, see 1983, 97–99.

can no longer elude the understanding that E is, in fact, himself.[9]

Film's final shots reveal to O (and to us) the shape of the shade that had pursued him: himself as E. But given the conventions that produce the art called cinema, E is the camera of *Film* as cheval-glass, a full-length mirror, now in front of O. Beckett himself uses the word "*investissement*" in his notes that led to the filming of *Film*. I have used the term "reintegration" to reinforce the idea that the two parts of being, designated in the scenario as O and E, are reunited to live, not to die. After all, the word for "eye" in French is written with O and E ligatured to each other: *œil*. The integration of the two parts of being, in what might have become a Berkeley horror story, has resolved the tense suspense and reestablished the workings of the imagination in the witnessworks. Warding off horror at the prospect of forever losing our self, the imagination accustoms us to being moved beyond our self for the sake of humanity.

It seems evident that in *Worstward Ho*, Beckett conjures the moment of integration between witness and martyr via the imagination in terms starkly reminiscent of *Film*:

> Stare clamped to stare. Bowed backs blurs in stare clamped to stare. Two black holes. Dim black. In through skull to soft. Out from soft through skull. Agape in unseen face. That the flaw? The want of flaw? Try better worse set in skull. Two black holes in foreskull. Or one. Try better still worse one. One dim black hole mid-foreskull. Into the hell of all. Out from the hell of all. So better that nothing worse say stare from now. [17.5]

In the drama of witnessness, imagining care for the other from the vantage of the skull can only come once the integration of self with self has been accepted. Then, rather than passively *seen*, the "skull [with] stare clamped to all [can serve actively as] *scene* and seer of all." With imagination in full action, engaged in a perpetual state of work, witnessness becomes a sort of rational consciousness of the irrational. Such a state is necessary for our witnessness to triumph over the aporia of "realist" silencing by the demand for proof. Imagination's force derives from its capacity to harness margins of error, setting aside those preserves for the differend between Levi's two types of witness, preventing a cleft from widening into an impassable abyss of evil while preserving it from being collapsed into illusory resolution. Thus the lone character pursued by his perceiver (himself) in *Film* is preserved from death when he accedes to and accepts his own perceivedness.

---

9 Both Beckett's notes toward the film (aka, "the scenario") and Alan Schneider's anecdotal information about the making of *Film* may be read in Beckett 1969.

The indolence of *Purgatorio*'s Belacqua, who served as model for most of Beckett's early dimmer wits, the apparent passivity of O before E, the weak force by which sensation communes with consciousness — these constants only underscore the power of imagination that Beckett implores us — however tacitly — to tap. On the centrality and the universality of imagination, Immanuel Kant was clear:

> The unity of apperception in relation to the synthesis of the imagination is the understanding, and this very same unity, in relation to the transcendental synthesis of the imagination, is the pure understanding. (1998, 238)

On this basis for pure reason, Kant would divine a judgment whose capacity for recovery when confronted with the experience of the sublime depends intrinsically on the resilience of the imagination and opens esthetics onto ethics. We can only imagine, along with Hannah Arendt (1982), that a critique of political judgment would have turned on these self-same powers.[10]

If we parse Sallis' definition of the image, viz. that it "name[s . . .] the occurrence, means, and locus in which the sensible becomes present to sensible intuition" (2000, 78), we encounter an object — the image — of the imagination that is *between* two forces. In terms of witnessness, this betweenness forms the "occurrence, means, and locus" of the permanent link between one and other, between witness and martyr. Between invention and imagination too. In the witnessworks housed in your mind's atrium, hardwired to your being as the extensive development of your imagination, you possess the artifice to develop your witnessness.

> On both sides imagination exceeds what is present, extending our gaze beyond the immediately visible (the sparse traces of spring), beyond to the stages to come (flowers, fruits, shade), opening to the future precisely in and through the profusion of sense to come. In this very movement imagination draws us beyond ourselves, displaces us from the simple feeling of self given in and through sensations, makes us exceed the bounds of the self-apprehension produced merely through sense and feeling. (Sallis 2000, 66)

Imagination is the "to come" in the now. Certainly not just reason and not even just sentiment and sensation. But imagination which is the product of images and witnesswork: the raw material of images — printed, framed

---

10   "How often it occurs that one can *only* imagine, which obviously doesn't imply the exhaustion of the truth of what one imagines?" (Didi-Huberman 2003, 83; 2008 64).

or virtual — subjected to the labor of witnessness in the witnessworks. Once one *one* has transformed a now into a "to come," that one has succeeded in beginning to operate (be alive) in the ethical mode, one has activated one's witnessness (and no further software updates would ever be necessary).

From the court of law are barred figments of the imagination or, if they make their way to the bar, they are ejected. However, just as there is no true understanding without imagination's power, so judgment of the highest forms — political and ethical — need the figment factory. For conventional witnessing, the imagination is anathema; for witnessness it is required.

3.4 figment

Sì ruminando e sì mirando in quelle,
mi prese il sonno; il sonno che sovente,
anzi che 'l fatto sia, sa le novelle.

Purgatorio XXVII, 91–93[1]

Although I have no desire to breathe new life into the old, tired reflex of associating Beckett with absurdism, reading his work fuels that temptation in the best of readers. What I *do* have a great desire to do is use Andy Warhol as cautionary tale against such temptations. When one of the most thorough commentators of *Worstward Ho* ventured to speculate about "what happens to the mind after death,"[2] I recognized that this venture had veered seriously toward the proverbial absurd. Beckett never thought that after death anything fancier than total decay happened to the "seat of all" and whatever it will have been capable of before the demise. He never expressed the slightest interest, therefore, in staging speculative fantasies that deviated from that view.

Far less absurd, and closer to what I'm certain Beckett thought about "what happens to the mind after death," were Andy Warhol's musings about his own mind and body and what might happen to them after his death. "I never understood why when you died, you didn't just vanish, everything could just keep going on the way it was only you just wouldn't be there. I always thought I'd like my own tombstone to be blank. No epitaph, and no name. Well, actually, I'd like it to say 'figment'."[3]

Figments populate the skulls of Beckett characters throughout. Beckett figured early on, somehow, that his whole quest would have to end up as a figment inside a head. To hold the other as a figment close by does

---

1   But while I watched the stars, in reverie,
     sleep overcame me — sleep, which often sees,
     before it happens, what is yet to be.
2   "[. . .] there is much less agreement about what happens to the mind after death. The answer to the question will depend largely on the definition of what mind is. As the thinking *substance* it would not seem in our contemporary estimation to have a high claim on deathlessness" (Hisgen 1998, 497).
3   Andy Warhol, quoted in Sean D. Hamill and Ian Urbina, "Remembering Warhol: A Tomato Soup Can and a Pocketful of Coins," *New York Times*, 27 February 2007, p. A12.

not have to happen too late. It's never too early. Murphy's mind turned into itself, bringing figments with it all the way up to *The Unnamable*, then beyond. The remnant of that sole Beckett character who dies finds itself in *The Unnamable* "inside of my distant skull, where once I wandered, now am fixed, lost for tininess" (1965, 18–19). Beckett will go on experimenting strategically with the word "figment," and the concept it's meant to ferry, all the way up through to the late prose texts, alternating it with "shades," of obviously Dantean inspiration. But whether as figment or shade, these English words for my imagined form in the head of my fellow man are more promising than the one Beckett had to use in French: *chimère*.

Avec dérisoire rampade et chimères vaines. (*Compagnie*)

With bootless crawl and figments comfortless. (*Company*)

As this juxtaposition shows, in some cases his English is incomparably better, if by "better" one means representative of the voice we recognize as that of the author. This voice, in English, is that of Beckett; in French, it is that of Racine. Conceptually better too: like nothingness, figments are marginally more substantial than chimera, which are more likely to be likened to the zero which, as we have amply seen, Beckett resists. As always, it is in that margin, that "edge" between two languages, two minds, that Beckett operates as witness of differends, hoping against hope that all others will as he does. Hopelessness aside, in *Lessness*, Beckett even manages to suggest comically a certain parallel between the idea of a witness and the importance of nurturing the figments of one's imagination. As Mary Catanzaro has pointed out, the word "genitals" in that spare text, appears "only twice, but emphatically, [and] is punctuated by the vigorous phrase, cadentially stated, 'Figment dawn dispeller of figments.'" (1993, 216). The odd but attested link between *testes* and *terstis*, the latter of which gives modern languages testimony and the quintessential third party, the witness, has been discussed thoroughly in this work. Witnessness by figments, of figments, is with us, as are balls, no matter how spent.

Calculating reason operating alone will transform the other into a disposable figure. This was *Auschwitz*, "reason-ridden" in the terminology of *Worstward Ho*. Brothers and sisters reduced to figures were marked for living no longer. But encourage the imagination in the newborn, never allowing it to die, and he will lend a future to his fellow sisters and brothers by carrying all of them within as figments.

There in the sunken head the sunken head. [8.3]

A figment is both remainder and supplement, both survivor and *memento* without *mori* — a sweet nothing that is not nothing. The energy to create it equals the minimal wherewithal, the knack that allowed Primo Levi to be lifted back up from the bottom. At the root of "figment" is *fig-*, the Latin short stem of *finger*, to feign, to make an artful maneuver. The figment is to the imagination what a remainder is in mathematics, in physics: the mind's correlate of the survivor, the other who is saved on your watch.

To put into words what the witnessable imagination does when the image to be met is a fellow human and not a tree about to bud in springtime, let us reverse the usual predicate. Let me ("I") be the other to be protected and let him ("he") be the clever protector. In my absence, he creates *me* as a figment. Multiplied by the myriad heads capable of imagining, my protection and survival are ensured.

With your witnessness, with your sunken head's doubling itself as other, that is, you'll be able to create me wholly figment, thus increasing twofold your noggin's capacity. Colluding with its offerings to the senses, your force of imagination meets my world halfway, where it forms that image of me called figment, for better or worse. For worse: that nothing so often deemed negligible, but which we know to be essential. For better: so that it serves *to* model and as model *for* our responsibility to the other. I do the same with you, in your absence. I, as figment, am that part of the event that occurs in your imagination: as shadily small as you might think me to be, the figment of me occupies the room.

Much ado about nothing in order to disprove the old saw that nothing is naught constitutes the mote motivating this meditation on imaginativeness and its central role in nurturing witnessness. Of all the insignificant, underrated things we've thus far misled ourselves into believing are intrinsic to humanity, what have we yet to redeem on the outside chance we can save ourselves from conventional stupidity and its concomitant inhumanity to man? The answer would be figments. Historically denigrated — at least in "our" cultures — these stand-ins that my imagination concocts for the others that surround me, that I carry with me into sleep (*Finnegans Wake*), but that occupy my wake as well, are crucial tokens to the care I take of their counterparts in tangible reality. In their absence, I carry with me my fellow creatures in the form of figments in order to counter any tendency to not give a fig.

To drive home the axiom that figment-making is originary, Molloy even mused about God's infancy, asking "*13° Que foutait Dieu avant la création?*" (Beckett 1951, 227). One might be tempted to translate the irreverent variation on Augustine's question, "What was God doing before he created heaven and earth?"[4] by "What the fuck was God doing before the creation?" but Beckett's own far more subtle solution suggests

---

4 For a detailed discussion of the concern with origins and the nature of creative activity that Beckett shared with Augustine, see Jones 2000 and Book XI of Augustine's *Confessions*.

both the certain pointlessness of solitary pleasuring and its proximity to the originary fabrication of figments: "What was God doing with himself before the creation?" (1951, 167). The moral of the rhetorical question, in any case, is that the way the child plays with his doll — whether he makes it a figbar of his imagi-Newton or a Fig Newton of his abomination — will determine how he treats his fellows when and if he makes it to adulthood. Ethical "development" is not necessarily a progression. It may well require a regression within our capacities as though we were God going back to whatever it was he was "doing with himself" before tackling the Big Job, but this step back to a time and a state in which we toy with our brainchild is necessary in order to foresee a future of survival for them. We *can* do better than God did.

When the force of imagination reconfigures one's mind as shared with the other, figments form. Two so-called minds in Beckett's imaginary will always simultaneously conjure each other as figments for mutual protection. Such is the only solution one can draw from the chiasmatically tongue-twisted rhetorical question posed by the narrator of *Company*: "Can the crawling creator crawling in the same create dark as his creature create while crawling?" (1982, 38).[5] Such also may be the geometric purity of poetry when, for example, in the example just cited, alliterative nodes correspond point for point with the coordinates maintaining *Company*'s two "named" characters in perfectly secure togetherness. Reduced to initial letters, those two nestle testy-beshy: W, the narrator (a witness, a Watt, a wit) speaks of his sounding board as M (a mott, a Molloy), both of whom create each other as figments.[6]

It is not just the imagination that extends into the future, as John Sallis writes, the figments that the imagination forges are pregnant with the future of their correlates in the out here and now. To the extent that they are the product of images perceived and images projected, figments are nows that merge the past and the future. And yes, making figments requires the same skills as those possessed by the poet Plato banned from his ideal republic and for whom there is no more reason to apologize. Only by this creative process (the imagination) and this processed critter (figment) can you envision, plan and implement a vivifying future for whoever I am in the world of flesh.

---

5 Finney discusses the significance of this tongue twister in Acheson, *et al.* 1987, 73.
6 He tries naming his hearer M and the narrator W (its mirror image) only to conclude: "Even M must go. So W reminds Figment" (1982, 63). All these split selves are figments of the imagination just as autobiography itself is shown to be an act of imagination" (Finney 1987, 71–73).

3.5   telltale

"He has been a very naughty boy," a voice of authority from Beckett's childhood utters in *Company* (1982, 28). Beckett took that scolding to heart, becoming the master of naught. So we now come to the knot of our tale of a Beckettian ethics, the tie that binds, the felicitous misapprehension of "naughty boy" as "knotty boy."

"Being beside oneself" is an idiomatic expression that has provided me with comfort of company as long as I've been thinking about and writing *Witnessness*. It occurred to me as a felicitous way to express conditions for ethics while I listened to Jacques Derrida reworking the work of *Politics of Friendship* and grapple aloud with what happens when we utter the statement, "I love you."[1] Not only does the person who says he's beside himself with joy or grief indicate his proximity to the feeling of the sublime, the vision of him standing outside himself — but right next to that one that *is* himself — approximates the vision that I have of the ethical relationship that one subject has with another. No wonder that with a title like *Becoming Beside Ourselves*, Brian Rotman's latest book was bound to entice me.

With *Becoming Beside Ourselves*, Brian Rotman extends his sweep-ing cultural analyses of zero and infinity to give us the most complete, concise, and convincing argument about the epistemological and ethical upheaval in the midst of which we have the good fortune to be living. As we mediate our existence less and less by our use of good old alphabetic or ideogrammic language and increasingly through reproductive imaging technologies, the less our very being is lettered and the more it becomes networked. Soon (perhaps already) it will no longer be necessary to advo-cate against the fiction of the monolithic self-sufficient subject each and every one of us will be severally interfaced with others in our minute-to-minute exercise of existence. Isolated geniuses like Arthur Rimbaud with his cry of "I is another!" have been announcing the end of singularity and the dawn of ontological multiplicity for quite a long time. But now, first with the telegraph, then the telephone, then the radio, then the television, the Internet, blogs, chat groups, IM, SMS, and iPhones, the whole lot going

---

1   The most profound and profoundly moving reading of this problematic in Derrida's thought is David Wills' "Full Dorsal" (2005).

wireless . . . we practice ever more minutes of our days *being* something quite *additional* to what, for example, I am at this precise moment: alone at least for now, forgotten momentarily by all others, unsolicited in the public sphere, with pen in hand, writing the first version of these words for me alone.

Critical thinkers among us are often Luddites. Many of us expend much energy deploring the power that our own technological inventions have over us, warning others about the dangers, calling for boycotts, while secretly logging in. Resistance to networked being, however, is futile because it would be resistance to what we are inexorably becoming. Inexorably and fortunately, because of the boon it will bring in the realm of empathy. Brian Rotman reminds us that this has happened before and we Luddites came to relish it. Just as we invented and mastered alphabets to make our world of speech into an inscribed and reproducible world, improve our memory, invent history, and so on, words themselves — graven words — have shaped and defined us. Humans may have invented writing, but writing has constantly reinvented us. We *are* (or at least have been, until very recently) as our writing is. So, too, today, networks of images and touching them form and will form what we are in the midst of becoming. We *will be*, along with and in varying degrees all others, logged in at the same time.

The world of names, our world of survivors, is an ancient wall that is cracked. The world cooled with man and fissures appeared with the shrinkage. But these cracks are our hope: they compel us forth. To plaster up the wall with the vain promises of universal peace and wealth is to fill up the abysses that keep us as in an archipelago. Yet it is our task to not allow this cracked world to collapse. How can this building maintenance conundrum be resolved?

The puzzle's solution is a world of witnesses to be read, one by the other, rather than be compelled to speak. The enigma is lifted by a witness who has no higher ambition than to *bear* witness — not by virtue of speech, but in the literal sense of *taking on* that burden — to the differend that asymptotically separates us. Rather than plaster over, we must learn to improvise or, to prolong the building metaphor, jury-rig with the help of a tool forgotten in the houses of today built, as they are, with wallboard, or sheetrock.

In days of yore, when cracks appeared, one placed on the walls of old buildings an instrument named, in English, a telltale — *témoin*, in French. These calibrated and dated plates bore testimony (if I may be allowed to exaggerate, for a moment, the solemnity of the situation) of the wall's continued shift, the movement between autonomous yet interconnected spaces. By their presence over the crack, constituting a third party joining the two separated entities, telltales provide a fragile passageway across the tiny abyss — the abyss that is nothing — between beings.[2]

Ooze on back not to unsay but say again the vasts apart. [13.7]

The betweenness that binds you to the other substantiates itself in a telltale that you both make. The figment that your imagination holds up for you is linked to you by means of a telltale.

Right now, at this extensible instant I call now, I see a fissure in the wall's plaster. It appeared before now, when I was looking elsewhere. In the next now I place a telltale on the fissure in order for the telltale to aid me in seeing what will have happened in future nows I cannot witness. Architects and builders know much of the silent eloquence of telltales. As the relay race baton guarantees the link from witness to martyr in Lyotard's *Differend,* so the telltale in the economy of witnessness. The telltale will be my surrogate witness of future nows. Analogously, responsibility is a knack naturally occurring in me, but that I'm meant to *apply.*

The human, with his ethical potential, is no longer an individual. "I," as island, has given way to awareness of being part of an archipelago. The other is here, linked with me, without my having to give up on *this*: my body that once shamelessly, unconsciously proclaimed "I." Now, forever "beside himself," careful for the other as he once was egoistically only for *ego,* the being for ethics extends himself into the being of the other as the other extends himself here. What is the nature of this extension? What differentiates the archipelago from a multiplicity of heteroclite and unbound islands? A sort of bridge has formed for the passage of affect and mutual protection to occur. But what sort of bridge makes plural being a network instead of schizophrenia?

If the driveling scribe can successfully teach himself to curb his verbosity in favor of readiness to witness in the form of enhanced legibility, with what expressive faculty is he left? For an expressiveness does subsist, at bottom, at the limit, if only "with worsening words" [10.16]. And what does an asymptotic yet vicarious relationship to the other — an approach tailor-made to protect him — entail if there is something yet predatory about it? "No stilling preying," the voice of *Worstward Ho* reminds us [16.3]. Preying is all right, as long as you prey on yourself as other, proving that you're still alive. Predatory vicariousness. A soundproof room only eliminates extraneous exterior noise that might interfere with my hearing the "good" sounds that I want to hear within a circumscribed space. But what of those faint noises emitted within my body? The model-wit's

2 These last two paragraphs are adapted from R. Harvey, "Telltale at the Passage" *Yale French Studies* 99 (Spring 2001), p. 110.

skull is a soundproof room for hearing and heeding the *one* that I form in cooperation with the other who remains within me.

A word. In Beckett's ultimate vocabulary, a worseless word. A "killer," as he wished for, already, in his *Texts for Nothing* of the early 1950s. *Telltale* is the nearest to perfection that language can offer to say (or, better, have written) the bridge to the *somewhere* where we're headed. Empathy flows to and fro across the telltale, the word for a witnessness that eschews the audacity of speech, to let itself be read. Aligned with the fundamental assertion that Maurice Blanchot made in *L'Entretien infini* that "to speak is not to see," the telltale across the gap between us utters not but is, rather, to be read. It therefore mutters volumes, infinitely. The mural telltale (inhuman although man-made) must be read by a human in order for its work to reach completion. The reading occurs after the event of movement that the telltale gauges. Belying its name, the telltale is mute. Yet it is a complete witness insofar as it registers everything that it is meant to register. Yes, here is the complete witness in the here and now. It "speaks" only through the proxy of that witness who was not present at the event of movement. As telltale between yourself and your other, you are both there and here, yourself and beside yourself. Yet no movement — *still*. Stillborn, you still go on. Your place is on that "vast apart."

Although Beckett's wit may claim that he can no longer go on, he discovers the knowhow to parry *no* with its palindromic antidote, *on*. He will tarry at the cusp of the two, as telltale, as surviving witnesses of *Auschwitz* taught themselves to do. Yes, even the most egregious crime harbors its telltale. And even Claude Lanzmann, who radically dismisses imagination's powerful legitimacy, has had to appeal to something like an "abstract bridge" to make sense of the relationship between before touching bottom and after and whose correlate in the mind affords responsibility a future (cf. Didi Huberman 2003, 124; 2008, 97). Witness, as we tarry at the threshold of empathy, Filip Müller who had the sense to imagine that the telltale to the other was worth preserving for a future purpose:

> Did we have the right to take such a risk and, in taking it, to gamble away our chance to go on living for the time being? What, at that moment, was more important: a few hundred men and women, still alive but facing imminent death from which there was no saving them, or a handful of eyewitnesses, one or two of whom might, at the price of suffering and *denial of self*, survive to bear witness against the murderers some day? (Müller 1979, 37; my emphasis)

Ordinary judgment cannot determine the ordinary moral valence of the bridge or telltale linking one "I" to another. This is witnessness *before* being a witness, in order to become one, perhaps.

3.6   empathy

Hand in hand with equal plod they go. In the free hands — no.
Free empty hands. Backs turned both bowed with equal plod they
go. The child hand raised to reach the holding hand. Hold the old
holding hand. Hold and be held. [5.5]

Alone together so much shared. (quoted in Knowlson 1996, 665)

It's all symbiosis [. . .] symbiosis (quoted in Knowlson 1996, 417)

Whereas a telltale is a mere soulless instrument, you and I together, form-
ing one with the telltale between, carry out the process that we still like to
call human life itself. Emotion of some sort if, in spite of all, we can remain
human, somehow inflects our betweenness-witnessness. Otherwise we
just sit there, inert and affectless. The way one gets one's capacity for
vicariousness to neutralize the death-dealing effect of event and shift its
occurrence fully into the realm of one's imagination is to transform it into
empathy. Empathy flows along the path of the telltale from one figment
to another, providing life blood to each of the surviving minds.

John Sallis envisions the imagination as an economy of which the
world outside the skull is as much a part as the faculty we traditionally
locate within the atrium between our shoulders. He thus positions one's
imagination as at once "here" — as one's own — and "elsewhere," there,
beyond the autonomous one that I think I am. The imagination is as much
somewhere on the side of one (and, in the temporality of that which one
imagines, with passion), as it is here and now.

On both sides *imagination exceeds what is present*, extending our
gaze beyond the immediately visible (the sparse traces of spring),
beyond to the *stages to come* (flowers, fruits, *shade*), opening to the
future precisely in and through the profusion of *sense to come*. (2000,
66; my emphasis)

Just as we can foresee what we know, we feel and feel *for* that which is
beyond us.

In this very movement imagination [. . .] displaces us from the simple feeling of self given in and through sensations, makes us exceed
the bounds of the self-apprehension produced merely through sense
and feeling. (2000, 66)

Thus a language discovered, then mastered, after the mother tongue — a
"foreign" language that becomes so apt to exceed the signifying expec-
tations laid in the first, allows the speaker to unveil far greater depths
of himself to the beloved. We thus imagine Beckett learning this from
his inventiveness with French. Thus, also, empathy, the great shareable
emotion that binds us, which is beyond us and with us simultaneously,
without contradiction.

A timid reading of Beckett would be one that conforms to the most
predictable orthodoxy and finds but little fellow feeling between pairs
or groups of characters. As fair example from the corpus to corroborate
such a safe interpretation, the interaction of the narrator-protagonist of
How It Is with Bim extends little beyond shoving a can-opener up his
bum at regular intervals. But what if empathy were not incompatible
with tension and strife? Is one empathetic simply in direct proportion
to one's demonstrations of feeling for one's fellow? What if, as Beckett's
inspirational Dante wrote:

> *e ora in te non stanno sanza guerra*
> *li vivi tuoi, e l'un l'altro si rode*
> *di quei ch'un muro e una fossa serra.*[1]

What if, as Didi-Huberman reminds us, the "anthropological meaning" of
Auschwitz were not only the "denial of the victim's humanity," which we
impute solely to the perpetrators, but also complete apathy and "incapacity for empathy" on the part of the survivor (2003, 58; 2008, 42)? After all,
is not a significant proportion of the guilt borne by survivors due to their
confusing the warring forces of inability and unwillingness to stop the
killing of others by non-humans disguised as men? If the humanity of the
other-than-victim, reduced nearly to ashes, can nevertheless be rekindled,
does it not maintain a residue of this coldness in survival? Beckett worked
to accept this nearly untenable duality. With a telltale as pathway for the
circulation of empathy, we are in ethical life, if only minimally. Beckett's

---

1   But those who are alive within you now
     can't live without their warring — even those
     whom one same wall and one same moat enclose
     gnaw at each other.
                                        Purgatorio VI, 82–84.

minimal verb for this minimal active similarity that survives between souls is "to eff," with which this node will conclude.

We have seen already how easy it is, sometimes, to bend a cautious reading Beckett's way. My own reading finds characters holding hands, closing the "egregious gap" between their bodies, showing mutual empathy everywhere. Everyone has seen or read *Godot* and knows the unabashed pleasure with which Beckett joins motley pairs in symmetry. His biographer, John Knowlson, is undoubtedly right to trace at least one of the origins of his apparent belief in fundamental empathy to his having learned that his good friend, Alfred Péron, was kept alive in a concentration camp thanks to the "solidarity [of] utterly dissimilar individuals" (1996, 381). On what must have been the rarest of occasions too, Beckett offered an explanation for *Godot* that jibes with fetching innocence with a belief in basic fellow feeling: "we are all waiting for Godot and do not know that he is already here. Yes, here. Godot is my neighbour in the cell next to mine. Let us do something to help him then, change the shoes that are hurting him!" (quoted in Knowlson 1996, 410). Martin Esslin sees Beckett's characters striving beyond themselves, in movements of unabashed vicariousness, in a practice of what he names with no lesser a term than the "original moral imperative" (1993, 19). As quintessence of Beckett's moral philosophy, *Worstward Ho* offers up the image of the empathetic ideal to which we all, apparently, strive: to "hold and be held."[2]

When Beckett, who adored the performing arts, elevates a gesture to a gracious dance movement, we know that he is prodding us toward it, imploring us to imitate it. Thus this tribute to the empathetic asymptotic touching of hands in *Ill Seen Ill Said*, which prefigures the hand-holding-hand-held in *Worstward Ho*: "Spreading rise and in midair palms uppermost come to rest. Behold our hollows" (1996 [1981], 67). H. Porter Abbott, duly enticed, rightly comments: "Reading the gap between these two sentences, we connect them with implicit words — 'as if they [the palms] were to say' — and in doing so imagine how her hands look held out in midair" (2004, 14). Further, we strain to feel the empathetic energies that pass between them.

Between them is the telltale scene of *Worstward Ho*. "Into this work Beckett builds a man, a woman, and a child, and it is from this primary family," writes Enoch Brater, "rather than from the flea in *Endgame*, that 'humanity might start from there all over again' (*Endgame*, 27). Even

---

2 "It was for his straightforwardly affectionate, uncomplicated, chummy relation-ship with his two sons and for the simple things that they shared that Beckett best remembered his father. [. . .] One of the most moving images in Beckett's late prose is that of an old man and a boy walking hand in hand across the foothills" (Knowlson 1996, 12).

though they may '[t]ry again', only to '[f]ail better', it is their frail endur-
ance, walking 'hand in hand', that keeps the life of language — and
life itself — going on" (1990b, 172). "Family" is the metaphor (just a
metaphor — not Aristotle's model for politics) for the terniary structure
of oneness through empathy. First (and, most often, last) there is the
one — you, say — who's sure he's sufficient unto himself; then there's
the other, the partner, the fellow — like him or not; then there's a third
that binds us, like a child does two adults, regardless of biological link.
That third is the imaginitiveness of the two at work across the bridge of
the telltale between them. This is what Beckett means in *Worstward Ho*
when he moves from "now the one. Now the twain" [6.2] to "All three
together" [10.16]. If such unapologetic fellow feeling could be converted
into pragmatic behavior, it would result in protective practices that might
just finally network us.

The distress that a bystander experiences upon witnessing pain (or
worse) inflicted on a fellow creature kindles empathy and its possible
actions.[3] But maybe empathy is like what neurobiologists are beginning
to find out about metaphor. Maybe empathy is to remorse as metaphor
is to language. Maybe empathy begins when my conscience is stung
— but stung before I know the pain of remorse, an ouchless sting.[4] The
separateness seemingly setting the rule of the witness-martyr couple
is inflected not by resolution, equilibrium, or even ultimate happiness-
despite-untogetherness, but by empathy. Empathy is a new name for the
sublime, which means negative pleasure.[5] Empathy is betweenness-as-
togetherness, acceptance of and respect for the thin veil of separation,
melancholy tamed.

With no training or licensing as a social psychologist, Beckett shows
through his work a conviction that we are grounded in empathy, an
innate need to go beyond ourselves empathetically, even in the absence
of another. In what may be her first scholarly article Elaine Scarry com-
mented beautifully on a passage in *Endgame*, paraphrasing thus X's
response to Y's claim that we are sometimes altogether alone, with no one
to feel for: "Then babble, babble words, like the solitary child who turns

---

3 Cf. Martin Hoffman, *Empathy and Moral Development*, 2000.
4 Again, Dante's *Purgatorio* as inspiration for elements in Beckett's worldview: "*Pur
vostra dignitate/mia coscïenza dritto mi rimorse.*" [. . .] "Your dignity / made conscience
sting me as I stood erect." Canto XIX, 132. Remorse is said "ayenbite of inwit" in
Joyce's *Ulysses*.
5 At the very beginning of the "Analytic of the Sublime," Kant writes, "as the mind
is not merely attracted by the object but is ever being alternately repelled, the satisfaction in the sublime does not so much involve a positive pleasure as admiration
or respect, which rather deserves to be called negative pleasure [*negative Lust*]"
(1951, 83).

himself into children, two three, so as to be together, and whisper together, in the dark" (1971, 282). This togetherness, despite all, is the motivation for Beckett's assertion of *company*. Empathy, indomitable as long as a heart is heard to beat, is the last rampart against meaninglessness.

Beside myself, beside one's self (where by "self" we mean consciousness), what can one say about what one finds? Nothing's more difficult to say. And no one has been more acutely aware of the challenge to writing in the survival of the word "ineffable," when "effable" has all but perished, but Beckett. Never one to become morbidly serious or maudlin about the worst, however, his attitude was "Eff it!"

The Irish, bidding unwanted company *adieu*, willingly ejaculate a sharp "Eff off!" We find the verb used here and there throughout Beckett's work and, wherever it's proffered, it hovers tantalizingly between its value as euphemism for "fuck" and appearance as abbreviation for the call to utter in the imperative "Eff it!" Moved by its importance in Beckett's vocabulary, one critic characterized the energy he mustered to write his final prose works as "a new strength to 'eff'" (Hisgen 1998, 433). But, if we are to understand empathy, the ambiguity Beckett meant by "effing" must not be ignored, or even underestimated. John Knowlson reported that in April 1984, during his recovery from a viral infection, Beckett wrote the following to Avigdor and Anne Arikha: "My old head nothing but sighs of expiring cells. A last chance at last, I'll try." And then he wrote lines reminiscent of *Ohio Impromptu* and prefiguring the first sentence of what would be his last text, *Stirrings Still*: "From where he sat with his head in his hands he saw himself rise and disappear," to which he added the final comment, "Ineffable departure. Nothing left but try — eff it" (Knowlson 1996, 697).[6]

While "Fuck it!" is undeniably meant, here, the impulse to struggle on, minimally, at the limit, against the ineffable, is equally patent. Man — one, *l'on*, me, you, Beckett — at the limit of life is not unlike his imagining God at least doing *something* with himself before the creation. Finding words to approximate in language the movements and actions enabled and spurred by empathy is very hard and more often than not renders awkward results, even from the most assiduous thinkers and best writers on the topic. Although "*deficiency* of information" hampers us "when facing these images we face the overwhelming *necessity* of a survivor's gesture," writes Didi-Huberman. Yet "when facing this we are facing the overwhelming *necessity* of an *empathetic* gesture, that is, of a kind of *active similarity* (2003, 63; 2008, 45). In this acting upon similarity that produces a minimal gesture of empathy, I find a rather satisfactory definition for

---

6 Cf. "In the prison cell of language, effability becomes an imperative: eff it, so that 'ineffability' is only a 'departure'. Eff it, say it: try inexpressively" (Locatelli 1999, 40).

Beckett's curiously truncated verb, to eff. *Effulgence* would be another word for our being beside ourselves for and with the other.

Meditating Kant's axiom found in the *Critique of Pure Reason* that "I exist as an intelligence" (1998, 260), Sallis rhetorically asks, "When one sees one's body reflected in the mirror, does one see anything of oneself beyond that which the eye, the window of the soul, renders visible?" (2000, 210). To which *Film* gives the emphatic answer, "yes and no": No, it is none other than I; Yes, it is I as another. A little further on, with a yet more emphatically rhetorical question, Sallis writes, "Would the discourse not need to become at least oriented to *one's own body* — indeed, not as something owned, possessed, by oneself, but rather as belonging to one's ownness as such?" (2000, 211). Later still, concerning the poetic imagination, Sallis finally shows his hand, exposing his position vis-à-vis these statements in the guise of questions, "It is not simply *as oneself* that one composes an artwork, but only through *an excess of oneself*, an excess that comes to be operative without ever becoming simply one's own, without ever being appropriated to one's ownness, to one's propriety. It is by this excess that artistic composition exceeds mere production (in the case of τεχνη), and it is on account of it that the pertinence of technique or technicity to art is limited" (2000, 218–19).

Empathy is one's work of art at the mind's limit, the creation that meets the eye and the soul of the spectator for whose hand the creator reaches out. In exceeding ourselves at the limit, we excel. If the endless lesson of *Auschwitz* has taught us anything, it is that if any remnant of ethical behavior can sustain itself when humanity threatens itself with its own annihilation, it is to our unflagging capacity for imagination. The first thing that one's imaginitiveness can do for one is to afford a dim glimmer of empathetic recognition for one's fellow creature: one's *one*, as the Irish say "your one." There is no one like her: she makes one one.[7]

---

7 Didi-Huberman limns the beginning of this process when he writes of the necessity of thinking from the position of "our own survival situation with respect to history [. . .]. [I]t is a question of engaging [the] *imagination*" (2003, 200; 2008, 161).

3.7 model-wit

So it is time to conclude by turning our piece of work — our sweatshop, our witnessworks, quintessence of dust — into our abode. No need to commute: you can work out of your home, your model-home. We've already intimated that a witnessworks is a place where witnessness develops. Now we'll insist that this industry be conducted in the cheese of your very own cottage.

> A place. Where none. For the body. To be in. Move in. Out of. Back into. No. No out. No back. Only in. Say in. On in. Still. [1.3]

Of what consists the wit of a witness? What if wit and witness were one and the same thing, precisely equivalent, of the same cloth, consubstantial? Would not everyone in possession of wit, who's got his wits about him, therefore have witnessness at their disposal? A whit of wit, a mote of mind: is that not what even Beckett's leastmost homunculi show us they possess by their narratives? — Not one wit (naught one whit), the white of the bright light versus the dimness (which is not night) of naught . . . naught, the cipher, the placeholder. The witness as telltale is positioned between infinite sets of integers, figures, people: he is the pivot point between negative and positive. Yet the wit of a witness is minimal, in no need of any particular training. Witnessness needs no more fitness than that afforded by wit ingrained. So let's move all of the furniture accumulated heretofore into the model-wit.

Beckett's vision for humanity — a way to get on — would not, notwithstanding the last glimmer of *Stirring Still*, be perfected further than *Worstward Ho*. There, our fitness for lessening the gap between two words for the same thing — witness and martyr — to develop the telltale in us and across which empathy flows, all comes in a kit tailor-fit for every one of us. Only a breakaway reading of *Worstward Ho* such as the one I've tried to propose, here, can ensure that one remains mindful of Beckett's twist on Hegel's "sense certainty." By lessening the visual dimension of the image — knee-jerkedly thought to be the only way to approach it — by deemphasizing the faculty to *envision*, by reducing asymptotically toward zero what Gaston Bachelard called imagining, and intensifying touch, Beckett's way would be to dwell in someone else's place, to crash his home gently, lend him the blind feeling that someone shares the room with him. Being the reader of his little vicious circle, you've already let yours be crashed by this reading.

Let us now, in conclusion, remind ourselves again of our mind's only true reminder: wit, with its *ness* to dwell where it is as well as beside itself, drawing my remainder, the other, within. I shade into you and you shade into me: this is the lesson Beckett drew from Dante's story of shades. This shading of one into the other for our one true safety that we call our spirit — an *esprit*, for the bilingual, bicephalous Beckett, a witless spirit, a spirit going on in witnessness, an *esprit-témoin*, a model-wit. The model-wit is the bilingual nexus where wit (*esprit*) and witness (*témoin*) settle together in the "seat and germ of all" for this to work for everyone.

Every person who has bought into "the American dream" knows what a model home is. Well, now, imagine that imagination in the service of empathy has a dwelling-place — or at least a staging area — for which no one even needs a mortgage. An English publication, our trusty OED, of course, points out that "model-home" is an American expression for the British "show house," for which we find the definition, "A house specially finished for exhibition as an advertisement, usually for others of similar construction, for example, on a housing estate." The idea being that these model-homes could be for anyone and everyone. Beckett, whose hovel in Ussy indicated he had no interest whatsoever in real estate, undoubtedly knew nevertheless that using "*témoin*" appositionally to another noun in French produces the same meaning as "model." Hence, for example, *un appartement-témoin*.

The model-wit described in *Worstward Ho* may be nothing to write home about, it's been the one thing philosophers have never been able to quite hammer out and that we've needed for as long as people have cared about whether we care or not. "Such the dwelling ill seen ill said. Outwardly. High time" proclaims the voice in *Ill Seen Ill Said* (1996 [1981], 74). Welcome, ladies and germs, to Beckett's model wit. We think you will enjoy the rest and remainder of your days in this humble abode. Oh my, George, just look! "What room for worse!" [10.1] "Never to be naught." [18.4]. Now are those expressions of deep-seated pessimism? Not in my book.

The model-wit — this witnessworks or factory for ethics that everyman, *l'on*, may understand he carries around with him all the time — has room for everyone. Here is how the narrator of *Ill Seen Ill Said* expressed the desire to welcome the woman who did nothing but call him "a naughty boy" when he was a youngster: "If only she could be pure figment. Unalloyed . . . In the madhouse of the skull and nowhere else" (1996 [1981], 20). Hisgen finds *Endgame* (1957) "early" in casting characters sequestered "in a skull-like interior world" (1998, 531). Yet in *The Unnamable* — originally published as *L'Innomable* in 1953 — the eponymous conscience knows himself "inside of my distant skull, where once I wandered, now [. . .] fixed, lost for tininess" (1965 [1958], 18–19).

Insufficiently adapted for the entirety of humanity are the extra-worldly courts of law invented by the likes of Sartre to punish those guilty of bad faith. Those are hells of the other. Beckett, *au contraire*, conceives of a purgatory for everyone in which ethics, ironically enough, has a chance. That purgatory is our own cranium, with its alleged mind. In fact, the intuition of the mind as first and foremost a space, which would later become more precisely a state, is found already in Beckett's earliest novel, *Murphy*, where the simplest of many formulations of the notion goes thus: "what he called his mind functioned not as an instrument but as a place" (1938, 178).[1]

One and the same, relentlessly resisting "no's knife," *Worstward Ho*, the model-wit "points nowhere but back to itself" (Brater 1980, 257). If it is a "mindspace" (Hisgen 1998, 453), a "completely self-contained universe" from which "conventional narrative detail referring to a recognizable real word" has been deleted (van der Weel 1998, 18, 20), "universe" is the operative term, for finally, undistracted by the compulsion to describe loquaciously, the model-wit can focus on the other within, which is all and all there is. Reading *Texts for Nothing* in reverse — jumping back from No. 12 to No. 1, we *almost* find the anxious question posed decades later in *Worstward Ho*: "who's this speaking in me, who's this disowning me, as though I had taken his place, usurped his life?" (1995, 150) — and *almost Worstward Ho's* answer: "we're of one mind [. . .] we're fond of one another, we're sorry for one another" (1995, 102). Almost, but not quite. For this answer at which he arrived in the mid-1950s is accompanied by a helpless "there it is, there's nothing we can do for one another."

While it is true that "the word *scene* is used only once [in *Worstward Ho*], in 'Scene and seer of all' [10.8], where it echoes *seen* so strongly that the reader is apt to mistake the one for the other" (Hisgen 1998, 442), the model-wit is nevertheless a stage, a *theatrum philosophicum*, but one whose elements — characters, props, lighting — require inner vision in order for empathetic representation to be arranged in such a way that it is operable. This "vision" must be understood most capaciously, to include the vision of the blind or the dumfounded with their blank stare. Beckett can then bring his idiosyncratic ideas for staging and filming to converge in monocular vision — at the pinhead's pinhole.

In paraphrasing Hannah Arendt's speculations concerning a fourth Kantian critique — of political reason — and the role that imagination would have undoubtedly played there, Myrian Revault d'Allonnes (2002)

---

1 Cf. Knowlson, "Precise topographical details do not ground his characters in an apposite world, let alone explain them away. They underline the attempted separation of the 'little world' of Murphy's inner self from the 'big buzzing confusion' of the outer world" (1996, 205); "Murphy pictures his mind as a closed system, 'a large hollow sphere, hermetically closed to the universe without'" (1996, 218).

writes the following: "We are neither in communal fusion, nor in consensual truth, nor in sociological proximity. We attempt, on the contrary, to *imagine* what our thought would resemble if it were elsewhere."[2] This *elsewhere* brought "home" by witnessness is the "seat and germ of all" oriented toward the other within, in the model-wit.

If it is emphatically hand in hand that I go on with my fellow figment within the model-wit, then it can only be that Beckett's believed fundamentally that the moral imperative indwells us. Not one reading of Beckett is recognizable in a world that affords you the luxury of reading this. To know what he wrote about is to have known the depths and to have returned. Beckett's wit both measures and is the measure of the infinitesimal distance between what we were when we could not know and what we are becoming now, as survivors in witnessness. Those are the parameters and obligations of one's model-wit.

---

2 Myriam Revault d'Allonnes, "Le cœur intelligent de Hannah Arendt," 56; quoted in Didi-Huberman 2003, 201; 2008, 162.

Thanks, from end to beginning

The final stages of writing *Witnessness* benefitted considerably from a sabbatical granted by the State University of New York at Stony Brook in Fall 2008.

Various forms of encouragement, material support, moral support, inspiration, intellectual rebound, and wit came to me as I wrote this book from François Noudelmann, Martin Crowley, Larry Schehr, Joe Litvak, Avital Ronell, David Bell, Michel Deguy, Florent Perrier, Haaris Naqvi, Ed Casey, Sophie Levent, Jacques Derrida, Georges Didi-Huberman, Fethi Benslama, Stuart Kendall, Tom Bishop, Martine Segonds-Bauer, Lourdes Carriedo, and all of the members of my Spring 2008 seminar.

They all know — or knew — how much.

The idea for it would not have emerged without the unflagging support of Hélène Volat whose gift it has been to lift her gaze upon me.

Bibliography

Abbott, H. Porter. "Farewell to Incompetence: Beckett's *How It Is* and *Imagination Dead Imagine*." *Contemporary Literature* 11 (1970): 36–47.
———. "Narrative." In Lois Oppenheim, *Palgrave Advances in Samuel Beckett Studies*: 7–29. Houndsmills and New York: Palgrave Macmillan, 2004.
Acheson, James, Kateryna Arthur, and Melvin J. Friedman, eds. *Beckett's Later Fiction and Drama: Texts for Company*: 65–79. Houndmills, England: Macmillan, 1987.
Ackerley, C.J. and S.E. Gontarski. *The Grove Companion to Samuel Beckett: A Reader's Guide to His Works, Life, and Thought*. New York: Grove Press, 2004.
Adorno, Theodor W. *Minima moralia: Reflections on a Damaged Life*. Translated. New York and London: Verso, 2006.
———. *Prisms*. Translated by Shierry Weber Nicholsen and Samuel Weber. Cambridge, MA: MIT Press, 1983.
Agamben, Giorgio. *Ce qui reste d'Auschwitz*. Translated as *Remnants of Auschwitz: The Witness and the Archive* by Daniel Heller-Roazen. New York: Zone Books, 2002.
Améry, Jean [Hans Mayer]. *Jenseits von Schuld und Sühne. Bewältigungsversuche eines Überwältigen* [*Beyond Guilt and Atonement*]. Munich: Szczesny, 1966. Translated as *At the Mind's Limits: Contemplations by a Survivor on Auschwitz and Its Realities* by Sidney Rosenfeld and Stella P. Rosenfeld. Bloomington and Indianapolis, IN: Indiana University Press, 1980.
Anidjar, Gil. *The Jew, the Arab: A History of the Enemy*. Stanford, CA: Stanford University Press, 2003.
Antelme, Robert. *L'Espèce humaine*. Paris: Gallimard, 1957. Translated as *The Human Race* by Jeffrey Haight and Annie Mahler. Marlboro, VT: Marlboro Press, 1992.
Aquinas, Thomas. *Summa theologiae*, v. III ("Knowing and Naming God"). Cambridge: Blackfriars, 1964.
Arendt, Hannah. *Lectures on Kant's Political Philosophy*. Chicago: University of Chicago Press, 1982.
Arsic, Branka. *The Passive Eye: Gaze and Subjectivity in Berkeley (via Beckett)*. Stanford, CA: Stanford University Press, 2003.
Badiou, Alain. *Beckett. L'increvable désir*. Paris: Hachette (Coup double), 1995.
———. "Être, existence, pensée: prose et concept." In *Petit Manuel*

d'inesthétique: 137–87. Paris: Éditions du Seuil, 1998. Translated by
Alberto Toscano as "Being, Existence, Thought: Prose and Concept." In
Handbook of Inaesthetics: 89–148. Stanford, CA: Stanford University Press,
2005.

——. *L'Éthique. Essai sur la conscience du mal*. Paris: Hatier, 1994.

Bartsch, Renate. *Consciousness Emerging: The Dynamics of Perception,
Imagination, Action, Memory, Thought, and Language*. Amsterdam;
Philadelphia: John Benjamin's Publishing, 2002.

Beckett, Samuel. *All That Fall*. New York: Grove Press, 1957.

——. *All Strange Away* [1964]. In *JOBS* 3 (Summer 1978): 1–9. Reprinted
in *The Complete Short Prose: 1929–1989*: 169–81. New York: Grove Press,
1995.

——. *Comment c'est*. Paris: Éditions de Minuit, 1961. Translated from the
French by the author as *How It Is*. New York: Grove Press, 1964.

——. *Compagnie*. Paris: Éditions de Minuit, 1980. Translated by the author
as *Company* [1980]. In *Nohow On*: 3–46. New York: Grove Press, 1996.

——. *Disjecta. Miscellaneous Writings and a Dramatic Fragment*. New York:
Grove Press, 1984.

——. *L'expulsé*. In *Fontaine. Revue mensuelle de la poésie et des lettres françaises*
10, no. 57 (décembre 1946–janvier 1947) 685–708. Translated by Richard
Seaver in collaboration with the author as *The Expelled. The Evergreen
Review* 6, no. 22 (January–February 1962): 8–20. Reprinted in *The Complete
Short Prose: 1929–1989*: 46–60. New York: Grove Press, 1995.

——. *Film*. [dir. Alan Schneider, 1964]. *Film: Complete Scenario/Illustrations/
Production Shots*. New York: Grove Press, 1969.

——. *Imagination morte imaginez. Les Lettres nouvelles* 13 (octobre–novembre
1965): 13–16. Translated by the author as *Imagination Dead Imagine. The
Sunday Times* (7 November 1965): 48. Reprinted in *The Complete Short
Prose: 1929–1989*: 182–85. New York: Grove Press, 1995.

——. *L'Innomable*. Paris: Éditions de Minuit, 1953. Translated as *The
Unnamable* [1958]. In *Three Novels by Samuel Beckett*. New York: Grove
Press, 1965.

——. *Mal vu mal dit*. Paris: Éditions de Minuit, 1981. Translated by the
author as *Ill Seen Ill Said* [1981]. In *Nohow On*: 49–86. New York: Grove
Press, 1996.

——. *Malone meurt*. Paris: Minuit, 1951. Translated from the French by the
author as *Malone Dies*. New York: Grove Press, 1956.

——. *Mercier et Camier* [1946]. Paris: Minuit, 1970. Translated as *Mercier and
Camier*. London: Calder & Boyars, 1974.

——. *Molloy*. Paris: Éditions de Minuit, 1951. Translated by Patrick Bowles
in collaboration with the author. Paris: Olympia Press, 1955.

——. *More Pricks Than Kicks*. London: Chatto & Windus, 1934.

——. *Murphy*. London: Routledge, 1938.

——. *Not I*. In *First Love and Other Shorts*. New York: Grove Press, 1974.

——. *Ohio Impromptu*. In *Rockaby and Other Short Pieces*. New York: Grove
Press, 1981.

——. *Sans. La Quinzaine littéraire* 82 (1 novembre 1969): 3–4. Translated by the author as *Lessness. The New Statesman* (1 May 1970): 635. Reprinted in *The Complete Short Prose: 1929–1989*: 197–201. New York: Grove Press, 1995.

——. *Still* [1973] ("Fizzle 7"). In *The Complete Short Prose: 1929–1989*: 240–42. New York: Grove Press, 1995.

——. *Stirrings Still. The Guardian* (3 March 1989): 5. Translated by the author as *Soubresauts*. Paris: Minuit, 1989.

——. *Texts for Nothing* [1950–1952]. In *The Complete Short Prose: 1929–1989*. New York: Grove Press, 1995.

——. *Watt*. Paris: Olympia Press (coll. Merlin), 1953; corrected edition, New York: Grove Press, 1959.

——. *Worstward Ho* [1983]. In *Nohow On*: 89–116. New York: Grove Press, 1996. Translated by Edith Fournier as *Cap au pire*. Paris: Éditions de Minuit, 1991.

Beer, Ann. "Beckett's "Autography" and the Company of Languages." *The Southern Review* 27, no. 4 (1991): 771–91.

Benjamin, Walter. *Passagen-Werk* [1927–1940]. Translated by Howard Eiland and Kevin McLaughlin as *The Arcades Project*. Cambridge, MA: Belknap Press of Harvard University Press, 1999.

Bennington, Geoffrey. *Late Lyotard*. Ebook, 2005.

Benslama, Fethi. "La Représentation et l'impossible." In Jean-Luc Nancy, ed. *L'Art et la mémoire des camps. Représenter. Exterminer*: 59–80. Paris: Seuil (Le genre humain), 2001.

Bettelheim, Bruno. *Surviving and Other Essays*. New York: Vintage, 1980.

Bishop, John. *Joyce's Book of the Dark: Finnegans Wake*. Madison: University of Wisconsin Press, 1986.

Bishop, Tom. "Samuel Beckett: Working Multilingually." *Centerpoint* 13 [4, no. 2] (Fall 1980): 140–42.

Blanchot, Maurice. *L'Arrêt de mort* [1948]. Paris: Gallimard, 1977. Translated as *Death Sentence* by Lydia Davis. Barrytown, NY: Barrytown/Station Hill Press, 1998.

——. *L'Entretien infini*. 1969. Translated by Susan Hanson as *The Infinite Conversation*. Minneapolis: University of Minnesota Press, 1993.

——. *L'Instant de ma mort*. Fata Morgana, 1994. Translated as *The Instant of My Death* in Derrida 2000.

——. *Le Pas au-delà*. Paris: Gallimard, 1973. Translated by Lycette Nelson as *The Step Not Beyond*. Albany: SUNY Press, 1992.

——. "La Solitude essentielle." In *L'Espace littéraire*. Paris: Gallimard, 1955.

Brann, Eva. *The World of the Imagination*. Lanham, MD: Rowman and Littlefield, 1991.

Brater, Enoch. *Beyond Minimalism: Beckett's Late Style in the Theater*. Oxford and New York: Oxford University Press, 1990a.

——. "Voyelles, Cromlechs and Special (W)rites of *Worstward Ho*." In Lance St John Butler and Robin J. Davis, eds. *Rethinking Beckett*: 160–72. New York: St. Martin's Press, 1990b.

———. "Why Beckett's *Enough* is More or Less Enough." *Contemporary Literature* 21, no. 2 (1980): 252–66.

Brienza, Susan D. and Peggy A. Knapp. "Imagination Lost and Found: Beckett's Fiction and Frye's Anatomy." *Modern Language Notes* 95 (1980): 980–94.

Brienza, Susan. "Imagination Dead Imagine: The Microcosm of the Mind." *Journal of Beckett Studies* 8 (Autumn 1982): 59–74.

Buber, Martin. *I and Thou* [1938]. Translated by Walter Kaufman. New York: Scribner, 1970.

Burke, Edmund. *A Philosophical Enquiry into the Origins of Our Ideas of the Sublime and Beautiful* [1757]. London: Penguin Books, 1998.

Cant, Sarah E. "In Search of 'Lessness': Translation and Minimalism in Beckett's Theatre." *Forum for Modern Language Studies* 35, no. 2 (1999): 138–57.

Caselli, Daniela. *Beckett's Dantes: Intertextuality in the Fiction and Criticism.* Manchester, New York: Manchester University Press, 2005.

———. "'God that old favourite': Issues of Authority in *How It Is.*" *Samuel Beckett Today/Aujourd'hui: An Annual Bilingual Review/Revue Annuelle Bilingue* 9 (2000): 159–72.

Casey, Edward S. *The World at a Glance.* Bloomington: Indiana University Press, 2007.

Catanzaro, Mary. "Song and Improvisation in *Lessness.*" In Marius Buning and Lois Oppenheim, eds., *Beckett in the 1990s*: 213–18. Amsterdam and Atlanta: Rodopi (Samuel Beckett today/aujourd'hui 2), 1993.

———. "The Space of the Couple in Beckett's *Imagination Dead Imagine.*" In Roger Bauer, Douwe Fokkema, *et al. Proceedings of the XIIth Congress of the International Comparative Literature Association/Actes du XIIe congrès de l'Association Internationale de Littérature Comparée: München 1988 Munich, III: Space and Boundaries in Literature (Continuation)/Espace et frontières dans la littérature (suite)*. Munich: Iudicium, 1990.

Celan, Paul. *Aschenglorie.* Translated by John Felstiner as "Ash-Aureole" in *Selected Poems and Prose of Paul Celan.* New York and London: W.W. Norton, 2001.

Clément, Bruno. *L'Œuvre sans qualités. Rhétorique de Samuel Beckett.* Paris: Éditions du Seuil (coll. Poétique), 1994.

Cohn, Ruby. "Samuel Beckett Self-Translator." *PMLA* 76 (December 1961): 613–21.

Collins, Christopher. *The Poetics of the Mind's Eye: Literature and the Psychology of Imagination.* Philadelphia: University of Pennsylvania Press, 1991.

Connor, Steven. *Samuel Beckett: Repetition, Theory and Text.* New York: Basil Blackwell, 1988.

———. *Theory and Cultural Value.* Oxford & Cambridge: Blackwell, 1992.

———. "'Traduttore, traditore': Samuel Beckett's Translation of *Mercier et Camier.*" *Journal of Beckett Studies* nos. 11–12 (December 1989): 27–36.

Coope, Ursula. *Time for Aristotle: Physics IV 10–14.* Oxford: Oxford University Press, 2005.

Critchley, Simon. *On Humour*. New York & London: Routledge, 2002.

Crowley, Martin. *L'Homme sans. Politiques de la finitude*. Paris: Lignes, 2009.

———. *Robert Antelme. L'Humanité irréductible*. Paris: Léo Scheer, 2004.

Currie, Gregory and Ian Ravenscroft. *Recreative Minds: Imagination in Philosophy and Psychology*. Oxford: Clarendon Press; New York: Oxford University Press, 2002.

Dante Alighieri. *Purgatorio* in *La Divina Commedia*. Translated by Allen Mandelbaum. 1982; and by Jean Hollander and Robert Hollander. New York: Anchor Books (Random House), 2003.

Davies, Paul. "The Ideal Real: Imagination and Knowledge in the Prose of Samuel Beckett." *Dissertation Abstracts International* 49, no. 12 (June 1989): p. 3731A.

Dearlove, J.E. "The Weaving of Penelope's Tapestry: Genre in the Works of Samuel Beckett." *Journal of Beckett Studies* 11–12 (1989): 123–29.

Deguy, Michel. *À ce qui n'en finit pas*. Paris: Seuil, 1995.

Delbo, Charlotte. *Aucun de nous ne reviendra*. Paris: Minuit, 1970.

Deleuze, Gilles. *Cinéma I. L'Image-Mouvement*. Paris: Minuit, 1983.

———. "L'Épuisé." In Samuel Beckett, *Quad*: 57–106. Paris: Minuit, 1992.

———. *Nietzsche et la philosophie*. Paris: Les Presses Universitaires de France, 2005.

———. *Le Pli. Leibniz et le baroque*. Paris: Minuit, 1988.

Deleuze, Gilles and Félix Guattari. *Kafka. Pour une littérature mineure*. Paris: Minuit, 1975.

Derrida, Jacques. "'A Self-Unsealing Poetic Text': Poetics and Politics of Witnessing." In Michael P. Clark, *Revenge of the Aesthetic: The Place of in Theory Today*: 180–207. Berkeley: University of California Press, 2000.

———. *De l'hospitalité*. Paris: Calmann-Lévy, 1997. Translated as *Of Hospitality* by Rachel Bowlby. Stanford, CA: Stanford University Press, 2000.

———. *Demeure. Maurice Blanchot*. Paris: Galilée, 1998. *Demeure: Fiction and Testimony* by Elizabeth Rottenberg. Stanford, CA: Stanford University Press, 2000.

———. "Des Tours de Babel" and "Appendix." In Joseph F. Graham, ed. *Difference in Translation*: 165–207; 209–48. Ithaca and London: Cornell UP, 1985.

———. *Donner la mort*. Paris: Galilée, 1999. Translated by David Wills as *The Gift of Death*. Chicago: University of Chicago Press, 1995.

———. "Living On: Border Lines." In Geoffrey Hartman, ed. *Deconstruction and Criticism*: 75–176. London: Routledge & Kegan Paul, 1979.

———. *Politiques de l'amitié*. Paris: Galilée, 1994. Translated by George Collins as *Politics of Friendship*. London and New York: Verso Books, 1997.

Didi-Huberman, Georges. *Être crane. Lieu contact, pensée, sculpture*. Paris: Éditions de Minuit, 2000. [translations mine]

———. *Images malgré tout*. Paris: Éditions de Minuit, 2003. Translated by Shane B. Lillis as *Images in Spite of All: Four Photographs from Auschwitz*. Chicago and London: University of Chicago Press, 2008.

Dolan, Terence Patrick, ed. *A Dictionary of Hiberno-English. The Irish Use of English*. Dublin: Gill & Macmillan, 1998.

Dowd, Garin. "'Vasts apart': Phenomenology and *Worstward Ho*." In Anthony Uhlmann, Sjef Houppermans, and Bruno Clément, eds. *Samuel Beckett Today: After Beckett*: 323–39. Amsterdam and Atlanta: Rodopi, 2004.

Duras, Marguerite. *Le Square* [1955]. Translated by Sonia Pitt-Rivers and Irina Morduch as *The Square* in *Four Novels*. New York: Grove Press, 1965.

Esslin, Martin. "What Beckett Teaches Me: His Minimalist Approach to Ethics." In Marius Buning and Lois Oppenheim, eds. *Beckett in the 1990s*: 13–20. Amsterdam & Atlanta: Rodopi (Samuel Beckett today/ aujourd'hui 2), 1993.

Faulkner, William. *As I Lay Dying* (1930). In *Novels 1930–1935*. New York: The Library of America, 1984.

Finney, Brian. "A Reading of Beckett's *Imagination Dead Imagine*." *Twentieth Century Literature: A Scholarly and Critical Journal* 17, no. 2 (April 1971): 65–71.

———. "*Still* to *Worstward Ho*: Beckett's Prose Fiction since *The Lost Ones*." In James Acheson, Kateryna Arthur, and Melvin J. Friedman, eds. *Beckett's Later Fiction and Drama: Texts for Company*: 65–79. Houndmills, England: Macmillan, 1987.

Fraser, Graham. "The Pornographic Imagination in *All Strange Away*." *MFS: Modern Fiction Studies* 41, nos. 3–4 (Fall–Winter 1995): 515–30.

Friedman, Alan Warren, Charles Rossman, and Dina Sherzer, eds. *Beckett Translating/Translating Beckett*. University Park: Pennsylvania State University Press, 1987.

García Landa, José. "'Till Nohow On': The Later Metafiction of Samuel Beckett." In Theo D'Haen and Hans Bertens, eds. *British Postmodern Fiction*: 63–76. Amsterdam: Rodopi (Postmodern Studies), 1993.

Gibbons, Sarah L. *Kant's Theory of Imagination: Bridging Gaps in Judgement and Experience*. Oxford: Clarendon Press; New York: Oxford University Press, 1994.

Gibson, Andrew. *Beckett and Badiou: The Pathos of Intermittency*. Oxford: Oxford University Press, 2006.

Goethe, Wolfgang. *Aus meinem Leben. Dichtung und Wahrheit* [1811–1833]. Translated by John Oxenford as *The Autobiography of Johann Wolfgang von Goethe*. Chicago: University of Chicago Press, 1974.

Gontarski, S.E. "Introduction: The Conjuring of Something out of Nothing: Samuel Beckett's 'Closed Space' Novels." In *Nohow On*: vii–xxviii. New York: Grove Press, 1996.

Grant, John E., "Imagination Dead?" *James Joyce Quarterly* 8 (1971): 336–62.

Guénoun, Denis. *Un Sémite*. Belfort: Circé, 2003.

Guérin, Thierry. "'Said nohow on': La Limite d'une traduction en français." *Samuel Beckett Today/Aujourd'hui* 7 (1998): 81–90.

Hansford, James. "*Imagination Dead Imagine*: The Imagination and Its Context." *Journal of Beckett Studies* 7 (Spring 1982): 49–70.

Harpur, Patrick. *The Philosophers' Secret Fire: A History of the Imagination*. Chicago: Ivan R. Dee, 2003.

Harvey, Robert. "Afterward." In *Afterwords: Essays in Memory of Jean-François Lyotard*: 85–94. Stony Brook: The Humanities Institute (Occasional Papers, 1), 2000.

——. "Droit de regard droit. *Film* de Samuel Beckett au regard de *Tu m'*" *Étant donné-Marcel Duchamp* 4 (2003): 84–93.

——. "Genet's Open Enemies: Sartre and Derrida." *Yale French Studies* 91 (1997): 103–16.

——. "'On' dans *Worstward Ho* (*Cap au pire*): fonction et valeur." In Lourdes Carriedo, Ma Luisa Guerrero, Carmen Méndez, and Fabio Vericat, eds. *A Vueltas con Beckett*. Alpedrete (Madrid): Ediciones de la Discreta (Colección Bártulos, 7), 2009.

——. "Passages." In Dolorès Lyotard, Jean-Claude Milner, and Gérald Sfez, eds. *Jean-François Lyotard. L'exercice du différend*: 113–28. Paris: Les Presses Universitaires de France (La Librairie du Collège International de Philosophie), 2001.

——. "Queneau/Dog/Man/Body: Coup de Dédé ou jeu de Descartes?" *Gradiva* 6, no. 2 (1996): 18–32.

——. "Telltale at the Passage." *Yale French Studies* 99 (Spring 2001): 102–16.

——. "Témoinité." *Europe* 984 (May 2008): 284–96.

——. *Témoins d'artifice*. Paris: L'Harmattan (coll. Esthétiques), 2003.

Heal, Jane. *Mind, Reason, and Imagination: Selected Essays in Philosophy of Mind and Language*. New York: Cambridge University Press, 2003.

Heidegger, Martin. "The Quest for Being." In Walter Kaufmann ed. and tr. *Existentialism from Dostoevsky to Sartre*: 233–79. New York: Meridien Books, 1956.

Herzog, Werner, dir. *Wo die grünen Ameisen träumen* [*Where the Green Ants Dream*], 1984.

Hilberg, Raul. *The Destruction of the European Jews*. New Haven: Yale University Press, 1961.

Hill, Leslie. "Poststructuralist Readings of Beckett." In Lois Oppenheim, *Palgrave Advances in Samuel Beckett Studies*: 68–88. Houndsmills and New York: Palgrave Macmillan, 2004.

Hisgen, Ruud and Adriaan van der Weel. "Worsening in *Worstward Ho*: A Brief Look at the Genesis of the Text." In Marius Buning, Matthijs Engelberts, and Sjef Houppermans, eds. *Samuel Beckett Today/Samuel Beckett Aujourd'hui: Crossroads and Borderlines*: 243–50. Amsterdam and Atlanta: Rodopi, 1997.

Hisgen, Ruud. "Interpreting Samuel Beckett's *Worstward Ho*." Doctoral thesis, Leiden University, 1998.

Hoffman, Martin L. *Empathy and Moral Development: Implications for Caring and Justice*. New York and Cambridge: Cambridge University Press, 2000.

Hopkins, Bryan Douglas. "The Modern Ascent of the Soul: Spiritual Progress in the Novels of Joyce, Beckett, and Nabokov" [University of

Texas, Austin, 1997]. *Dissertation Abstracts International* 59, no. 1 (July 1998): 165.

Houpert, Jean-Marc and Paule Petitier, eds. *De l'irreprésentable en littérature.* Paris: L'Harmattan, 2001.

Hume, David. *A Treatise of Human Nature* [1739]. Edited by Ernest C. Mossner. London: Penguin, 1985.

James, William. *Pragmatism.* Cambridge: Harvard University Press, 1975.

Johnson, Mark. *The Body in the Mind: The Bodily Basis of Meaning, Imagination, and Reason.* Chicago: University of Chicago Press, 1987.

Jones, David Houston. "'Que foutait Dieu avant la création?': Disabling Sources in Beckett and Augustine." *Samuel Beckett Today/Aujourd'hui: An Annual Bilingual Review/Revue Annuelle Bilingue* 9 (2000): 185–98

Joyce, James. *Finnegans Wake* [1939]. New York: Viking, 1976.

Kafka, Franz. "Before the Law" and "In the Penal Colony." Translated by Willa and Edwin Muir in *The Complete Stories.* New York: Schocken, 1971.

Kant, Immanuel. *Kritik der Reinen Vernunft* [1787]. Translated as *Critique of Pure Reason* by Paul Guyer and Allen W. Wood. Cambridge and New York: Cambridge University Press, 1998.

——. *Kritik der Urteilskraft* [1790]. Translated by J.H. Bernard as *Critique of Judgement.* New York: Hafner Press, 1951.

——. *Logik. Ein Handbuch zu Vorlesungen* [1800]. <http://www.textlog.de/kant-logik.html>

Kearney, Richard. *Poetics of Imagining: Modern to Postmodern.* New York: Fordham University Press, 1998.

——. *The Wake of Imagination: Toward a Postmodern Culture.* Minneapolis: University of Minnesota Press, 1988.

Kieran, Matthew and Dominic Lopes. *Imagination, Philosophy, and the Arts.* New York: Routledge, 2003.

Klossowski, Pierre. *Nietzsche et le cercle vicieux.* Paris: Mercure de France, 1975.

Knowlson, James. *Damned to Fame: The Life of Samuel Beckett.* London: Bloomsbury, 1996.

Krance, Charles. "*Worstward Ho* and On-words: Writing to(wards) the Point." In Lance St. John Butler and Robin J. Davis, eds. *Rethinking Beckett: A Collection of Critical Essays*: 124–40. New York: St. Martin's Press, 1990.

Kurosawa, Akira, dir. *Dodesukaden*, 1970.

——, dir. *Rashomon*, 1950.

Lakoff, George and Mark Johnson. *Philosophy in the Flesh: The Embodied Mind and Its Challenge to Western Thought.* New York: Basic Books, 1999.

Lanzmann, Claude. "Parler pour les morts" *Le Monde des débats* (May 2000): 14–16.

Laplanche, Jean. *Problématiques VI. L'après-coup.* Paris: Les Presses Universitaires de France, 2006.

Laplanche, Jean and Jean-Bertrand Pontalis. *Vocabulaire de la psychanalyse.* Paris: Presses Universitaires de France, 1967.

Laub, Dori. "Bearing Witness or the Vicissitudes of Listening." In Shoshana Felman and Dori Laub, M.D. *Testimony: Crises of Witnessing in Literature, Psychoanalysis, and History*: 57–74. New York and London: Routledge, 1992.

Leibniz, Gottfried Wilhelm. *La Monadologie* [1714]. Précédé d'une étude de Jacques Rivelaygue. Paris: La Librairie Générale Française (Le Livre de Poche), 1991.

Lescourret, Marie-Anne. *Emmanuel Levinas.* Paris: Flammarion, 1994.

Levi, Primo. *Se questo è un uomo* [1947]. In *Se questo è un uomo. La Tregua.* Torino: Giulio Einaudi (Einaudi Tascabili), 1989. Translated by Stuart Woolf as *If This Be a Man.* New York: Orion Press, 1959. Aberrantly retitled as *Survival at Auschwitz.* New York: Touchstone, 1996.

——. *I sommersi e i salvati.* Torino: Giulio Einaudi, 1986. Translated as *The Drowned and the Saved* by Raymond Rosenthal. New York: Vintage, 1989.

——. *La Tregua* [1958]. In *Se questo è un uomo. La Tregua.* Torino: Giulio Einaudi (Einaudi Tascabili), 1989. Translated by Stuart Woolf as *The Truce: A Survivor's Journey Home from Auschwitz.* London: Bodley Head, 1965.

Levinas, Emmanuel. *Autrement qu'être, ou au-delà de l'essence.* Dordrecht: Martinus Nijhoff, Kluwer Academic, 1978. Translated by Alphonso Lingis as *Otherwise Than Being, or, Beyond Essence.* Pittsburgh, PA: Duquesne University Press, 1998.

——. *Du sacré au saint. Cinq nouvelles lectures talmudiques.* Paris: Minuit, 1977.

——. *Totalité et infini.* Translated by Alphonso Lingis as *Totality and Infinity: An Essay on Exteriority.* Dordrecht and Boston: Kluwer, 1991.

Levy, Eric P. "The Beckettian Mimesis of Seeing Nothing." *University of Toronto Quarterly* 70, no. 2 (Spring 2001): 620–32.

Llinás, R.R. *I of the Vortex.* Cambridge, MA: MIT Press, 2001.

Locatelli, Carla. "Samuel Beckett's *Stirrings Still.*" *The American Poetry Review* 28, no. 5 (September/October 1999): 32–39.

——. *Unwording the World: Samuel Beckett's Prose Works After the Nobel Prize.* Philadelphia: University of Pennsylvania Press, 1990.

Lyotard, Jean-François. *Chambre sourde. L'antiesthétique de Malraux.* Paris: Galilée, 1998. Translated by Robert Harvey as *Soundproof Room: Malraux's Anti-Aesthetics.* Stanford, CA: Stanford University Press, 2001.

——. *Le Différend.* Paris: Minuit, 1983. Translated by Georges Van Den Abbele as *The Differend: Phrases in Dispute.* Minneapolis: University of Minnesota Press, 1988.

——. "Emma" [1989]. In *Misère de la philosophie*: 57–95. Paris: Galilée, 2000.

——. "La Force des faibles" *L'Arc* 64, 1976, pp. 4–12. Translated by Fred J. Evans as "The Strength of the Weak" in Robert Harvey and Mark S. Roberts, eds. *Toward the Postmodern*: 62–72. Amherst, NY: Humanity Books, 1999.

——. *Heidegger et "le juifs."* Paris: Galilée, 1988. Translated by Andreas Michel and Mark Roberts as *Heidegger and "the jews."* Minneapolis: University of Minnesota Press, 1990.

——. *L'Inhumain. Causeries sur le temps.* Paris: Galilée, 1988. Translated by Geoffrey Bennington and Rachel Bowlby as *The Inhuman: Reflections on Time.* London: Polity, 1991.

——. *Leçons sur l'Analytique du Sublime.* (Kant, *Critique de la faculté de juger,* §§23–29). Paris: Galilée, 1991.

——. *Un trait d'union.* Sainte-Foy, Québec: Le Griffon d'argile, 1993.

McMillan, Dougald. "Worstward Ho." In S.E. Gontarski, ed. *On Beckett: Essays and Criticism*: 207–09. New York: Grove Press, 1986.

Malraux, André. *La Condition humaine* [1933]. Translated by Haakon M. Chevalier as *Man's Fate* [1934]. New York: Random House, 1961.

Mesnard, Philippe and Claudine Kahan. *Giorgio Agamben à l'épreuve d'Auschwitz. Témoignages/Interprétations.* Paris: Kimé, 2001.

Michaux, Henri. *La Vie dans les plis.* Paris: Gallimard (Poésie), 1990.

Milne, Drew, "The Dissident Imagination: Beckett's Late Prose Fiction." In Rod Mengham, ed. *An Introduction to Contemporary Fiction: International Writing in English Since 1970.* Cambridge: Polity, 1999.

Modell, Arnold H. *Imagination and the Meaningful Brain.* Cambridge, MA: MIT Press, 2003.

Müller, Filip. *Eyewitness Auschwitz: Three Years in the Gas Chambers.* New York: Stein and Day, 1979.

Myskja, Bjørn K. *The Sublime in Kant and Beckett: Aesthetic Judgement, Ethics and Literature.* Berlin and New York: Walter de Gruyter (Kantstudien, 140), 2002.

Nietzsche, Friedrich. *Die frölische Wissenschaft.* Translated by Walter Kaufmann as *The Gay Science.* New York: Vintage Books, 1974.

Noudelmann, François. *Beckett ou la scène du pire. Étude sur En attendant Godot et Fin de partie.* Paris: Honoré Champion Éditeur, (coll. Unichamp, 75), 1998.

Piette, Adam. "Beckett, Early Neuropsychology and Memory Loss: Beckett's Reading of Clarapède, Janet and Korsakoff." In Marius Buning and Lois Oppenheim, eds., *Beckett in the 1990s*: 41–47. Amsterdam and Atlanta: Rodopi (Samuel Beckett today/aujourd'hui 2), 1993.

Queneau, Raymond. *Le Chiendent.* Paris: Gallimard, 1933. Translated by Barbara Wright as *The Bark Tree.* London: Calder & Boyars, 1968.

Rabelais, François. *Gargantua* [1534]. Translated by M.A. Screech in *Gargantua and Pantagruel.* London: Penguin, 2006.

Ramachandran, V.S. and E. Hubbard. "Hearing Colors, Tasting Shapes." *Scientific American* 288, no. 5 (May 2003): 53–59.

Ravez, Stéphanie, "Tombeau du regard/Regard du tombeau: Place de l'imagination chez Ignace de Loyola et Samuel Beckett." *Samuel Beckett Today/Aujourd'hui: An Annual Bilingual Review/Revue Annuelle Bilingue* 6 (1997): 329–41.

Readings, Bill. *Introducing Lyotard: Art and Politics.* London and New York: Routledge, 1991.

——. "Pagans, Perverts, or Primitives? Experimental Justice in the Empire of Capital." In Andrew Benjamin, ed. *Judging Lyotard*: 168–91. London: Routledge, 1992.

Renton, Andrew. "*Worstward Ho* and the End(s) of Representation." In John Pilling and Mary Bryden, eds. *The Ideal Core of the Onion: Reading Beckett Archives*: 99–135. Reading: Beckett International Foundation, 1992.

Revault d'Allonnes, Myriam. "Le cœur intelligent de Hannah Arendt" in *Fragile humanité*. Paris: Aubier, 2002.

Ricks, Christopher. *Beckett's Dying Words*. Oxford: Oxford University Press, 1993.

Riquelme, John Paul, "The Way of the Chameleon in Iser, Beckett, and Yeats: Figuring Death and the Imaginary in The Fictive and the Imaginary." *New Literary History: A Journal of Theory and Interpretation* 31, no. 1 (2000 Winter): 57–71.

Rotman, Brian. *Becoming Beside Ourselves: The Alphabet, Ghosts, and Distributed Human Being*. Durham and London: Duke University Press, 2008.

——. *Signifying Nothing: The Semiotics of Zero*. Basingstoke, Hampshire: Macmillan, 1987.

Rousset, David. *L'Univers concentrationnaire*. Paris: Minuit, 1965.

Sallis, John. *Force of Imagination: The Sense of the Elemental*. Bloomington: Indiana University Press, 2000.

Sardin-Damestoy, Pascale. *Samuel Beckett, auto-traducteur ou L'art de l'empêchement. Lecture bilingue et génétique des textes courts auto-traduits*. Arras: Artois Presses Université, 2002.

Sartre, Jean-Paul. *L'Imaginaire. Psychologie phénoménologique de l'imagination* [1936]. Paris: Presses Universitaires de France, 1949. Translated as *The Imaginary: A Phenomenological Psychology of the Imagination* by Jonathan Webber. London and New York: Routledge, 2004.

——. *L'Imagination. Psychologie phénoménologique de l'imagination* [1940]. Gallimard (Idées), 1966.

Scarry, E.M. "Six Ways to Kill a Blackbird or Any Other Intentional Object: Samuel Beckett's Method of Meaning." *James Joyce Quarterly* 8, no. 4 (Summer 1971): 278–89.

Schäfer, Uwe, "Fleshing the Cannibal's Bones: Samuel Beckett's *Imagination Dead Imagine* and Wilson Harris's *Jonestown*." *Commonwealth Essays and Studies* 18, no. 2 (Spring 1996): 1–12.

Schnabel, Julian, dir. *Le Scaphandre et le papillon* [*The Diving Bell and the Butterfly*], 2007.

Sedgwick, Eve Kosofsky. *Touching, Feeling: Affect, Pedagogy, Performativity*. Durham and London: Duke University Press, 2003.

Self, Will. *Liver: A Fictional Organ with a Surface Anatomy of Four Lobes*. New York, Berlin, and London: Bloomsbury, 2009.

Smith, Anna. "Proceeding by Aporia: Perception and Poetic Language in Samuel Beckett's *Worstward Ho*." *Journal of Beckett Studies* [Tallahassee] 3, no. 1 (1993): 21–37.

Spiegleman, Art. *Maus I: A Survivor's Tale: My Father Bleeds History*. New York: Pantheon, 1986.

Stoppard, Tom. *Rosenkrantz and Guildenstern Are Dead*. London: Faber and Faber, 1967.

Thobo-Carlsen, John. "Beckett's Dialogic "Design" and Rhetoric of Impotence." *Samuel Beckett Today/Samuel Beckett Aujourd'hui* 11 (2001): 245–52.

Toumayan, Alain. "'I more than others': Dostoevsky and Levinas." *Yale French Studies* no. 104 (2004): 55–66.

Trezise, Thomas. *Into the Breach: Samuel Beckett and the Ends of Literature*. Princeton, NJ: Princeton University Press, 1990.

Vaihinger, Hans. *The Philosophy of "As If": A System of Theoretical, Practical, and Religious Fictions of Mankind* [1911]. Translated by C.K. Ogden. New York: Barnes & Noble, 1968.

van der Weel, Adriaan. "The Genesis of Samuel Beckett's *Worstward Ho*." Doctoral thesis, Leiden University, 1998.

Vico, Giambattista. *La Scienza nuova* [1774]. Translated by Thomas Goddard Bergin and Max Harold Fisch as *The New Science of Giambattista Vico*. Ithaca, NY: Cornell University Press, 1968.

Wall, John. "A Study of the Imagination in Samuel Beckett's *Watt*." *New Literary History: A Journal of Theory and Interpretation* 33, no. 3 (Summer 2002): 533–58.

Weller, Shane. "The Anethics of Desire: Beckett, Racine, Sade." In Russell Smith, ed. *Beckett and Ethics*: 102–17. London and New York: Continuum, 2008.

Wills, David. "Full Dorsal: Derrida's Politics of Friendship." *Postmodern Culture* 15, no. 3 (May 2005). <http://www.iath.virginia.edu/pmc/>

Wolosky, Shira. "The Negative Way Negated: Samuel Beckett's *Texts for Nothing*." *New Literary History* 22 (1991): 213–30.

Zamiatin, Evgenii Ivanovitch. *Mbi* [1925]. Translated as *We* by Mirra Ginsburg. New York: Viking Press, 1972.

Index